Technology, Institutions,
and Economic Growth

Technology, Institutions, and Economic Growth

RICHARD R. NELSON

HARVARD UNIVERSITY PRESS

Cambridge, Massachusetts

London, England

2005

Library of Congress Cataloging-in-Publication Data

Nelson, Richard R.
Technology, institutions, and economic growth / Richard R. Nelson.
p. cm.
Includes bibliographical references and index.
ISBN 0-674-01916-4 (alk. paper)
1. Economic development.   2. Technology—Economic aspects.
3. Institutional economics.   I. Title.

HD75.N455 2005
338.9′001—dc22   2005050353

Contents

Introduction

The 1950s saw a renaissance of interest among economists in economic growth. There were several reasons for this. One was the availability of the new GNP statistics, which gave economists an aggregate measure of a country's economic size, and hence the ability, through analysis of time series, to measure economic growth rates. A second was the development of neoclassical growth theory, which suggested or justified a particular way of analyzing such time series. As a result of research since that time, we now possess a wealth of empirical understanding about economic growth.

Ironically, what we have learned suggests strongly that the neoclassical theory of economic growth, which clearly was an important source of interest in the subject among economists, and which provided considerable focus to their research, is hopelessly inadequate as a growth theory. On the one hand, the theory is blind to many of the important variables and processes involved. On the other hand, certain fundamental assumptions of the theory would seem to be just wrong. Also, what we have learned suggests that using an aggregate measure, like increase in GNP of GNP per capita, as a measure of economic growth tends to take attention away from what is going on beneath the aggregate, where differing rates of advance in different sectors, and the birth and death of industries, seem to be an essential part of the economic growth story. The essays in this volume are motivated by these issues.

I have been among a group of scholars who, for some years, have

1

been trying to call attention to the problem with neoclassical theory, and to build a more satisfactory theory of economic growth. For the most part the reaction of my colleagues in economics has been to cover their ears.

There clearly are important things that neoclassical growth theory has got right. One is that technological advance is the central driver of growth, as we have experienced it. That part of standard growth theory is strongly supported by the empirical evidence. However, the theory treats economic growth in terms of a moving equilibrium of the economic system. And it is very clear that technological advance, and economic growth driven by technological advance, involve disequilibrium, indeed continuing disequilibrium, in a fundamental way. Economic growth needs to be understood as an evolutionary process.

The standard growth theory in economics focuses on the roles of business firms, and the incentives and the constraints provided by competition in a market setting. Firms operating, interacting, and competing in a market context surely are an important part of the institutional structures that have spurred and oriented the economic growth experience. However, the standard theory is blind to a wide range of other institutions that have played key roles, like universities and public laboratories, scientific and other professional associations, and government agencies and programs.

Some of my colleagues in economics recognize the difficulties with prevailing dominant economic growth theory but then argue two things. First, that it is in the nature of a theory to simplify the reality greatly, to strip the picture down to its essence. Second, that in any case, there is no real alternative to a neoclassical formulation of economic activity, including the activities that generate economic growth.

But my argument to the first claim above is that prevailing growth theory does not just "simplify" the growth experience, it oversimplifies it, distorts it, and leaves out essential elements. My response to the second remark is that there indeed is an alternative. There long has existed in economics a tradition of evolutionary theorizing about economic change that is comfortable with contexts that are out of equilibrium, and a rich institutional economics strand that has recognized the complexity of modern capitalist systems. These traditions were strong in economics from the beginnings of the modern discipline up until World War II, after which they were pushed to the boundaries and almost disappeared. Over the past quarter century, however, both evolutionary and institutional economics have shown new life, and they are beginning to join together again, as they were joined earlier in the history of economic thought. My own work has been very much part of this intellectual renaissance.

In my 1996 book, *The Sources of Economic Growth,* I collected a set of my earlier writings that sought to advance the agenda of evolutionary and institutional economics. This book includes essays mostly written since that time.

Part I contains two chapters that flesh out my argument that neoclassical growth theory is not simply an oversimplified, and hence inadequate, characterization of economic growth as we have come to understand it empirically. An even more serious problem is that it provides a very misleading view of the key processes at work. The chapters in Part II develop an evolutionary theory of economic growth within which prevailing institutions both strongly affect the rate and direction of change, and themselves evolve. Here I provide a broad view of the different strands of evolutionary and institutional theorizing that have been developing over the past quarter century, and attempt to pull those strands together.

Part III is concerned with the fact that, while the economic growth we have experienced has dramatically lifted the living standards of peoples fortunate enough to live in areas where growth has been significant, once one looks beneath the aggregate, the evolution of human capabilities has been extraordinarily uneven. The advance of productivity, broadly defined, has varied greatly from sector to sector. This has been reflected in the continuing rise in the relative cost of certain basic services, like education, which has been the source of a variety of economic and political problems.

Another manifestation of our uneven ability to advance various economic activities and mechanisms is that institutional change is both much more sluggish and more difficult to evaluate than technological advance. An important reason for this is that the body of understanding bearing on institutions and how they work is much weaker than the body of understanding underlying modern technologies. As a result, institutional change is strongly tied up with ideologies. In recent years a major component of prevailing ideologies has been that market organization almost always is the most effective way to govern economic activity. The two chapters in Part IV are concerned with this fact, and with some of the consequences.

The view of economic growth that I present recognizes, highlights, that an economy consists of many different sectors, providing a vast variety of goods and services, and focuses on variables like the strength of scientific knowledge and the character of prevailing institutions as key factors affecting how progress is made in different fields. This view has two implications that are strongly reflected in the way I have written the various chapters, that I want to put up front and in clear view.

First, it is misguided to look for a simple formal model, or a few simple empirical laws, that will capture the essence of what we know about economic growth. It may be useful to build and explore simple models for the purpose of learning to think through the implications of various processes we have reason to believe are at work. I myself have, in other places, done a considerable amount of formal modeling, particularly formal evolutionary modeling. However, it is a mistake to think that one can achieve a broad theory of economic growth that has a simple mathematical form. As in biology (which long ago Marshall argued was the future form of economic analysis), our basic understandings, our broad theory, must mostly be expressed verbally.

Second, it certainly is useful if portions of what we know about growth—the phenomenon itself, the causal factors—can be described quantitatively. However, many of the most important variables defy simple quantitative characterization (the state of scientific knowledge, for one; the nature of prevailing institutions, for another). Various quantitative indicators can be devised to provide measures of aspects of these kinds of variables, just as a GNP measure was devised to provide an indicator of the overall size of an economy. But scalar measures almost always are inadequate. As I indicated above, the tendency of many economists to see economic growth strictly in terms of what has been happening to GNP or GNP per person has blinded analysis to the fact of dramatic intersectoral differences. And in many cases, even multiple indicators provide only a partial summary of what we know about an important variable. Thus we know much more about the nature of research in the fields of medicine, and in education, than we can describe in numbers. Numbers help greatly in description and comparison, but they are only a part of what we know empirically. Just as much of theorizing in economics needs to be verbal, with formal analysis playing a supporting but not dominant role, much of our empirical knowledge can be described only qualitatively, with quantitative measures in a supporting but not exhaustive role.

I know well that these two positions fly in the face of current orthodox thinking on these matters. But I propose that they need to be considered seriously.

PART I

Neoclassical economic growth theory is a cramped and awkward way of abstracting what economists know about the processes of economic growth. This is not simply because much of consequence is omitted, although this is important. It also is because the interpretation of prevailing configurations of outputs and inputs, and the specification of the processes through which they change over time, are basically inconsistent with what we know empirically. As a result, the theory provides at best an inadequate, and in some cases a downright misleading, explanation for the economic growth we observe.

Economists working with and developing neoclassical growth theory are not totally unaware of this. The first chapter in Part I is concerned with efforts over the past fifteen years to develop a "new" neoclassical growth theory. These new growth models bring into the formal theoretical structure certain important aspects of technological advance that long have been known to empirical scholars but that were absent, even implicitly denied, in older neoclassical growth theory. For example, a number of the new neoclassical growth models break from the assumption of perfect competition that was a standard feature of the old models, to recognize that in capitalist economic systems, the process of innovation involves the creation of at least temporary positions of market power. Some of the authors of the new theory even claim their models to be "Schumpeterian."

The argument I present in Chapter 1 is that these accommodations simply are not sufficient to enable a theory of economic growth that encompasses what we know empirically. A viable economic growth theory must recognize the evolutionary nature of the processes of technological advance, and of the ways in which the structure of inputs, outputs, and institutions is molded by and molds the advance of technology. And it must recognize the institutional complexity of modern capitalist economies. Both of these themes are developed further in subsequent chapters of this book.

Chapter 2, drawn from an article written with Howard Pack, is concerned with the misleading interpretation of experienced economic growth that neoclassical growth theory can give. The context is the extraordinary economic growth achieved over the past forty years by Korea, Taiwan, and the other Asian Tigers. In the 1990s several empirical investigations, based on neoclassical growth theory, attacked the standard view that innovation and technological learning had played the central role in lifting productivity and incomes in those countries, and proposed that, rather, their growth was simply the result of high investment rates. Pack and I propose that a good way of thinking about the alternative interpretations of growth is to contrast an "accumulation" theory, which is what the authors we criticize propose, with an "assimilation" theory, in which innovation and learning are central, which we argue in fact captures the key driving forces. The case for the latter is overwhelming, once one takes off the blinders afforded by neoclassical growth theory.

CHAPTER 1

The Agenda for Growth Theory:
A Different Point of View

1. Introduction

From the time they were first developed in the mid-1950s (Solow 1956, Swan 1956), almost all formal neoclassical models of economic growth have recognized technical advance as the key driving force, and thus have been consistent with a central conclusion of the empirical research on the sources of growth. However, most of the earlier formal models were mute or incoherent regarding the sources of technical advance. A new generation of neoclassical growth models began to emerge in the late 1980s and early 1990s, in which technical advance was endogenous, being the product of the profit-seeking investments of business firms (among the important early models see Aghion and Howitt 1990, Grossman and Helpman 1989, Romer 1990). These models captured in stylized form several of the understandings about technical advance that for many years have been well documented by empirical scholars. (For a good survey of these understandings, see Freeman 1982.)

To build in features that make R & D profitable for firms, these models departed from the earlier ones in one or both of the following ways. First, firms are able to keep proprietary at least a portion of the value of the increased productivity or better product performance won through their R & D. Second, to square with the recognition that

---

* Based on Richard R. Nelson, "The Agenda for Growth Theory: A Different Point of View," *Cambridge Journal of Economics* 22, July 1998.

technology is in some degree proprietary, and also that support of R & D is feasible only if price exceeds production cost by some margin, markets are assumed to be imperfectly, not perfectly, competitive. (For a good statement of this, see Grossman 1994.)

The endogenizing of technical advance in this way was complemented by the building in or deduction of other phenomena. Thus some of the models treat technical advance as a process of "creative destruction," in which new technologies make obsolete older ones (see Grossman and Helpman 1989). In many of the models there are "externalities" from investments in R & D (as in Romer 1990) or from other activities, for example, education (see Lucas 1988). Up-front R & D investments and, in some models, other factors such as differentiation of intermediate products, which enables varied production needs to be better met as an economy gets larger, generate economies of scale. In some of these models the rate of investment in new plant and equipment affects the steady-state growth rate, because of scale economies or externalities or both, whereas in the older generation of models the steady-state growth rate was independent of the investment rate.

The characterization above does not do justice to the elegance of some of the new neoclassical growth models, nor does it lay out their variety. (For more extended and systematic reviews, see Romer 1991 and 1994, and Verspagen 1992.) And it does not treat neoclassical growth models of a more recent vintage (largely because these have stayed pretty much in the mold described above). However, the account suffices to bring out several points.

First, these new-generation neoclassical growth models are different from most of the earlier generation in ways that appear to make them more "realistic," in the sense of capturing, in stylized form, at least some of the features of growth fueled by technical advance that many economists studying the topic empirically have long known to be important. Incorporation of these features almost certainly makes it somewhat easier for formal growth theorizing to engage effectively with the empirical work of economists trying to come to grips with the puzzling features of experienced economic growth.

Second, this brief review also suffices to highlight that the phenomena incorporated in the new formal models, and neglected in many of the old ones, scarcely represent novel new insights or ideas. The basic notions that "technical change is largely endogenous," "technology is to at least some extent proprietary, and market structures supporting technical advance are not perfectly competitive," "new technology often makes obsolete old technology," "growth fueled by technical advance involves externalities and economies of scale," and "the investment rate may matter in the long run" scarcely smack of novelty. All have been part of the body of understanding of those studying economic growth and technical advance for a long time (Freeman 1982, already cited, is a good reference). Indeed, as I shall show in the next section, Abramovitz put forth most of these propositions in his review article on the economics of growth, written more than fifty years ago, in 1952.

The authors of the new models might respond that a causal argument is not well posed until it is articulated formally. Indeed, formalization of previously unformalized ideas about growth seems to be an important part of the agenda of the new growth theorists. However, it certainly is relevant to ask just what is gained by formalization of existing unformalized understandings.

It is also important to note that, while the new models have picked up pieces of the understanding about technical change and economic growth made by economists who have studied the subject empirically, the models neglect or misspecify what seem to be equally important parts of that understanding. Thus virtually all detailed empirical studies of major technological advances have highlighted the inability of the actors involved early in the game to foresee the path of development, even in broad outline, and the major surprises that often occurred along the path (see Rosenberg 1996). In contrast, the new models assume perfect foresight, or if they admit less than that, they assume that uncertainty about the future can be treated in terms of a well and correctly specified probability distribution of possible future events.

As another example, several recent writers have argued that differences across nations in the way firms are organized and managed has significantly influenced their economic growth performance. Thus Chandler (1990) and Lazonick (1990) ascribe a good portion of the reason why the United States surpassed Great Britain in economic performance in the last part of the nineteenth century and the first part of the twentieth to differences in management and organizational structure between American and British firms. A number of authors (see, for example, Womack, Jones, and Roos 1990) view the organization of Japanese firms in the post–Second World War era as a major factor explaining Japan's extraordinary growth performance. The past two decades also have seen a resurgence of interest among economists in differences in national institutions—for example financial systems (Gilson and Roe 1993), universities (Nelson 1993, Rosenberg and Nelson 1994), or more generally (North 1990)—as important aspects of the explanation for differential national growth performance. The new neoclassical growth models, in contrast, treat firms in a highly stripped-down way, and have little in them about institutions, aside from "the competitive (or monopolistically competitive) market."

To the extent that formalization of important and previously unformalized understandings about technical change and economic growth defines an important part of the agenda for the new growth theorists, it seems useful to ask why certain ideas have been picked up and formalized and others not. The salience of the understanding certainly would seem to be one operative criterion. Thus the incompatibility of the assumption of perfect competition with the facts of endogenous technical advance called attention to an obviously serious limitation of earlier formal growth models. But uncertainty, in the sense of Knight (1921), would also seem highly salient to realistic modeling of economic growth fueled by technical advance. Why has imperfect competition been taken aboard but not Knightian uncertainty? And if imperfect competition for some reason has proved attractive or easy to build in, why has the understanding that firms differ significantly in their capabilities and their strategies proved unattractive or undigestible for the new growth theorists? Why the failure to treat national economic institutions, like financial institutions or the university research system?

The answer, I believe, is that another part of the agenda of the new growth theory, or a constraint on that agenda, is to hold the modeling as close as possible to the canons of general equilibrium theory. Romer (1990) states this explicitly, and the form of the models that have been developed by others suggests that they too hold this as an objective or constraint. However, it certainly seems relevant to think a little about what is gained and what is lost by operating under this constraint.

The central arguments are these. First, it does matter whether or not the understandings of empirical scholars working in an area—in this case, on technical advance and economic growth—are incorporated in formal models, although for reasons that have as much to do with the culture in economics as with the particular power of formal modeling. Therefore, second, it is consequential, and in my view unfortunate, that understandings of the sort I have mentioned above, about technological advance, about firms, and about supporting institutions, have not yet been taken on board in formal models, or at least not in the formal models that now are in fashion. And third, constraining formal growth theorizing to the canons of equilibrium theorizing makes formalizing these understandings unnecessarily difficult.

These propositions need to be understood in the context of a particular point of view regarding the nature of theorizing in economics. Sidney Winter and I (Nelson and Winter 1982) have argued that theorizing, perhaps because the subject matter and operative mechanisms in economics are so complex, tends to proceed on two levels at least. What we called appreciative theorizing tends to be close to empirical work and provides both interpretation and guidance for further exploration. Mostly it is expressed verbally and is the analyst's articulation of what he or she thinks really is going on. However, appreciative theory is very much an abstract body of reasoning. Certain variables and relationships are treated as important, and others are ignored. There generally is explicit causal argument. On the other hand, appreciative theorizing tends to stay quite close to the empirical substance.

In contrast, formal theorizing almost always proceeds at some intellectual distance from what is known empirically, and where it does appeal to data for support, the appeal generally is to "stylized facts," or reasonably good "statistical fits." If the hallmark of appreciative theory is storytelling that is close to the empirical details, the hallmark of formal theorizing is an abstract structure set up to enable one to explore, find, and check proposed logical connections. Good formal theorizing is less likely than appreciative theorizing to contain logical gaps and errors. The logical inferences tend to reach further. And there is greater self-consciousness about assumptions and analytic argument.

We proposed that, when the intellectual enterprise in economics is going well, empirical research, appreciative theorizing, and formal theorizing work together or, rather, empirical work and appreciative theorizing work together, and appreciative and formal theorizing work together. Empirical findings or facts seldom influence formal theorizing directly. Rather, in the first instance they influence appreciative theorizing—that is, what the empirical researchers want to highlight and draw from their work. In turn, appreciative theorizing provides challenges to formal theory to encompass its understandings in stylized form. This may identify gaps or inconsistencies in the verbal stories, and suggest new mechanisms and connections to explore. In turn again, the empirical and appreciative theoretical research enterprise may be reoriented.

By this account, formal theory must be understood as far from exhausting the body of theoretical understanding possessed by economists working in a field, but rather as touching on only a portion of that broader body, and as addressing what it does in highly stylized form. At the same time, formal theory is the most rigorously worked out part of theory. One important role of formal theorizing obviously is to discipline and sharpen appreciative theory, and to lend a helping hand in its development. In so doing, it may or may not break new ground. But often the attempt to formalize a verbal argument will identify some logical problems in the causal exposition, and thus help to straighten out the argument.

However, the formalization of verbal, appreciative theoretic arguments may introduce elements not present in the latter, or distort them significantly, or leave out important ones. Thus while the new growth theory is advertised as taking in the Schumpeterian proposition that technological advance involves firms with some market power, that theory also builds in an assumption of moving equilibrium that is antithetical to appreciative theorizing within the Schumpeterian tradition.

I want to argue that another important (and limiting) role of formal theorizing in contemporary economics is, somewhat paradoxically, to bring the understandings it contains into the view of the profession at large. For whatever reasons, graduate training in economics tends to emphasize formal models. When graduate students take a first course in a field, mostly what they are taught are the models. Formal models in a specialized field, if they are analytically interesting, also have a much easier time getting into the more general and widely read economic journals, particularly if they are accompanied by some econometrics, than do looser form, appreciative theoretic discussions. The latter, therefore, tend to be read and known principally by the specialists in a field.

For both of these reasons, the state of formal theory in a field serves as a constraint on, as well as a help to, appreciative theorizing. It is not simply that the state of formal theory limits the confident reach of appreciative theorizing. Formal theory provides the starting place and guide for young scholars entering a field of inquiry. And economists generally (not always) evidence unease when their appreciative theorizing takes them far outside what they can at least rationalize in the language of formal theory.

This brings me back to the basic arguments that motivate the title of this chapter. I want to argue here that the new growth theory, while advertising its break from tradition, in fact has stayed very close to the status quo ante. In the words of Abramovitz (1952), the new formal modeling is focused on the "immediate source of growth" and provides little help for appreciative theorizing aimed at understanding the factors behind these immediate sources. Yet, in my view, this is where the most promising research avenues lie. The new formal growth models pull attention away from these routes. Moreover, the kind of formal theorizing that can facilitate these kinds of explorations very likely will require a focus on variables and relationships that have been ignored or denied by neoclassical formal growth theory, new as well as old, and a break from the canons of equilibrium theorizing. This task defines my proposed agenda.

I shall develop my case as follows. In Section 2 of this chapter, I present a brief history of research on economic growth from the early 1950s to the early 1980s, focusing on two matters. One is the nature of the interaction among appreciative and formal theorizing and empirical research during this period. The other is the growing sense of malaise in the intellectual enterprise that set in after the 1970s, as conventional theoretical ideas were perceived as having little grip on the puzzles associated with growth slowdown. Then, in Section 3, I will discuss various pieces of new appreciative theory that have come into view since the late 1970s. In particular, I will describe recent theorizing about technology, firms, and institutions. In the concluding section, I will suggest some implications should these issues come to be at the top of the agenda for growth theory.

2. Postwar Theorizing about Economic Growth

Economic growth, of course, was a central interest of Adam Smith and many of the classical economists of the nineteenth century. However, during the first half of the twentieth century the topic dropped out of vogue, as microeconomic analysis increasingly came under the sway of partial and general equilibrium theory, and, with the Great Depression, macroeconomic analysis became obsessed with unemployment. After the Second World War, a number of economists again became interested in economic growth. The new surge of research on economic growth was not kindled by any arresting new theory in economics. However, much of the new research was designed to exploit the availability of new economic statistics, particularly the national income and product statistics, which Simon Kuznets pioneered and which for the first time enabled economists to measure growth at a national level.

2.1. The State of Growth Theory as of 1952

In 1952 *A Survey of Contemporary Economics* was published, which attempted to assess the state of the discipline at the time. It contained a chapter on the economics of growth by Moses Abramovitz, who was very much involved in this new research. For my purposes there are two important features of that chapter. First, Abramovitz begins with a statement about the absence at that time of any coherent modern growth theory to guide empirical research. "Unlike most of the topics treated in the *Survey,* the problem with economic growth [is that it] lacks any organized and genuinely known body of doctrine whose recent development might illuminate the subject of this essay." The reader will, of course, note that Abramovitz was writing a few years before the publication of the Solow and Swan pieces (1956) that are reputed to have established modern growth theory, and be tempted to take his statement as an indication that those articles filled an intellectual vacuum.

But the other noteworthy aspect of Abramovitz's essay is the up-to-date character, by contemporary standards, of the issues and relationships he discusses. It is as if most of what formal neoclassical growth theory would later teach was already known. Thus there is a clear statement of the logic behind modern growth accounting, a logic that was being used in the empirical work with which he was involved. Abramovitz notes that economists have long professed a theory that the level of output is determined by the quantity of inputs (land, labor, and capital) and factors that affect their productivity (the state of the arts, industrial and financial organization, the legal system, and so on). Therefore, on one level at least, economic growth can be understood as the result of changes or improvements in these "immediate determinants of output." Abramovitz also proposes that analysis of growth simply at this level is not deep enough, and that a satisfactory theory of growth must come to grips with the forces behind changes in the immediate determinants.

His essay goes on to analyze the forces affecting the expansion of the traditional factors of production—land, labor, capital—and of their contribution to growth. Among other features of his discussion, Abramovitz refers to the view, then common in economics, that the marginal productivity of capital will be high or low depending on the ratio of capital to other factors, and will diminish as capital grows relative to them—clearly this characteristic of the "old" neoclassical growth theory did not come as news. But he then goes on to argue that increases in economic efficiency as the scale of output grows may offset diminishing returns—a feature built in to some of the "new" neoclassical growth theory.

Abramovitz states that, in his view at least, "technical improvement" must account for "a very large share, if not the bulk, of the increase in output." Thus, while the growth-accounting empirical evidence that persuaded others of the economics community on this was not yet in, Abramovitz would not have been surprised by it. Abramovitz clearly sees technical advance as "endogenous," resulting largely from investments aimed to create and exploit it, and anticipates the concept of "knowledge capital" as follows: "And insofar as new applied knowledge results from the deliberate direction of revenues to its discovery and use, the stock of knowledge is increased by a process identical with that which produces increases in the stock of material equipment." Referring to Schumpeter (1942), he observes that "with the development of industrial research departments of corporations . . . almost all engineering work is undertaken only in conjunction with the deliberate entrepreneurial decision." Some proponents of the new growth theory have argued that, until recently, analysts of growth were hung up on a growth theory that assumed perfect competition, but Abramovitz clearly had no such hang up. Abramovitz recognized as well that the investments that yield new proprietary technology also generate externalities, at least with time, "as experience is gained and knowledge of the new art becomes widespread."

Abramovitz highlights the interdependence of technical progress and the expansion of other factors as sources of growth. Vintage models would not have come as news to him. "The actual exploitation of new knowledge virtually always involves some gross investment (in material equipment)."

Abramovitz goes on to imbed his analyses of expansion of the traditional inputs to production, and of technical advance as the major factor augmenting their productivity, in a discussion of "enterprise" and "institutions." He had already focused on modern corporations as key actors in technical progress, and in investing in material equipment. He then observes that "the role of enterprise has been slighted by traditional theory because of the theory's generally static character which leads easily to assumptions about perfect knowledge, and rational calculation of profit." He goes on to suggest that, if one finds Schumpeter's analysis persuasive, one is compelled to recognize that "the marginal productivity of capital depends on enterprise to such a degree" that to neglect it is to miss the whole point of capitalist economic development. Here Abramovitz, in the view I shall espouse, is far ahead of developments in even the "new" neoclassical growth theory, at least as that work has developed to date.

He is also far ahead in his discussion of the broader cultural and institutional factors surrounding and supporting enterprise. Here he expresses the judgment that the broader context is key, and also his concerns that the general conclusion suggested by this survey of the factors controlling the vigor of enterprise is that a vast deal of emphasis must be placed on forces that, in the ordinary conception of the bounds of economics, would have to be classed as political, psychological, or sociological. Abramovitz thus flags the challenge for economists, and stresses that, to unravel the mysteries of economic growth, economists must focus on these issues. Mostly, of course, we have not done so. The focus of almost all research on economic growth since Abramovitz wrote has been on his "immediate determinants."

I have dwelt at some length on Abramovitz's essay, pointing to its modern tone as well as to its richness. Abramovitz clearly was a remarkable scholar. But in his 1952 essay he does not present his theorizing about growth as being particularly original. Indeed, he writes as if he were recounting notions long held in economics, and held at the time he was writing by other scholars focusing on empirical study of economic growth, for example, Simon Kuznets.

2.2. Empirical Research on Growth during the 1950s and 1960s

At the time Abramovitz wrote, a number of economists were hard at work doing empirical research on growth using the new National Income and Product accounts and other new data. By the early 1950s the results of that research, probing the immediate determinants of growth, began to come in. Studies by Schmookler (1952), Fabricant (1954), Kendrick (1956), and Abramovitz himself (1956) all reported that the growth of output experienced in the United States had been significantly greater than reasonably could be attributed to input growth alone.

In these papers the contribution of total input growth was estimated by weighing the different inputs by their prices, a practice apparently considered so reasonable and obvious that few of the authors even bothered to rationalize it explicitly. (While not recognized by many at the time, an earlier paper by Tinbergen [1942] had anticipated much of the methodology.) The excess of output growth over input growth was attributed to a variety of factors. Technological advance, increasing returns to scale, investments in human capital, the allocation of resources from lower to higher productivity activities, all were recognized as parts of the story, but these authors clearly put heavy stress on technological advance. It is interesting that Solow's 1957 piece, which most economists not immersed in research on economic growth regard as the seminal article calculating the "residual" and interpreting it as a measure of technological advance, was published after the studies noted above. The reason for the impact of Solow's piece, I would argue, is that his analysis was structured by a "formal" theory, whereas the theorizing in the earlier articles was more "appreciative" and looser.

Edward Denison's research and writings, which started to be published in the early 1960s, elaborated and enriched the growth-accounting methodology, and significantly increased our understanding of the sources of economic growth, at least at the level that Abramovitz had referred to as the immediate determinants. Regarding growth in the United States, Denison's (1962) conclusions basically were consistent with those published earlier by the scholars cited above, and his contribution mainly involved an ingenious and painstaking attempt to break down the sources of total factor productivity growth into the various components mentioned above. Other economists followed along the same track, developing other kinds of disaggregation and exploring different measures of factor-marginal productivity (see, for example, Jorgenson and Griliches 1967).

Later in the 1960s, Denison (1968) extended his framework to examination of growth in the European economies, with findings that were quite similar to those about the United States (see also Domar 1963). However, Denison also probed the reasons why European worker productivity was significantly lower than American (in the early 1960s it was roughly half). The key finding here was as remarkable as the earlier finding that growth of total factor productivity accounted for the bulk of productivity growth. It was that differences in inputs per worker could account for only a small share of the difference between American and European productivity levels, and that European nations were apparently operating at significantly lower levels of "total factor productivity" than the United States.

Studies of this sort directed the attention of a number of economists to the study of technological advance. This research proceeded in a number of different styles, from econometric (Griliches 1957; Mansfield 1968, 1971, 1977) to historical (Rosenberg 1976, 1982a, 1982b; Freeman 1982). Jacob Schmookler (1966) did pioneering work using patents as a measure of inventive input. The research in this field covered a range of topics, from those stimulated by Schumpeter (do industries where the firms are large and have considerable market power experience more rapid technical advance than more fragmented industries?), to more general factors that are associated with interindustry differences in technical advance, to the connections between science and technology, to the difference between private and social returns to R & D (the gap seemed to be large).

My discussion above of the renaissance and consequent blooming of empirical research on economic growth during the 1950s and 1960s hardly mentions developments in formal growth theory. As I noted, the enterprise was well on its way before the publication of Solow's and Swan's theoretical essays that are widely regarded as having provided the basic ideas for analyses of growth. My point is that most of the basic appreciative theoretical ideas that guided empirical analyses of growth were already there.

However, some of the empirical research, particularly on technological advance, seemed to signal that there was something wrong with the translation of those appreciative theoretic ideas into the formal neoclassical growth theory that, after Solow's landmark work, was becoming broadly accepted as the right way to theorize about economic growth. Thus Griliches's work on the diffusion of hybrid corn, Mansfield's on the advantages that innovation or early adoption of a productive new technology seemed to give the firm in question, and the broad sweep of Rosenberg's work, all pointed to Knightian uncertainty, differences in belief among the relevant actors, and disequilibrium as essential features of economic growth driven by technological advance. While economists doing empirical research on technological advance engaged in lively argument about what kind of industrial structures were associated with rapid technological advance, it was clear that those structures were often oligopolistic and were almost never perfectly competitive. Why did these discrepancies with the assumptions of formal neoclassical growth theory not cause major controversy, or at least wide discussion, about the "general competitive equilibrium" built in to neoclassical growth theory? (Of course, recognition of the latter discrepancy has strongly influenced the new formal neoclassical growth theorizing, but that development occurred with a lag of more than a quarter of a century.)

The reason, I would argue, was that the appreciative theory that interpreted and guided research on technological advance had a life of its own, and if the researchers did not call attention to discrepancies they found with formal growth theory, no one else was particularly bothered by them. In some cases this required a certain obeisance on the part of the empirical researchers. But the appreciative theory did not presume any tight equilibrium, or perfect competition. If the empirical researchers made no fuss, what the formal theory said had only a minor influence on the empirical research and appreciative theorizing, and vice versa.

By that I certainly do not mean that the works of Abramovitz and Kendrick, or Denison, or Mansfield, or Griliches, proceeded independently of economic theory, or even neoclassical theory. But the production function idea had been around for a long time, as had the idea that the change in output could be explained in terms of changes in the inputs of the production function and changes in productivity. Abramovitz treats these ideas as essentially "old hat" in his 1952 essay. The notion that, in growth accounting, the output increase stemming from an increase in an input might be approximated by the price of that input was a simple application of neoclassical factor remuneration theory. Those who believed in this approximation certainly were not wedded to the assumption of perfect competition or of perfect equilibrium, but felt the calculation was illuminating in any case. The idea that the difference between output growth and the factor price-weighted growth of inputs measures growth of "total factor productivity" did not depend on formal neoclassical growth theory. Nor did the notion that technological advance was a key driving force, and largely endogenous.

As the various citations from the Abramovitz 1952 article show, one does not need a formal model to have a theory that new technology often needs to be embedded in new physical capital. The ideas that technical advance often is the result of prior investments in R & D, and that education is reflected in human capital, similarly were around long before they were incorporated in formal models.

What, then, did the advent and development of formal neoclassical growth theory contribute to the enterprise? In a few cases it added ideas and techniques that were distinctly new. Indeed the basic proposition in Solow's first growth model, that if diminishing returns to capital are strong, the steady-state growth rate is independent of the savings rate, certainly came as something of a surprise to most economists, although many did not believe it. The development and application of duality theory to analysis of growth almost certainly would not

have occurred in the absence of formal theoretical work (see, for example, Gollop and Jorgenson 1980; Jorgenson 1986). The putty-clay
model (Solow, Tobin, and von Weizacher 1966) is another example of
formal theorizing developing ideas far beyond the stage where appreciative theorizing alone could carry them. However, I think it is fair to
say that, for the most part, what formal growth modeling did was to
shape up and sharpen appreciative theoretic ideas that had been in
the community for some time.

As my earlier discussion about research on technological advance
suggests, the shaping and sharpening provided by formal theory sometimes involved imposing assumptions that were not there in the appreciative theory, and that impeded understanding. I have proposed that,
where that was the case, the formal theory was mostly simply ignored.
This is not to say, however, that in those cases the misspecification in
the formal theory was benign. In the first place, it slowed down or even
blocked the ability of new researchers entering the field to come to the
understandings reached by the earlier empirical researchers. And it
certainly shaped the research on technological advance that was considered right-headed by the wider profession, and determined what
was recognized and cited outside the small circle of economists doing
research in that field.

I would propose that the most important contribution of the old
neoclassical formal growth theory was to make the research on economic growth more legitimate than it had been, even sexy, and thus to
attract many more young economists to its pursuit than would have
been the case without the development of formal neoclassical growth
theory. One of the tones of Abramovitz's 1952 review piece is that of
isolation from the contemporary mainstream of economics. Reading
the article, it is difficult to imagine the surge of young economists
coming into the field in the late 1950s and 1960s. It is quite possible,
without Solow's 1957 article, which expressly grounded the empirical
calculations in formal neoclassical growth theory, that the empirical
work of Kendrick and Denison, which involved vastly more digging
and calculating, would have received much less attention.

In retrospect, it is fascinating that the few attention-gaining explicit
arguments about formal growth theory proceeded on grounds relatively distant from where most of the empirical work was going on.

This was largely so, for example, regarding Kaldor's theoretical challenge to neoclassical growth theory (see, for example, Kaldor 1957; Kaldor and Mirrlees 1962).

In any case, empirical studies conducted in the 1950s, 1960s, and early 1970s enormously increased our understanding of economic growth. Most of their findings have not been overturned by subsequent studies. The other side of this coin is that subsequent studies following the same line seem to be adding little that is new. By the early 1970s there were indications that research of the sort I have described was experiencing sharply diminishing returns.

2.3. Sharp New Questions, Inadequate Answers

It seems fair to say that the research described above was partly driven by the development of new data on growth, and partly by the energy lent by a theory of growth that, if not new in many of its basic conceptions, did provide a formalization of some ideas that many economists found exciting and promising. The researchers involved were, basically, trying to find out and order empirical facts about growth and to develop a persuasive interpretation for what they found. There were few nagging puzzles at the forefront of attention, crying out to be explained.

By the early 1970s certain aspects of the growth experience began to attract attention as puzzles to be explained and problems to be solved. There was, first of all, the sharp fall in growth rates in the United States and Western Europe that occurred in the late 1960s and early 1970s. Early in the era of slower growth, the problem was ascribed to the oil price shock and related developments, but as slower growth continued, the search began for more systematic reasons (see, for example, Denison 1979; Griliches 1980).

Research concerned with the broad economic growth slowdown in the United States, Western Europe, and, later, Japan, soon identified another phenomenon that was interesting in its own right—that the quarter century after the Second World War was marked by a significant narrowing of the large productivity and income gap between the United States and the other advanced industrial nations that had existed at the start of the period. While some economists first ascribed the original gap to the destruction caused by the Second World War, empirical studies soon made it evident that the United States had gained a significant productivity and income lead over the countries of Western Europe even before the First World War. During the interwar period that gap had, if anything, enlarged. The post–Second World War era came to be seen as a period when "convergence" began to occur strongly. Attention turned to the twin questions, "What are the basic processes involved in convergence?" and "Why has convergence been so much stronger since the Second World War?" (See Abramovitz 1986; Nelson and Wright 1992; Baumol, Nelson, and Wolff 1994.)

Closer looks at the data raised another set of questions. While convergence seemed to be a phenomenon broadly applicable across the economies that had achieved significant technological sophistication at the time of the Second World War, since the end of the war some of those economies had grown significantly more slowly and some more quickly than others of apparently comparable initial conditions. The sluggish growth performance of Great Britain attracted a lot of attention, particularly (of course) from British scholars (for example, Bacon and Eltis 1976), but also from others (such as Lazonick 1990). Meanwhile, Japan's economic growth performance came to be widely recognized as extremely impressive. Indeed, by the mid-1980s Japanese industry appeared actually to be forging ahead of American industry in a number of fields. A number of scholars turned to trying to explain Japan's striking success in economic growth (for example, Dertouzos, Lester, and Solow 1989; Aoki 1990; Womack, Jones, and Roos 1990).

The closer empirical look also revealed the "convergence club" to be relatively narrow. In particular, of the economies that could be regarded as quite backward after the war, only a few had achieved rapid sustained economic growth. Here Korea and Taiwan stood out. A considerable body of research began to focus on the factors that seemed to lie behind the remarkable surge of Korea and Taiwan, from very poor and backward economies as of the early 1960s to economies that, by the 1990s, had more than quadrupled their per capita incomes and were the home of companies that in a number of fields were quite capable of competing with firms from the United States, Europe, and Japan (see Amsden 1989; Kim and Lau 1994; Pack and Westphal 1986; World Bank 1993).

Given the research traditions that had grown up during the 1950s and 1960s, it was natural for the economists' first cut at these questions to focus on the immediate determinants of economic growth. And much of the research on these questions continues to proceed along those lines. One can question, however, how much useful understanding can be gained by studies that focus on the immediate determinants of growth and do not probe very far behind them.

Thus research on convergence relatively quickly made clear that the economies that were catching up with the United States most rapidly—for example, Japan—had achieved a combination of rapid growth of total factor productivity, relatively high rates of growth of the physical capital stock, and relatively high and growing investments in "human capital" (see Baumol, Nelson, and Wolff 1994). These three characteristics all seemed to be complementary features of economies that were rapidly and effectively taking on board advanced technologies, often pioneered in the United States. But this proposition only posed the deeper question of why some economies were able to put this package together and others were not.

In a similar vein, economists quickly came to recognize that Korea and Taiwan had unusually high rates of investment in physical and human capital. While there continues to be considerable argument about the contribution of growth of total factor productivity to the rapid development of these economies, everyone recognizes that the process has involved the progressive adoption of sophisticated technologies that were new to these countries, if not to the world. But the question then becomes: "How were these economies able to do that, while other economies have not been able to do so?" (Nelson and Pack 1999; see Chapter 2 of this volume).

In the mid-1990s economic growth began to pick up rapidly in the United States, and to a lesser extent in Europe. At about the same time, Japanese economic growth slowed down significantly. Korea, Taiwan, and the other Asian Tigers also experienced significant growth slowdowns, and several of the Latin American countries that earlier had been experiencing fairly rapid growth began to have economic difficulties. As with earlier analyses of economic slowdown in the United States and Europe, and rapid growth in Japan and Korea, most economic analyses have involved a growth accounting or an equivalent. As Abramovitz argued many years ago, an explanation at that level doesn't explain much.

I would like to propose that the attempt to probe more deeply leads inevitably to three topics that continue to be repressed, or misspecified, in standard growth theory, including the new neoclassical growth models. These are, first, technology as a body of understanding and practice, and the processes involved in mastering and advancing technology. Second, the nature of the organizations, principally business firms, that employ technology and produce output. And, third, the nature and role of a wide variety of economic institutions that establish the environment within which firms operate.

The question of what technology is, and how it is advanced and mastered, shows up just below the surface of analyses of all of the phenomena discussed above. It shows up in the puzzle of why total factor productivity growth slowed in the United States in the early 1970s and picked up again in the mid-1990s. Questions about the nature of technology and how it is mastered come naturally to mind when one is trying to understand the processes of convergence, and particularly the rapid growth of Korea and Taiwan, or stagnation in the former Soviet Union and many of the other former communist countries.

As Abramovitz noted in his 1952 review article, the search for understanding of technology and technical advance quickly leads to the need to understand what goes on in business firms. Scholars from outside economics, seeking to understand the sources of Japanese economic strength, relatively quickly focused on what they saw as special features of Japanese firms. While economists have been slower to try to look inside firms, in recent years the theory of the firm has become a lively topic in economics. To date, however, very little of our growing understanding of firms has percolated into growth theory.

It is clear that strong firms require a supportive external environment, including an effective financial system, labor markets that meet their needs, educational and training institutions that provide the needed skills. Several economists have proposed that one of the reasons for Japan's economic success is that productive institutional transformations have occurred there more rapidly than they have in the United States and Europe. More generally, the studies of Japan, and more recently of what has been going on in Russia and Eastern

Europe, have focused the attention of economists on economic institutions. But again, what we have learned has yet to find its way into formal neoclassical growth theory.

3. Teachings of Appreciative Theorizing on Technology, Firms, and Economic Institutions

Griliches (1994) has argued persuasively that there are severe data constraints on our ability to improve our understanding of economic growth fueled by technological advance. In the preceding section I began my argument by saying that there also are severe "theory" constraints. My argument contains both a negative and a positive element. The negative element is that prevailing formal growth theory is limiting, both because it is largely focused on the immediate sources of growth, and because the way it is structured makes it difficult for that theory to incorporate effectively the appreciative theory that is taking shape and that bears on some of the key factors behind the immediate sources of growth. In this section I shall briefly highlight some of the more interesting and provocative appreciative theorizing that is taking shape regarding technology, firms, and institutions. My positive argument will be that these provide the basis for a more satisfactory growth theory.

In the preceding section I argued that one of the limitations of analysis focused on the immediate sources of growth is that these sources seem to come in packages. Thus, during the era when the U.S. economy was surging ahead of the European economy, American investment rates were high, the American education system was turning out significant numbers of people capable of taking on managerial posts in the new industrial enterprises, and technological advance was obviously proceeding at a rapid rate. In the early post–Second World War era, the countries that have moved toward the frontier most rapidly have been marked by a combination of high rates of physical investment, large investments in human capital, and rapid acquirement of superior technologies. The growth boom of the late 1990s was marked by both high investment and rapid technological advance. Once one recognizes these interdependencies, one naturally is led to the deeper question: What seems to generate or support the cluster of activities that appears to be associated with rapid growth?

For many scholars the search for an answer to this question has led to research to deepen understanding of technology and technological change. While it is obviously hazardous to single out as key any one element of a package of associated and complementary ones, a strong case can be made for taking technological advance as the basic driving force, its effects emerging not only in growth of total factor productivity but also as the enabler of the productive increases in physical capital and other inputs per unit of labor that, in conventional treatments, are considered as independent sources of growth. Similarly, a strong case can be made that the large productive increases in human capital that have occurred were closely linked with the technological advance that was taking place. (For a rich discussion, see Abramovitz 1986.) Elaboration of this kind of argument, of course, sooner or later forces attention to the question: What is technology anyway?

There are a few simple metaphors about technology. One is that prevailing technology is like "a set of blueprints," suggesting the conception of a "technology library," albeit one in which some of the "books" are proprietary. The notion that technology is "knowledge" has also been around for some time, suggesting something more embodied in human minds.

Research by economists on technology and technological change supports the idea that much about modern technologies indeed is described in blueprints, texts, pictures, equations. However, in many fields it takes a highly trained professional to make sense of the blueprints. Further, even for professionals, access to the documents about most technologies provides only a start toward what is required to make a technology work. A great deal of learning by doing and using is often necessary to gain real mastery of a technology. And it is increasingly apparent that for many technologies much of the "knowledge" that is needed to command a technology is "know-how," which is in the fingers as well as in the head. (For good discussion, see Pavitt 1987 and Dosi 1988.)

These elements of appreciative theory regarding command over technology carry over to understandings about how technical advances occur. Scholars of technical advance have long known the importance of investments in R & D, generally involving the employment of professionals trained in the relevant underlying engineering and scientific disciplines in the generation and development of new technologies.

However, they have also long understood that many technologies seem to experience a continuing stream of improvements that reflect understandings gained and changes wrought through learning by doing and using (see, for example, Rosenberg 1982b). In many technologies it is apparent that both processes are involved, and that they interact strongly. Thus, while what is learned in experience sometimes directly results in changes in practice and design, in many cases this learning has its impact largely by feeding back to influence the problems and targets addressed through R & D.

A number of studies have documented the fact that broad new technologies tend initially to be brought into practice in crude form, representing a bundle of potentialities, rather than a practice that is operationally ready (see, for example, Enos 1962, Nelson and Rosenberg 1993). The car, the airplane, the transistor, the computer, and the laser all surfaced as new technologies of potentially wide applicability, but requiring considerable work and ingenuity before they would be worth anything in economic use. It took a long time, and a lot of investments, and much learning, and learning how to learn (Stiglitz 1989) before these new technologies became major contributors to economic growth.

A common feature to the development paths taken by major new technologies is that quite unforeseen capabilities and uses are discovered along the route. Different new technologies often interact in complex and surprising ways. In the early days of the electronic computers, no one foresaw the vast use by business that came later, partly because no one foresaw the advent of the transistor, the integrated circuit, and the microprocessor. AT&T, which in the early days had control of intellectual property rights to the laser, did not foresee its use in telecommunications through the vehicle of fiber optics.

In many cases, the evolution of a technology displayed apparent path dependencies, with early developments that seemed to involve some element of chance shaping the path of further development of the technology and, in particular, turning it down a particular route when another might have been possible. David (1985) argues that this is the case with respect to the layout of the typewriter keyboard, and Arthur (1988a, 1988b) gives several other examples. Whether "path dependency" has in fact locked technological and economic development into tracks yielding outcomes that are significantly inferior over the long run to what could have been achieved had the early direction been different is a matter of some dispute. But the evidence that technological advances today are significantly shaped by what has (and has not) been achieved earlier is very persuasive.

To a considerable extent the rate and direction of technological advance is shaped by the activities of business firms, and business firms are the repositories of extant technological capabilities. Long ago most economists took on board the notion that firm investments in R & D were an important source of technical advance, and now this is incorporated in some of the new formal models. However, recent research has suggested that issues of firm organization and strategy are at least as important to technical advance as the quantity of their investments in R & D.

While there are changes in the air, until recently few economists have shown much interest in what actually goes on in firms. There are a number of reasons for the neglect. An important one is that, unlike scholars of business management and strategy, the interest of economists is mostly in variables at a level of aggregation well above that of individual firms, often macroeconomic variables, and even our "microeconomics" is about industry-level rather than firm-level variables. But perhaps a more basic reason is that we economists tend to work with theories that suggest, at the levels of aggregation we are interested in, that what firms do can be presumed to be determined by constraints, opportunities, and incentives provided by their environment. Thus, there is no call to look carefully at firms, per se. They are simply puppets dancing to the tune played by the market.

However, under the appreciative theory sketched above, mastery of a technology is more like a skill that needs to be learned and requires more practice than most neoclassical theorizing is wont to admit, and the entity that learns and practices is the firm. The practice of complex technologies inherently involves organization and management. The way a firm organizes the implementation of a common broad technology can make an enormous difference. This is a key finding of much of the recent work comparing U.S. and Japanese car production.

Studies of the sort mentioned earlier of American and Japanese firms have been an important stimulus to new thinking about firms. Several recent studies of how Korea and Taiwan managed to take on board advanced technology so rapidly have also stressed the effective entrepreneurship and learning of firms (see, for example, Amsden 1989, Hobday 1995, Kim 1997, Nelson and Pack 1999).

Another major stimulus, also mentioned earlier, has been Chandler's pioneering historical work on the rise of the modern corporation (1962, 1977, 1990). Particularly, Chandler's work has led to the development of a small body of writings in which key firm capabilities are seen as dynamic rather than static, involving the ability to learn, adapt to changes in the environment, and innovate, and not simply to perform well given prevailing practice and conditions (see Winter 1988; Dosi, Teece, and Winter 1992; Teece and Pisano 1994). This new body of writings on firms is, of course, quite conformable with the new theorizing about cumulative technical advance, sketched above.

While there are signs lately that economists are paying more attention to firms (for example, Williamson 1985; Holmstrom and Tirole 1989), few yet seem able to see firms as the key actors in economic growth in the sense that Schumpeter did, or more recently Chandler. Chandler's theory of the growth of modern capitalism, particularly in the United States, stresses how firm strategies called for large-scale investments in plant and equipment, R & D, and the training of management. For the most part, these investments were made out of retained or forgone profits. (For a good summary of the Chandlerian theory, see Teece 1993.) Under Chandler's theory, the "immediate determinants of growth" are, as Abramovitz observed in his discussion of Schumpeter's growth theory, largely a function of "enterprise."

Of course, what firms do, and the technologies they employ and develop, are influenced to a considerable extent by the environment they are in. Economists are inclined to define the environment in terms of markets. In turn, behind markets are demanders of products and suppliers of inputs (who may be individuals or organizations like other firms), and their preferences, and the constraints they face.

However, in recent years at least some economists have become cognizant of aspects of the environment not really considered in the simple treatment. (In a way, the new awareness of institutions represents a renaissance of earlier thinking. For a discussion, see Hodgson 1988.) There is increasing recognition among economists that there are entities out there such as universities that do research that feeds into technical advance in industry, and whose teaching programs affect the supply of scientists and engineers; government agencies financing certain kinds of R & D, and others setting standards; banks and banking systems; and a variety of organizations and laws that affect labor supply and demand. Patent, regulatory, and liability law are part of the environment. And so are a variety of widely shared beliefs and values and customs that affect common expectations about what should be done, and what will be done, in a particular context.

This is an extraordinarily complex group of things, and it may be foolhardy to give a name to the collection. But as I have noted, many scholars have called them all "institutions."

One can question what is common about them. Some economists and other scholars have employed the language of game theory and attempted to define institutions as "the rules of the game" that, given the motivations of the players, constrain the way the "game" will be played (see, for example, North 1990, 1994). Other economists, stressing that many repeated games have multiple equilibria, have proposed that the concept of "institutions" needs to include not only the formal rules of the game (the "law"), but also the particular equilibrium or self-sustaining pattern of play that has evolved (the "custom"). Schotter (1981) was among the first to argue this way. The notion that institutions define both rules and customs seems to incorporate both statute and common law, and government policies, including the particular ways they have come to be enforced. More generally, it seems to fit the durable parts of "public environment" within which individual actions proceed, and which constrains and frames such actions.

It does not directly seem to fit the "organizations" in the environment, such as dominant firms, like IBM, and universities and banking systems. However, while, according to the definition above, particular organizations would not be considered as institutions, generally accepted forms of governance and structure of kinds of organizations might be. Thus, to the extent that either Harvard or the University at California is taken as a model of what a research university should be, and other universities model themselves on that, one can speak of research universities like Harvard or Berkeley as institutions. In this same sense, one can also see corporate forms widely prevalent in an economy as institutions, to the extent that there is a belief that these forms are right and appropriate (Williamson 1985).

While recently there has been a surge of interest among economists in economic institutions, in fact the interest is almost ancestral. Much of Adam Smith's *The Wealth of Nations* is about differences in institutional structures, and how these explain the different economic performances of nations. The new work examining the role of differences between the United States and Japan in financial institutions, and how these differences mold and support firm differences, is in fact a throwback to older forms of economic growth theory.

The orientation to the key factors driving economic growth developed thus far in this chapter would lead one to focus on national institutions supporting the technological and organizational capabilities of business firms. Thus historians like Landes (1970) have argued that an important reason why British industry did poorly in the new chemical products industries of the late nineteenth century, and performed very unevenly in the new electrical equipment industries, was the failure of British universities to develop strength in the teaching of science and engineering. A recent study (see Nelson 1993) compares the institutional structures supporting industrial technical advance in a number of different countries, and argues that differences in the systems explain a great deal about differences in national economic performance. Perez (1983) has argued that, for rapid growth to proceed, a nation's institutions must be tuned to the dominant technologies of the era.

But, of course, institutions are not constant. They do change, if perhaps slowly. The question of how they change would appear to be a fundamental challenge for growth theory. In the 1970s a few intrepid economists put forth the hypothesis that "institutions evolve optimally" (see, for example, Demsetz 1967, Davis and North 1971). Just how this was supposed to happen was, however, never set out. Since that time more modern economists have become aware again of major differences across nations in institutions—differences that seem to make a big difference—and thus are more aware that in some countries the processes that guide the evolution of institutions seem to be more effective than in other countries. They also have come to understand that these processes are very complex, and poorly understood (see, for example, North 1990, 1994; Nelson 1993).

In his 1952 article Abramovitz flagged broad national institutions, either supporting or constraining industry, as something economists need to understand if they are to understand growth, and as a topic whose exploration will require them to step over the traditional boundaries of their discipline. In my view, getting a good intellectual grip on institutions is going to be harder than achieving a better model of technological change, or of firm capabilities and their dynamics, simply because "institutions" are so diffuse. But, as Abramovitz said more than fifty years ago, if we are to understand growth we will somehow have to understand institutions. Several of the following chapters are aimed to advance our understanding of institutions and institutional change.

4. An Agenda for Growth Theory

Understanding economic growth better surely should be a top priority for economic research. There is so much that we do not understand. The slowdown in growth in the United States and in Europe after the 1960s remains something of a puzzle, as does the reason for the sharp increase in growth rates in the mid-1990s. The notion that technological advance comes in the form of long waves is interesting, but we have only the beginning of an understanding of why this might be so. Nor do we have a solid understanding of why certain nations take the technological lead in certain eras, or why other nations, with a lag, catch up rapidly. And the appreciative theoretic understanding of why, for example, the United States became the leader in the surging information technologies and biotechnologies that accelerated growth in the 1990s has no place in standard formal growth theories. Neither does our appreciative understanding of why Japan moved from the bottom of the pack of advanced industrial nations in the early 1960s to close to the top by 1990. The extremely uneven performance among nations that were very poor as of 1960 remains a nagging puzzle. Some, like Korea and Taiwan, have grown rapidly and seem to be becoming sophisticated industrial powers. The less-developed nations that have not had that successful experience naturally look to Korea and Taiwan, but it is not clear exactly what went on in those economies that others can readily imitate. And while some economists view the future of the ex-communist economies optimistically, these economies continue to struggle to find the secret of rapid catch-up to the frontiers.

The surge of writing called "the new growth theory" reflects the growing awareness among economists that much about economic growth remains a puzzle. Some of the new models have effectively incorporated a number of the understandings about growth, and particularly about technical advance, that have been gained over the years by those doing empirical research. This is at once a gain for the formal modeling part of the research enterprise and a gain for the appreciative theorizing part, enriching the former and bringing new rigor to sharpen the insights of the latter.

At the same time, as I have stressed in the foregoing discussion, the new formal growth models, like the earlier ones, focus on "immediate sources of growth" and, to some extent, the factors just behind them. While they may give new life and power to exploration of these variables and their contribution to growth, there are strong reasons to believe that many of the important insights that can be gained by exploring in this vein have been mined, and the returns are much higher from research that looks at the factors further behind the immediate sources.

And I am concerned that the goal of formalization per se focuses efforts on understandings that are relatively easy to formalize, or on formalizations of those understandings that are relatively easy but that miss or deform important parts of the understandings. Earlier I referred to the treatment in the new formal growth models of uncertainty in technological advance as if it were calculable risk. It is evident, I believe, that the failure of the new neoclassical growth theory to open up the formal treatment of firms, or even to try to take on board institutions, reflects the fact that these things are not easy to treat formally. This is especially so if the formal modeling is constrained by the canons of general equilibrium theory.

It is interesting that most of the formal theorizing that has interacted creatively with appreciative theorizing in the domains I have tried to highlight has stood outside the arenas that have been incorporated in the new neoclassical growth theory. Thus the recent work of Milgrom and Roberts (1990) formalizes intuitions that appreciative theorists have identified regarding the implications of strong complementarities in firm practice. Recognition by game theorists of multiple equilibria and the sensitivity of the equilibrium reached to the vagaries of the dynamic time paths has certainly clarified the thinking about institutional evolution by scholars like North. (A good survey review along these lines that is quite consistent with North's point of view is Sugden 1989.) And, of course, there has developed an extensive body of formal evolutionary modeling of technological advance that has been expressly motivated by the appreciative theorizing of empirical scholars of the subject. Chapter 3 reviews this literature.

But the interaction between formal and appreciative theorizing on the key topics on my agenda has been limited. This has been a problem not only because the former has not given much help to the latter. Perhaps more important, because most of the appreciative theory emanating from research along these lines has so little contact with formal theory, the broad economics community tends not to see this work and, when it does, to consider it "atheoretical." This discourages young scholars from working along these lines.

I am virtually certain that useful formalization in these areas will require not only the treatment of variables and relationships that have seldom been considered in standard neoclassical theory, but also a breaking away from the canons of standard equilibrium theorizing. The constraining nature of these canons is revealed sharply by the attempts in models bound by them to treat the uncertainties involved in economic growth driven by technological advance as risk. The "rationality" of the actors facing Knightian uncertainty has to be modeled as a "bounded rationality." Such a formulation seems absolutely necessary if formal theory is to make better contact with what empirical scholars know about technological change, and to deal in a nonmechanical way with the fact that firms do differ in their strategies and the bets they lay, and not simply in their fortunes. Institutions need to be understood as strongly constraining the realm of rational choice by defining rather closely which actions are appropriate. They cut down on the need for conscious decision making. I survey this body of analysis in Chapter 5.

There are no particular analytic problems involved in formal specification of behavior that is boundedly rational, nor do economists need to learn new mathematics to treat systems that may not be in equilibrium. The tethers here are a particular set of methodological prejudices that need to be recognized as such and perhaps as getting in the way of fruitful formal modeling. In my view, although I confess to not being unbiased, formal evolutionary models have amply proved their ability to generate, hence to explain, the macroeconomic paths of output and inputs that traditionally have been treated as what a growth theory needs to explain, and at the same time are consistent with many of the microeconomic patterns and processes that scholars of technological advance have documented.

However, formal evolutionary growth models have been no better than neoclassical ones in taking on board the characteristics of the key institutions that certainly lie behind the parameters assumed or estimated in these models. The key intellectual challenge to formal growth theory—whether the basic dynamic structure be evolutionary or neoclassical—lies, I believe, in learning how formally to model entities that are not easily reduced to a set of numbers, like the character of a nation's education or financial system, or the prevalent philosophies of management. But the gains here certainly seem to warrant the effort.

More than fifty years ago Abramovitz flagged technical advance, the role of enterprise, and the broader cultural and institutional factors surrounding and supporting enterprise, as the factors behind the "immediate" sources of growth, and said that understanding all three was a challenge. It still is. Appreciative theorizing for some time has been struggling with questions about technology and technical advance, and recently has begun to focus on firms. Appreciative theorizing about institutions is experiencing a welcome renaissance. But if my arguments about the relationships between appreciative theorizing and formal theorizing are correct, to be fully effective appreciative theorizing needs help from formal theorizing. To provide that help, however, requires that formal theory try to break some new ground, and shake loose from conventional constraints. A principal purpose of this chapter has been to inform formal growth theorists where the most interesting and promising research on growth is located, in the hope of luring some to where the action is.

CHAPTER 2

The Asian Miracle
and Modern Growth Theory

1. Different Theories of Economic Development

The debate about how to explain the "Asian miracle" puts a spotlight on a more general theoretical debate about how to explain long-run economic growth. The broader debate is between theorists who, in effect, attempt to explain economic growth in a way that is consistent with the canons of general equilibrium theory, and theorists who argue that growth must be understood as an evolutionary process driven by technological advance. The former case is, of course, familiar; see Romer (1990) for a strong statement. The latter was articulated in Nelson and Winter (1982), and is in the spirit of Schumpeter's well-known criticism of equilibrium theory as a vehicle for understanding economic growth.

The focus of this chapter is not on the general debate but on its particular manifestation in explaining the Asian miracle. Between the 1960s and the 1990s, Korea, Taiwan, Singapore, and Hong Kong transformed themselves from technologically backward and poor to relatively modern and affluent economies. Each has experienced a more than fourfold increase in per capita income, and each now has a significant collection of firms producing technologically complex products and competing effectively against rival firms based in the United States, Japan, and Europe. The growth performance of these

---

* Based on Richard R. Nelson and Howard Pack, "The Asian Miracle and Modern Growth Theory," *Economic Journal* 109 (1999): 416–436.

countries has vastly exceeded those of virtually all other economies that had comparable productivities and income levels in 1960. On these grounds alone, the question of how they did it is obviously of enormous scientific and policy importance.

It has been less well noted that their growth has been unprecedented historically. The development of Japan in the half century after the Meiji Restoration is widely regarded as being comparable. However, Japan's growth rate over this period was less than half that of the Asian newly industrialized countries (NICs) since 1960. Of course, growth rates in general were slower during this earlier period. But the rate of catch-up by the NICs is still remarkable. It certainly would seem that there is an "Asian miracle" crying out for explanation.

Of course, economists have not been blind to or unattracted by the challenge. Over the 1980s and 1990s a number of theories have been put forward purporting to explain the phenomenon (see Westphal, Kim, and Dahlman 1985; Pack and Westphal 1986; Amsden 1989; World Bank 1993; Young 1995; Kim and Lau 1994; Krugman 1994; Rodrik 1994). There is unanimity among the different theories regarding the identity of some of the key causal factors. All the Asian NICs have experienced rapid growth in their physical capital stock. All have been marked by very high rates of investment in human capital. Virtually all theories about how they did it place these investments at center stage in the explanation.

However, there are significant differences in the causal mechanisms stressed. At the risk of doing some violence to the actual diversity, for our purposes we find it useful to divide up theories of the Asian miracle into two groups. One group, which we shall call "accumulation" theories, stresses the role of these investments in moving these economies "along their production functions." The other group, which we call "assimilation" theories, stresses the entrepreneurship, innovation, and learning that these economies had to go through before they could master the new technologies they were adopting from the more advanced industrial nations; it sees investment in human and physical capital as a necessary but far from sufficient part of the assimilation process.

The accumulation theory has been pushed hard by several economists, in a way clearly designed to strip away most of the "miraculous" from the "Asian miracle." They say that what lies behind rapid development is, simply, very high investment rates. Economists who support this point of view do not deny that the adoption and mastery of new technology and other modern practices was an important part of the story. Rather, their position is that one should try to explain as much as one can in terms of investments that enable movement along a production function, and then see if anything much is left over that requires an explanation on other grounds. Several economists who have followed this path find that, according to their calculations, the lion's share of increased output per worker can be explained simply by increases in physical and human capital per worker. Thus there is little need to assign much of the credit for the growth "miracle" to entrepreneurship, innovation, or learning, except insofar as these are terms given to the shift to more capital- and education-intensive methods of production (see Young 1995, Kim and Lau 1994, Krugman 1994).

To assimilation theorists, this point of view seems odd. The technologies that the NICs came to master progressively during the 1970s and 1980s were ones with which, in 1960, they had no experience at all. To learn to use them effectively required the development of new sets of skills, new ways of organizing economic activity, and familiarity with and competency in new markets. To do this was far from a routine matter; it involved risk-taking entrepreneurship as well as good management (see Pack and Westphal 1986, Amsden 1989). What makes the Asian miracle miraculous is that these countries did these things so well, while other countries were much less successful. To be sure, adopting the technologies of the advanced countries required, among other things, high rates of investment in physical and human capital, and the NICs achieved these high rates. But to say that these investments simply enabled the economies to "move along their production functions" seems a strange use of language. At the least, it poses the question of just what is meant by "moving along a production function."

Are we drawing a distinction without a real difference? We do not think so. The accumulation account stresses, simply, investments. The message is that other countries could have done as well as the successful NICs if they had made a similar investment effort. If a nation makes the investments and marshals the resources, development will follow. In contrast, the assimilation account stresses learning about, risking to operate, and coming to master technologies and other practices that are new to a country, if not to the world. The marshaling of inputs is part of the story, but the emphasis is on innovation and learning, rather than on marshaling. Under this view, if one marshals but does not innovate and learn, development does not follow.

A convinced accumulationist might respond by saying that, if one educates the people and provides them with modern equipment to work with, they will learn. An assimilationist might respond that the Soviet Union and the Eastern European communist economies took exactly that point of view, made the investments, and didn't learn. There is nothing automatic about the learning business. The response of the accumulationist might be that the old communist countries provided an economic environment in which there was no incentive to learn to be efficient, either in a technological or an economic sense, much less to innovate. The assimilation theorist might agree, but then propose that it is important to understand, therefore, just how the successful NICs did it. The accumulationist would reply that they got the prices right and made the necessary public investments. Economists who stress entrepreneurship, innovation, and learning would reply that it is not all that simple, and point to countries such as Spain that have had high investment rates, and have got most of the prices right, but that are developing at far lower rates than the Asian NICs.

The difference between the theories shows up strikingly in the way they treat the following four matters: what is involved in entrepreneurial decision making, the nature of technology, the economic capabilities lent by a well-educated workforce, and the role that exporting plays in rapid development.

Accumulationists pay little explicit attention to firms, seeing their behavior as being determined basically by the environment—the incentives and constraints—they face, which determines the actions that are most profitable. Assimilation theorists, on the other hand, see entrepreneurial firms, and their ability to learn rapidly, as a critical factor behind the success of Korea and Taiwan, with their behavior supported by their environments but only partially determined by external forces (see Hobday 1995, Kim 1997). For an assimilation theorist, at least our brand, when firms contemplate venturing onto ground that is new to them, the profitability of such venturing is highly uncertain, in the sense of Knight. Some firm managers will dare to venture; others will choose to stick close to the familiar. Thus, what firms do is determined by the daring of their decision makers, as well as by their environment. And whether an entrepreneurial venture will succeed or fail is also only partly determined by environmental factors. It depends, as well, on the zeal, smartness, and learning abilities of firms' management and workers.

Part of the difference here resides in how the different theories see technology. Accumulationists seem to believe that the state of technological knowledge at any time is largely codified in blueprints and associated documents, and that adopting a technology that is new to a firm, but not to the world, primarily involves getting access to those blueprints. In contrast, assimilationists argue that only a small portion of what one needs to know to employ a technology is codified in the form of blueprints; much of it is tacit, and learning is achieved as much by doing and using as by reading and studying (see Nelson and Winter 1982, Rosenberg 1982b). Further, while many economists believe that technology is defined in terms of engineering and physical science, in fact the lines between the engineering aspects of technology and the organizational aspects are blurred, and controlling a technology often involves knowing how to manage a very complex division of labor as much as it involves knowing the relevant physics and chemistry.

Both of these differences show up in terms of how the two theories go about explaining the fact that the NICs were able to increase greatly and rapidly their capital-labor ratios (by more than fourfold over the years in question) without experiencing a significant decline in the rate of return to capital. The accumulationist would tend to invoke the concept of the elasticity of substitution, which refers to innate technological opportunities, and propose that the phenomenon in question indicates that the elasticity of substitution was high. The assimilationist, on the other hand, would argue that there is no such thing as a set of technological possibilities that can be defined independently of decision makers' ability to search out, see, and effectively take on board new technology. That is, what the accumulationist would explain in terms of the nature of the parameters of a conventionally defined production function, an assimilationist would explain in terms of skillful entrepreneurship and learning.

Along the same lines, the two theories also differ regarding how they see the effects of the rapidly rising education levels in these countries. For the accumulationist, rising human capital is treated simply as an increase in the quality or effectiveness of labor. Assimilationists, on the other hand, tend to see the effects of sharply rising educational attainments, in particular the creation by these countries of a growing cadre of reasonably well-trained engineers and applied scientists, in ways similar to that sketched out many years ago by Nelson and Phelps (1966). A good technical education facilitates seeing new opportunities and effectively learning new things. Thus the growing human capital of the NICs was a very important support for successful entrepreneurship.

The difference between the two theories also shows up sharply in how they treat the strong export performance of the NIC manufacturing firms. The accumulationists tend to see the steep rise in manufacturing exports as just what one would expect in economies where the stocks of physical and human capital were rising rapidly, and were shifting comparative advantage toward the sectors that employed these inputs intensively. From this perspective, there is nothing noteworthy about the surge of manufacturing exports, save that it is evidence that the economic policies of these countries let comparative advantage work its ways. In contrast, the assimilationists, while not denying that the NICs were building a comparative advantage in various fields of manufacturing, tend to highlight the active efforts by government to induce—almost force—firms to try to export, and the entrepreneurship, innovation, and learning the firms had to do to compete effectively in world markets, even with government support.

Several economists of the assimilation school have argued that exporting stimulated and supported strong learning in two ways (see Pack and Westphal 1986, Pack 1987). First, being forced to compete in world markets made the managers and engineers in the firms pay close attention to world standards. Second, much of the exporting involved contracting with American or Japanese firms that demanded high performance and provided assistance to achieve it. The story here is clearly different from one that sees the development of these new competencies as simply the more-or-less automatic result of changing factor availabilities that called them into being.

We have noted that the assimilationist's position (at least the one we espouse) sees the high rates of investment by the NICs in physical and human capital as a necessary, if not a sufficient, component of the assimilation process. These high rates themselves are remarkable, even if not miraculous. Under the argument of the assimilationists, these investments were at least partially induced by, and sustained by, the rapid innovation and learning that was going on.

Successful entrepreneurship in the NICs was certainly facilitated by the growing supply of well-trained technical people. On the other hand, it was not automatic that newly trained engineers would find work in entrepreneurial firms. There had to be entrepreneurial firms in which to work, or the opportunity to start new ones. Thus aggressive entrepreneurship supported and encouraged rapidly rising educational attainment.

The successful manufacture of new products almost always requires that firms acquire new physical capital. There is no question that policies in these countries encouraged saving. But what made saving and investment profitable was the strong and effective innovative performance of the firms that were entering new lines of business.

We think it is apparent that the two broad theories differ both in their causal structures and in the hints they give about "how to do it." The emphasis of the accumulationists is on getting investment rates up and prices right. The message of the assimilation theorists is that successful industrial development requires innovation and learning to master modern technologies; effective innovation and learning depend on investment and a market environment that presses for efficient allocations, but they also involve much more. And, indeed, to a considerable extent, the investment needed is induced by successful entrepreneurship.

Section 2 of this chapter considers the argument that careful attention to the numbers and rigorous calculation support the accumulationist theory, and that there is little evidence that innovation and learning played much of a role. We argue that the commonly used calculations do not do what their proponents claim. In Section 3, we propose a different way to discriminate between a change in output accompanied by changes in inputs that can be considered simply "a movement along the production function," and a change that seems to involve innovation and learning. In the light of the argument we develop there, in Section 4 we consider the evidence. We propose that that evidence supports strongly the assimilationist's case. Section 5 considers in what ways the differences between the two theories matter.

2. Why the Standard Calculations Do Not Discriminate

The case put forward by proponents of the accumulationist theory is based on calculations of two kinds. One is a growth accounting. The other involves fitting a dynamic production function. In both methods, the strategy is, basically, to try to calculate the effect of input growth on output growth, holding the production function constant, and then to see (under growth accounting) if anything much is left over as a "residual," or (under production-function fitting) whether the passage of time itself seems to contribute to output growth over and above what is explained by input growth over time. We argue here that, contrary to widespread views in economics, neither kind of calculation can separate out growth that "would have occurred without technical advance" from growth that involved technical advance.

Often it is not recognized adequately that the simple logic of growth accounting is applicable to the analysis of only small changes in inputs and outputs (see Nelson 1973). The procedure basically involves making estimates of the marginal productivities (or output partial elasticities) of the various inputs that have changed and, in effect, using these to calculate the contribution of input expansion to output growth by using a first-order Taylor series. However, in the case of the Asian Tigers, the investments whose contribution to growth is being estimated have cumulatively been very large. While repressed by the format of growth accounting, which usually sets up the calculations in terms of average yearly changes and thus makes the changes appear relatively small, in the countries in question capital per worker increased more than four times after the 1960s, and years of average educational attainment also increased greatly.

The calculations in standard growth accounting take marginal productivities as estimated by factor prices (or output elasticities as estimated by factor shares) as being exogenous. But under the assumptions of neoclassical production function theory (which lie behind the growth accounting logic), large finite changes in inputs can lead to large finite changes in marginal productivities. For this reason, the factor prices (or factor shares) that are treated as being exogenous in growth accounting need to be understood as endogenous. Thus a growth accounting of the standard sort does not provide a way to calculate growth that would have occurred had there been no technical advance, if input changes are large. Sustained high marginal productivities (output elasticities) of the most rapidly growing factors, which lead a growth accountant to propose that most of the growth is explained by their expansion, could be largely the result of the fact that technical advance offset the diminishing returns that otherwise would have set in.

We know that, in the countries in question, despite the large changes in their quantities, the rates of return on physical capital and on education stayed high. We noted earlier that one explanation is that technologically determined elasticities of substitution, in the sense of standard production function theory, were quite high, and thus significant increases in these inputs relative to others had only a modest effect on marginal productivities as the economy moved along its ex ante production function. Under this explanation, a good share of output increase would indeed have occurred without any technical advance. This seems to be the implicit argument of the proponents of the accumulation theory. However, another explanation is that the elasticities of substitution, defined in the standard way, were quite low, and that only the rapid taking on board of new technologies prevented the sharply diminishing returns that one would have observed had these economies stayed with the production functions that existed at the start of the development traverse.

Consider the latter explanation, which we believe is the correct one. Under it, innovation and rapid learning are driving growth. However, a growth accounting of a standard sort might show a very small residual, or even a negative one. The factor shares of the more rapidly growing factors—physical and human capital—would be, and would remain, high, as a consequence of the rapid learning that made their continued expansion productive. These investments themselves would be and would remain high because rapid technical advance kept their returns high. Thus a growth accounting might "attribute" the lion's share of output growth to input growth. There would be little left to explain in terms of innovation and learning, despite the fact that these are the basic factors driving growth.

The use by some scholars of the Tornqvist index for the weights applied to input increases represents acknowledgment that, if one is interested in the impact on output of finite changes of inputs along a production function, output elasticities can change along the way. But the use of such an index (as in Young 1995) does not deal with the problem highlighted here. The index uses actual shares, at the end as well as the beginning of the period. But the actual shares at the end of the period can be, and in the case in question almost surely were, affected by the technological changes that occurred over the period. In general, they are not what the shares would have been at the new input quantities, had the production function stayed constant over the traverse.

We want to underline this point because many economists seem to believe that the absence of a large residual in growth accounting is strong evidence that the lion's share of growth resulted from movements along a prevailing production function. This is not so if the input changes involved are large. Growth accounting alone cannot tell whether the relevant elasticities of substitution were large or small, and thus cannot distinguish between the two stories sketched above about the sources of growth. There is an "identification" problem.

One might think that the fitting of a dynamic production function can avoid this logical limitation of growth accounting, when input changes are large and finite. However, in practice, the identification problem cannot be resolved in this way.

Thus, consider the two explanations depicted in Figure 2.1 for a large increase in output per worker, between time one and time two, associated with a large increase in capital per worker. In each picture, point 1 refers to output per worker and capital per worker in time one, and point 2 refers to these variables in time two.

In the explanation on the left, much of the experienced labor productivity increase would have occurred even had the economy stayed with its production function of period one (the curve that goes through point 1). The way the production function is drawn depicts only a weak diminishing return to increasing capital intensity. The firm or economy in question is presumed to know, at time one, how to operate effectively at much higher capital intensities than were employed then, but chooses not to do so because prevailing factor availabilities made it necessary to operate at low capital intensity. Between

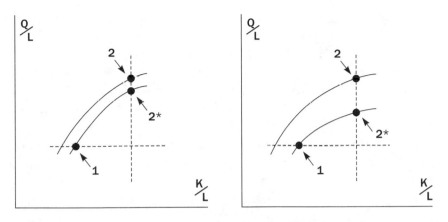

Figure 2.1 Movements of the production function (Q/L = product per worker; K/L = capital per worker).

time one and time two, factor availabilities changed. Had the production function not changed at all, output per worker would have increased to the level denoted by point 2* simply because of the employment of more capital per worker. In fact output per worker increased more than that because the production function shifted (to the curve through point 2), but not very much more.

In contrast, in the explanation on the right, very little productivity growth would have occurred had the economy remained with its old production function and simply increased capital intensity. Output per worker at point 2* is significantly below output per worker at point 2. A large share of the productivity increase, therefore, must have been accounted for by a shift in the production function.

Both explanations (the one on the left and the one on the right) fit the data at time one and two. The "levels" and the "slopes" of the old production functions are the same at time one, and the levels and slopes of the new production functions are the same at time two. This point was highlighted by Diamond, Macfadden, and Rodriguez (1972), and Nelson (1973), more than thirty years ago. It seems to have been forgotten.

When one fits a dynamic production function statistically (through many rather than just two points and slopes), how does one discriminate between these two explanations? Obviously, one needs to place some restrictions on the form fitted (for example, that the rate and direction of technical advance be constants over the period, or that the underlying production function must always have a particular "kind of general shape"). Most of the econometric exercises we are concerned with here have imposed relatively loose restrictions, although sufficient to enable a best fitting equation to be calculated. However, even if an equation that looks like the left-side explanation in Figure 2.1 wins the "maximum likelihood" contest (as in Kim and Lau 1994), if the constraints on functional form are relatively loose, it is a good bet that an equation that looks like the right-side explanation is not very far behind. Standard regression techniques of the sort that have been employed do not enable confident acceptance of one explanation and rejection of the other.

The graphs drawn in Figure 2.1 are in fact constructed from regressions estimated from the actual data for Korea's manufacturing sector for the years 1962 to 1991. The dynamic production function fitted to the data is a standard constant elasticity of substitution (CES) production function, with two inputs—capital and labor—and constant returns to scale. To keep the analysis simple and transparent, we constrained technological advance to be neutral and constant over the period in question. The key parameters to be estimated are r, the rate of technological progress, and e, the elasticity of substitution.

In the graph on the left we forced e to be large, 0.9. Since growth of capital per worker (K/L) then "explains" a lot of the growth of gross product per worker (Q/L), the estimated rate of technological change, r, comes out low, 0.16. (For regression runs in which we set e as greater than one, the estimated rate of technological change was even smaller, and for large values of e, it came close to zero.) In the graph on the right, we constrained e to be low, 0.2. Since under this constraint the growth of K/L cannot "explain" much of the growth of Q/L, the estimated rate of technological progress, r, came out high, 0.045. Both of these regressions, and one in which all parameters were chosen by least squares, yield values of R^2 of 0.99, leaving little to choose among the regressions on a statistical basis.

Again, we want to underline the point. The fact that the best fit of a dynamic function provides an explanation for growth in which technological advance plays a small role, and input growth accounts for the lion's share of growth, does not itself provide strong evidence against the argument that, in fact, growth would have been far less if there had not been significant technological advance. Only the imposition of particular constraints on the dynamic production function enables econometric techniques to choose between the explanation on the left and the one on the right in Figure 2.1. These constraints are basically arbitrary. And the imposition of somewhat different ones can change radically the estimated contribution of technical advance in the attribution.

The authors in question certainly have been careful with their data, and in the use of their methods. The problem is that the methods employed just do not do the job they are thought to do. Nor, at this stage of our argument, are we introducing new data, although we agree that the issue is an empirical one. Before considering new evidence, it would seem important to do some rethinking about the kind of data that would discriminate between growth where entrepreneurship, innovation, and learning were central, and growth where they were not.

3. Back to Basics

How is one to decide between two different explanations, each broadly compatible with the macroeconomic data, when one explanation stresses "movements along a production function" and the other emphasizes "entrepreneurship, innovation, and learning"? We propose that, to get an empirical answer, one must first ask some conceptual questions. What might one mean when one says that an observed change in inputs and outputs simply reflects a move along a production function? What might one mean if one argued it was not that simple, but that entrepreneurship and innovation were in fact involved? If we agreed on answers to these conceptual questions, we might be able to agree on what kind of empirical evidence would be relevant.

Regarding what we economists seem to mean by a move along the production function, reflect on the simple treatment in undergraduate microeconomics texts. The production function, there, is said to be the "efficiency frontier" of the "production set"—the set of all input-output combinations from among which a firm can choose. One way of explaining the set to students is to say that a firm "knows" a certain set of production techniques or activities, and the production set is generated by different levels and mixes of those activities. In any case, the firm is viewed as both "knowing about" each of the alternatives, and "knowing how" to do whatever is associated with achieving the input-output vector associated with each.

The verbal articulation may admit that there might be modest set-up costs associated with marshaling and organizing to shift operations to a point within the set that is different from what the firm is doing currently, and that some adjustments (another form of set-up cost) might be required to get the new choice operating smoothly, although these shift costs are generally repressed in the formal modeling. However, it seems inconsistent with the "operating within the production set" idea if the set-up costs for shifting to a new point involves doing a lot of exploratory "search and study" to identify and get a better feel for alternatives that, up to then, had been unfamiliar to the firm, and the "adjustment" involved a lot of trial-error-try-again learning by doing and using. At least it would seem inconsistent if the results of searching and learning were highly uncertain, both to the firm ex ante and to an economist trying to predict what the results would be.

Of course, a plausible interpretation of the production set idea might admit a certain amount of statistical uncertainty regarding inputs and outputs, particularly if there were unknowable outside forces, such as the amount of rainfall, that had a bearing on the process. But if the decision maker in question has only very rough ideas about the consequences of trying to do something, and initially about how to do it, that something does not seem to be an activity that can be regarded as within the unit's production choice set. The production set of a firm would appear to be limited at any time to those things the firm knows about and knows how to do with confidence and skill. At least, that is how economists implicitly define the concept.

On the other hand, a move that involves a lot of study of initially hazy alternatives, or R & D where even the nature of the outcome is not clear in advance, would, according to these criteria, be regarded as a "technological" change or "innovation" for the firm in question. We do not see how such a move possibly can be regarded as one "along a prevailing production function," if economists adhere to what they teach about the meaning of choice sets.

We call attention to the fact that, under the way we are proposing the distinction be drawn, a firm's production set in principle could be very extensive. Indeed, much of what some versions of the new neoclassical growth theory treat as technological advance would, under the principles suggested here, be regarded as moves along a firm's prevailing production function. In these models (see Romer 1990), investments in R & D are strictly up-front costs required to make a product or technique operational. But in these models (if not in fact) R & D is strictly a set-up cost to make an activity the firm always knew about available for use. There are no Knightian uncertainties involved.

However, once we get away from particular abstract models, most economists who have studied the processes empirically understand that the introduction into the economy of products or processes significantly different from any employed before does not look like a move along a prevailing production function. It is well documented empirically that, while theoretical engineering calculations at any time encompass a wide range of techniques not yet brought to practice, the bringing to practice of new technology invariably involves up-front research and development costs, with Knightian uncertainties at least early in the process (see Nelson and Winter 1982, and Rosenberg 1996). While R & D can resolve some of these uncertainties, there are uncertainties in the R & D process itself. Further, even after R & D there almost always are "bugs" at the start, and it usually takes some time before the operation is really under control. In many cases, the attempts at innovating prove to be unprofitable and need to be abandoned, or radically revised.

Of course, in this chapter we are dealing with the adoption of technologies that, while new to the firm or country, are not new to the world. The issue, then, is whether such changes in the behavior and performance of firms in the NICs can be explained meaningfully as changed choices within largely unchanging choice sets.

The accumulationists clearly have in mind that, if a technology is in effective use in one country, there are methods that firms in other countries can use to take on board that technology at relatively low cost, and without significant uncertainties regarding the outcome of their efforts. Quite often, detailed descriptions are available. Consultants can be hired who are familiar with the practices involved. In many cases, assistance can be gained from the firms who are operating the technology, although some license fees may be required.

The assimilationist, in contrast, is skeptical about easy "technology transfer." To be sure, for many of the technologies that the firms in the NICs adopted, there were available engineering texts, articles, and so on. Blueprints and specific handbooks could often be obtained. There were many consultants for hire.

However, the assimilationist would stress that such a move invariably involves not only up-front costs of identifying, learning about, and learning to master the technique in question, but also significant uncertainties. The range of options is hazy. Things often do not work out as expected. Consultants can seldom guarantee success. Inevitably there is a lot of learning by doing and using. The costs, and the uncertainties, are greater the further the technique being adopted is from those the firm has in fact employed. In many cases, major changes in firm organization may be required. The firm may need to learn to sense new markets. Firms attempting these changes can and often do fail. Those that succeed do so because they learn to do things successfully that they simply could not do before; that is, they succeed by expanding their production sets.

4. What Does the Evidence Indicate?

We can return now to the question of what kind of evidence one would need to determine whether an observed change was within a prevailing capability or choice set, or required an expansion of the set of things the organizations in question knew how to do. In the previous section we argued that the standard data and techniques for deciding simply do not do the job. We propose here that the kind of evidence that is relevant involves examination of process, not simply time paths of inputs and outputs, and that the persuasive data are to be found at a quite low level of aggregation.

A major problem with highly aggregated economic data is that it masks the magnitude and even the nature of the allocational changes going on. Thus, earlier, we noted that in the 1990s Korean and Taiwanese manufacturing firms were heavily engaged in producing products that in the 1960s they were not producing at all. This is illustrated strikingly by Table 2.1 for Taiwan. In particular, note Taiwan's production of electronic goods, which by the late 1980s accounted for roughly 21 percent of Taiwanese manufacturing exports. In 1960 virtually no electronic goods were produced in Taiwan. Such a change in the allocation of activity within the manufacturing sector almost certainly would be associated with considerable turnover of firms, with companies go-

Table 2.1. Changes in physical production levels of selected industrial products Taiwan, 1960–90

Product	1960	1990
Artificial fibers (million tons)	1,762	1,785,731
Polyvinyl chloride (million tons)	3,418	920,954
Steel bars (million tons)	200,528	11,071,999
Machine tools	0	755,597
Sewing machines	61,817	2,514,727
Electric fans	203,843	15,217,438
Television sets	0	3,703,000
Motorcycles	0	1,055,297
Telephones	0	1,055,297
Radios	0	5,892,881
Tape recorders	0	8,124,253
Electronic calculators	0	44,843,192
Integrated circuits (1,000s)	0	2,676,865
Electronic watches	0	5,115,695
Shipbuilding (tons)	27,051	1,211,607

Source: Taiwan Statistical Data Book (1992), Council for Economy Planning and Development, Republic of China, Taipei, table 5-6c.

ing out of business in the declining sectors, and new firms entering the expanding fields. And within the expanding areas one would expect to see a certain amount of turnover as some firms try and fail, while others succeed. Unfortunately, we do not have the firm turnover data that are directly relevant to the phenomena we are characterizing.

However, there are data on the number of firms of different sizes in Korea and Taiwan for several years, and a summary of these data is presented in Table 2.2. The pattern is roughly what one would expect under the assimilationist's story. There was a striking decline in the number of very small firms, most of which were probably locked into old technologies and producing traditional products, and a sharp rise in the number of middle-size or larger firms; we conjecture that a large share of these were new firms entering the new product fields, or older firms that succeeded in taking on board modern technology. In the early 1970s, the productivity of these larger firms was strikingly higher than that of the small firms they were replacing (according to the story we are proposing).

Table 2.2. Percentage distribution of employment by firm size

	Number of employees					
	4–9	10–19	20–49	50–99	100–499	500+
Taiwan						
1954	18	13	14	9	16	31
1961	18	10	14	8	17	34
1971	8	7	11	9	29	37
Index of value per worker, 1971		100	91	100	117	259
Korea						
1958	17	16	21	13	21	12
1963	15	14	16	12	21	22
1975	4	5	8	9	30	44
Index of value per worker, 1971		100	133	193	256	304

Source: Ho (1980), tables 3.1, D2, D3.

However, to get at the details of what was going on would seem to require the study of individual firms. Only by studying firms can one see just what was involved when they came to master new technologies and learn what was needed to operate in new product fields.

Happily, during the 1980s and 1990s several scholars developed detailed studies of Taiwanese and Korean manufacturing firms, tracing the sources of the firms' rapidly growing range of manufacturing competencies. Thus, Alice Amsden (1989) has provided a detailed history of a Korean textile firm, which describes what was going on over a period of time when it achieved very significant productivity gains. Table 2.3 shows what happened to machine and labor productivity during the decade after 1977, when it purchased most of its capital equipment. The reduction in worker hours per unit of output was considerable, particularly in spinning. Amsden explains the productivity growth in terms of active learning. Early in the period, its foreign equipment suppliers provided technical assistance. Later in the period it employed its own engineers to help it increase productivity. Note that, in 1986, while it had become much more efficient than it had been a decade earlier, its labor productivity was still lower than that in comparable plants in advanced industrial countries, a phenomenon not consistent with a move along a freely available international production function.

For our purposes, some of the most interesting sets of firm studies

Table 2.3. Learning in a Korean textile factory

	1977	1986	1986*
Labor productivity			
Ring spinning (kg per manhour)	52.4	78.5	156.25
Open-end spinning** (kg per manhour)	137.1	210.3	324.30
Weaving (meters per manhour)	216.2	224.1	360.36
Machine productivity			
Ring spinning (kg per spindle)	0.20	0.23	0.21
Open-end spinning** (kg per rotor)	0.91	1.26	1.11
Weaving (meters per loom)	36.1	35.4	39.8

Notes: * Relative to international best practice.

** Initial year is 1979.

Source: Cols. 1 and 2 adapted from Amsden (1989), table 10.4, Col. 3 calculated from col. 2 plus coefficients from Pack (1987), tables 3.1 and 3.2, and the calculations underlying those tables.

are those undertaken by Michael Hobday (1995) of Korean and Taiwanese electronics companies. Hobday describes in detail how these firms started out, usually producing quite simple products, and moved on progressively to more complex ones. In most of the cases Hobday studied, these new complex products were first made to order for foreign customers who, in the early stages, provided detailed engineering instructions and assistance. Gradually, however, many of the companies became able to do their own design work. In a number of cases they moved on to sell under their own brand label. Throughout the history of these firms, one can see them actively working to learn to do better the things they were doing and to be able to do more sophisticated and profitable things. In the early stages, this learning involved reverse engineering. As the companies began to do their own design work, this engineering effort began to be counted as R & D.

Linsu Kim (1997) provides a set of analyses of Korean firms, in several different industries, that show much the same phenomena as does Hobday's (1995) study. The firms started out using relatively unsophisticated technologies and learned, over the years, to master progressively more sophisticated ones. By the 1990s many of these firms were approaching the technological frontier. But the paths they took were not simple, and success never was guaranteed.

The story about the development of Korean and Taiwanese firms

Table 2.4. R & D and patenting activity in Taiwan

Year	R & D/GDP	Total patents	Taiwanese nationals' patents	Foreign patents
1981	0.95*	6,265	2,897	3,368
1986	0.98	10,526	5,800	4,726
1991	1.65**	27,281	13,555	13,726

* 1984.
** 1990.

Source: Taiwan Statistical Data Book (1992), tables 6.7, 6.8.

told by Amsden, Hobday, and Kim, is strikingly similar to that told by Odagiri and Goto (1997) in their study of how Japanese industry learned about and learned to master the technologies of the West in the years between the Meiji Restoration and the advent of the Second World War. They find that a major amount of searching, exploring, trying, failing, and learning was required before Japanese firms acquired proficiency in the Western technologies they were adopting and adapting. The decisions of company managers to adopt the new ways involved major uncertainties. Odagiri and Goto stress their entrepreneurial nature, and the innovation and learning involved. Our argument is that Korean and Taiwanese firms went through much the same process half a century later.

Table 2.4 shows the rise in accounted R & D and patenting by nationals in Taiwan. A similar progression—from engineering work focused largely on mastering and adapting foreign technology, to work on designs sufficiently new that the effort could legitimately be called R & D—occurred in Korea. And, of course, the same phenomenon occurred in Japan in the early postwar period.

To return to our basic analytical argument, we do not think that the industrial development of Korea and Taiwan since the 1950s, or of Japan a half century earlier (see Saxenhouse 1974, as well as Odagiri and Goto 1997), can be interpreted as moving along production functions, at least if that term connotes changing choices within a largely unchanging choice set. On the other hand, if the kind of entrepreneurship, innovation, and learning on the part of firms revealed in the case studies is considered to be perfectly consistent with the notion of moving along a production function, we do not know what that concept would exclude, and hence it becomes meaningless.

5. Do the Differences Matter, and If So, How?

The differences between the two theories would appear to matter for two different reasons. The first is, simply, regarding how one understands what happened. What lies behind the Asian miracle? The second is that the two theories might imply somewhat different things regarding appropriate economic development policy. What kinds of government policies are helpful, and what are the lessons for other countries?

It is apparent that, for many economists, one of the strongest attractions of the accumulation theory is that it is clean and simple, and its basic outlines conform with the general theory about economic activity that one finds in modern economics textbooks. It is at once delightfully iconoclastic, and comfortably conservative, to take the miraculous out of the Asian miracle by proposing that it all was a simple matter of moving along a production function. No appeal is needed to the idea of entrepreneurship or innovation, the sources of which might very well lie outside the effective province of neoclassical economics.

It also is clear that a major source of resistance to the assimilation theory is that it seems to be a complex theory that raises as many questions as it answers. This raises suspicions that the assimilation theory cannot be formulated cleanly. It is a comfort, therefore, that a simpler, more familiar theory seems capable of providing all the explanation needed.

And yet, what is at odds intellectually may be only a small part of the corpus of traditional economic theory. Moreover, that particular part, which proposes that production sets can be defined sharply and that there is a clear distinction between moving along the production function and having the production function shift, came into economics a relatively short time ago. Perhaps these particular conceptions are not needed for most standard economic arguments, and maybe they have been accepted too uncritically in any case.

A strong argument can be made that the assimilationists' perspective is quite consistent with an older set of ideas in economics. The idea that economic growth can be explained by increases in the factors of production, and by improvements in their productivity, goes back at least as far as John Stuart Mill. However, a striking feature of the earlier analyses of economic growth, as contrasted with the more contemporary treatments, is that there was no compulsion to make a sharp separation between the contributions of different sources of growth. For Adam Smith, increases in the size of the market, discoveries of better ways to perform a task, growing mechanization, and changing organization of work all go together. They would seem to also do so in Mill. The early post–Second World War growth accountants, in particular Moses Abramovitz, also stressed the interaction of technological advance, growing physical-capital intensity of production, increasing exploitation of scale economies, rising educational attainments, and changes in the organization of production as factors behind experienced economic growth. The question of which of these factors should be interpreted as moving the economy along a production function and which should be regarded as shifting it seems not to have been of major concern to these authors.

In the second section we argued that standard techniques do not permit a clear separation between movements along and shifts in the production function. Now we would like to argue that the very notion that one can make such clear splits, even in principle, may not be a useful theoretical premise.

In particular, we would like to argue that "innovation" in practice is a matter of degree, not kind, and that our growth theory ought to recognize this explicitly. For any firm or organization at any time, there are some activities that are under practiced control, some that are not so at present but seem easy to learn, others harder, and others at present impossible but perhaps with research and experimentation achievable over the long run. The problem with now-standard production theory is that it does not recognize these continuities, but rather presumes a sharp rift between the known and the unknown.

The case studies of firms, briefly discussed in the third section, show them moving from the known to the unknown, but cautiously, and drawing from the known as much as they can. Yesterday's unknown becomes today's known, and the firms venture further. An effective theory of what has been happening requires, we believe, abandonment of the notion that production sets at any time are sharply defined, and thus that there is a clear distinction between moving to another perceived point and innovation. Rather, there is a continuum.

If it is recognized explicitly that that distinction is in fact fuzzy, does it mean that this is a fuzzy theory? Not at all. One of the striking features of the various "evolutionary models" of economic growth that have been built since the 1980s is that, within them, innovation is treated as a matter of degree; firms move step by step into the unknown, and in so doing seldom move very far from the known.

Abandoning the sharp distinction between moving along a production function and innovation is clearly a big step analytically. Such a step involves placing learning and adaptation at center stage in the behavioral analysis, and relinquishing analytical techniques and arguments that presume that "profit maximization" is something that managers are in fact able to achieve, rather than something they strive for intelligently. Yet it is arguable that most of the important and useful propositions about the role of markets and competition depend on the latter rather than the former.

The notion that competition tends to force prices down toward costs, and to stimulate reform or elimination of high-cost producers, goes far back in economics. The argument does not depend on the existence of sharply defined production sets, or the achievement by firms of policies that maximize profits, given the full set of theoretical alternatives. It is intelligent striving that does the job. Similarly, the argument that a change in factor prices will induce behavior that economizes on the factor whose cost has risen does not require either sharply defined production functions or maximization, but only intelligent striving.

What are the policy implications of taking an assimilationist, or evolutionary, view on what happened in the Asian miracle? Are the policy prescriptions under an assimilationist theory fundamentally different from those under an accumulationist theory? In many ways, the policy prescriptions are in fact quite similar, although the reasons behind the arguments differ somewhat.

Both neoclassical and assimilationist theories put considerable weight on investments in human capital. By stressing the importance of innovation and learning, and the role of an educated workforce in these processes, the assimilationist might push even harder on the education front than would a modern neoclassical economist.

No disagreement exists on the importance of investment in physical capital. However, the assimilationist would highlight the role of such investments as a vehicle for taking aboard more modern technologies, and would stress that, if capital formation is not linked to effective entrepreneurship, the returns to investment are almost certain to diminish greatly after a point. On the other hand, the assimilationist would point to effective entrepreneurship as a key vehicle for keeping investment rates of return high, and would put less emphasis on simply trying to lift up the savings rate.

Both theories stress the importance of exporting. However, here too the reasons for the emphasis are somewhat different. The assimilationist sees exporting as an extremely important vehicle for learning, as well as a way of exploiting evolving comparative advantage. Thus the assimilation theorist might be especially strong on the importance of exporting, and willing to bias the incentive system to induce firms to try to export.

Both theories stress the essential role of private enterprise, profit incentives, and an environment that stimulates managers to make decisions that enhance economic development. A neoclassicist would focus on getting the prices right and making necessary public infrastructure investments. The assimilationist would take a somewhat more complex line on both of these matters. In particular, an assimilationist might stress the role of government funding and organization in building up a national scientific and technological infrastructure from which firms can draw assistance. But under both theories, it is the energy of private enterprise that is key, and under both there is deep skepticism about the value of detailed government planning.

Both neoclassical and evolutionary theorists stress the great importance of competition. However, here too the reasons differ somewhat, with the proponents of evolutionary theory pushing competition, especially in contexts where innovation is both important and risky. From this point of view, competition is valuable largely because choice sets are not clear, or not clearly defined, and it is highly valuable, therefore, to try a lot of things.

So, the policy differences between the theories may be significantly smaller than the conceptual or analytical differences. This should not be a surprise. Economists were stressing the importance of profit incentives, and competition, and the dangers of government planning, long before the idea of a sharply defined production set came into fashion. Indeed, one can find these basic arguments in Adam Smith's *Wealth of Nations*.

PART II

If one considers the curricula for doctoral students at top-rated economics departments, or browses through the articles in the most prestigious economics journals, one surely comes away with a strong impression that, today, neoclassical economics is dominant in the discipline. Evolutionary conceptions are hardly mentioned, at least not explicitly. And yet, these first impressions are somewhat misleading. There is a long and honorable tradition of evolutionary theorizing in economics. And after a relatively long dormant period, there are signs that evolutionary economics is coming to life again.

From the beginnings of the modern discipline up until recently, economists have tended to understand economic processes as dynamic, developmental, and historical. In the introduction to this volume, I noted the implicit evolutionary theorizing of Adam Smith, and of Karl Marx. Alfred Marshall, who generally is considered to be a founding father of neoclassical economics, was an evolutionary theorist, both implicitly and explicitly. While he was uncomfortable with analogies to biological evolution, Joseph Schumpeter also clearly was an evolutionary theorist; consider his articulation of the concept of "creative destruction." Friedrich Hayek espoused an evolutionary theory of the development of contemporary economic institutions.

In the mid-twentieth century, evolutionary theorizing in economics seemed to diminish, or at least to be pushed to the side. There was a certain elegance, and a mathematical tractability, to an economic theory that assumed that the actors "maximize" and that the system as a whole was in "equilibrium." As noted in Chapters 1 and 2, these notions even were carried over to the neoclassical theory of economic growth that developed during the 1950s and 1960s, where, I have argued, they were particularly inappropriate and blocked understanding.

In recent years there has been something of a rebirth of evolutionary theorizing in economics. Whether the new evolutionary economics will thrive and prosper is an open question. A central purpose of this book is to get some of that theorizing, and the arguments for it, into broader view.

Chapter 3 explores a wide range of recent evolutionary theorizing in economics. Evolutionary theorizing seems particularly appropriate as a vehicle for understanding how human know-how has developed, and Chapter 4 is concerned with that topic. In Chapter 5, I begin to develop a central theme I have been arguing over the years—that the processes of long-run economic growth are largely driven by the co-evolution of technologies and institutions.

CHAPTER 3

Recent Evolutionary Theorizing about Economic Change

1. Introduction

"The Mecca of the economist lies in economic biology . . . But biological conceptions are more complex than those of mechanics; a volume on Foundations must therefore give a relatively large place to mechanical analogies, and frequent use is made of the term equilibrium which suggests something of a static analogy" (Marshall 1948, p. xiv). This famous passage from Alfred Marshall's *Principles of Economics* (it first appeared in the fifth edition, which came out in 1907) nicely brings out two issues that are as germane to economics today as they were when Marshall wrote. The first is the heavy reliance by economists in their formal theorizing on the notion of "equilibrium." The other is the appeal that "biological conceptions" have for many economists, particularly when their focus is on economic change.

Marshall clearly believed that our science should aim to understand economic change and not simply the forces molding and sustaining the current configuration of economic variables. His "mechanical analogies" and equilibrium concepts included those of Newtonian dynamics as well as those associated with the balancing of forces on bodies at rest. Since the time of Marshall, and following his lead, economists have developed their own equilibrium concepts. While until recently they were mostly associated with analysis of situations presumed

---

* Based on Richard R. Nelson, "Recent Evolutionary Theorizing about Economic Change," *Journal of Economic Literature* 33 (March 1995): 48–90.

to be at rest, in recent years much of economic theorizing has been concerned with dynamics, and the equilibria, like those of Newtonian dynamics, are ones in which the variables under study change over time. But Marshall might observe that the equilibrium concept in these models still somehow has a static feel to it.

Few economists confuse the formal equilibrium theory with the reality. Most readily acknowledge that at least some economic situations need to be understood as involving significant elements of novelty, so the actors should be regarded as searching for a best action, as contrasted with actually having found it. In their analysis of certain economic phenomena, for example technological advance, many economists recognize that frequent or continuing shocks, generated internally as well as externally, may make it hazardous to assume that the system ever will get to an equilibrium; thus the fixed or moving equilibrium in the theory must be understood as an "attractor" rather than a characteristic of where the system is.

However, until recently at least, there has been a resistance to building these complications into formal models. Partly the reason is a belief that to do so would make the models intractable, or at least complex and difficult to understand. This seems to have been Marshall's concern. But nowadays this predilection seems more than simply a matter of analytic tractability and convenience. When expressly doing or talking theory, unlike Marshall most contemporary economists seem to be drawn to equilibrium concepts as a matter of aesthetics. General equilibrium theories are seen as elegant, and theories that depart from these canons are seen as somewhat ad hoc.

It is interesting, therefore, that when economists are describing or explaining particular empirical subject matter in a context that does not demand that they write or talk theory explicitly, they often eschew equilibrium language, and reveal the same inclination as did Marshall to make use of "biological conceptions" or metaphors. I noted above the proclivity of many economists to consider individuals and organizations as entities that search and "learn." Industrial organization economists sometimes characterize certain industries as "young" and others as "mature," with the connotation that various things naturally happen as an industry gets older (see, for example, Mueller and Tilton 1969). Evolutionary or developmental language is used quite widely by economists to describe how technologies, or institutions, or the structure of an economy changes over time. Writings in economic history almost invariably are full of such biological metaphors.

It might be argued that this difference between the language of informal description and explanation and the language of formal theory is just what one might expect, and does not signal a problem. After all, describing and explaining in a context in which it is important to be sensitive to the details is one thing. Theorizing is quite another.

However, this proposition is problematic on at least two counts. First, the further the language of a particular explanation is from the logic of formal theory, the less analytic structure the latter can provide the former. Economists who would eschew equilibrium language, and use "biological conceptions" in describing and explaining, must pay an analytic price. Those who do implicitly are taking a position that the analytic structure of equilibrium theory misses elements they regard as essential to their story, and thus they are willing to pay that price.

Second, the argument draws too sharp a line between formal theorizing and verbal economic explanation. Winter and I have argued that, because the real economic world is so complex, theorizing about it tends to proceed on at least two different levels of abstraction (Nelson and Winter 1982, pp. 46–48). Formal theorizing is one level. By formal theorizing, I mean what economists do when they are self-consciously putting forth a theoretical argument.

But economists also need to be understood as "theorizing" when they are trying to explain what lies behind the particular phenomena they are describing, even when they are not advertising their account as a "theory." While starting with the empirical subject matter, the accounts put forth by economists of the development of an industry, or the evolution of a technology, focus on certain variables and ignore others, just as is the case with formal theory. Quite complex causal arguments often are presented as parts of these accounts, if generally in the form of stories. (For a more extended discussion focusing on implications for formal modeling, see Malerba et al. 1999.)

Thus the difference between the language and the logic of economists' less formal explanatory stories, which often involve evolutionary or developmental concepts, and that of formal equilibrium theory, cannot be shrugged off as simply a difference between description and theory. The difference is between two different kinds of theories, in the sense that the mechanisms and relationships treated as causal are different, or at least appear to be.

One could respond by arguing that, while the language may be different, in fact the substance of theories using biological conceptions and equilibrium theories is not very different. In particular, the theories predict much the same things. There is no real difference between saying that firms literally maximize and saying that their behaviors have been learned through trial, error, and correction, and in some cases have been selected through the competitive process. Thus extant actors behave "as if" they maximize. (The classic statement of this position is, of course, Milton Friedman's [1953].)

Economists are not alone in putting forth this argument. A number of evolutionary theorists in biology do also. Both the economists and the biologists who take this position admit that, at any particular time, the actual system may not be precisely in equilibrium, but they propose that it generally is close enough so that the characteristics of equilibrium tell one a lot about the actual situation.

However, economists who use the language of development and evolution in telling their stories apparently do not believe that concepts like optimization and equilibrium can explain adequately the phenomena they are addressing, and these economists have kindred souls in biology. Many students of biological evolution strongly deny the proposition that "optimization" provides a meaningful explanation for the character of extant living forms, even when the observed configuration seems relatively durable and stable (see, for example, Gould 1980). It has been argued that the process of evolution is strongly path dependent and there is no unique selection equilibrium. Any "optimizing" characteristics of what exists therefore must be understood as local and myopic, associated with the particular equilibrium that happens to obtain. The heart of any explanation of extant living forms thus must be evolutionary analysis of how the particular equilibrium, and not a different one, came to be. Further, often there is good reason to suspect that evolution presently is going on at a relatively rapid rate, and thus equilibrium of any kind is not an appropriate concept for analysis.

It would appear that many economists who use developmental and evolutionary language have in mind notions like these. While, as we shall see, the economists using evolutionary language in their theorizing are not of one ilk, almost all are, in effect, positing that to say that actors behave "as if" they were maximizing does not tell us much about why they are doing what they are, and provides only a start on any prediction of what they will end up doing if conditions change. Many clearly believe that path dependency is important in economics, and a number argue that the phenomena in which they are interested must be understood as associated with continuing disequilibrium, not equilibrium.

Until recently economists have used the language of evolution almost exclusively in their appreciative theorizing, but not in their formal theorizing. However, in recent years evolutionary concepts have been employed increasingly in formal evolutionary theorizing. The book published by Sidney Winter and myself just over two decades ago (Nelson and Winter 1982) has been followed by a number of other works also exploring formal evolutionary theorizing in economics. (See, among others, Clark and Juma 1987; Silverberg, Dosi, and Orsenigo 1988; Anderson, Arrow, and Pines 1988; Day and Eliasson 1986; Chiaromonte and Dosi 1993; Magnusson 1994; Anderson 1994; Kwasnicki 1996; Saviotti 1996; Metcalfe 1988, 1992, 1998.)

In 1991 the *Journal of Evolutionary Economics* was founded, and several other new journals have advertised an interest in evolutionary economics. Over the past decade many articles using the language and concepts of evolutionary economics have been published in the *Journal of Economic Literature* and in such other journals as *Research Policy* and *Industrial and Corporate Change*. While the main-line economics journals, and the standard courses taught in economics departments, continue to shy away from evolutionary economics, the community of evolutionary economists is growing rapidly.

The recent work on formal evolutionary economic theories has had several distinct, if connected, sources. Over the past quarter century a number of scholars, principally coming from biology, or philosophy, have been developing the long-standing argument (it goes back to Darwin) that Darwinian mechanisms are highly relevant to understanding the emergence and development of human cultures. The prominent writers here include Wilson (1975), Dawkins (1976), Campbell (1965), Dennett (1995), Plotkin (1982, 1994), and Hull (2001). I do not believe that this strand of theorizing has had a major influence on the economists whose evolutionary theorizing I will describe later, although perhaps it should have. But it certainly has had a major influence on the theorizing of anthropologists and other scholars studying primitive cultures.

Evolutionary game theory has had more of an influence on the economists whose writings I will describe here. In particular, the proposition that many games have multiple equilibria, and that the equilibrium arrived at is sensitive to initial conditions and the "evolutionary" processes of learning and adjustment, is strongly in the minds of many of them. However, while most of the writings in evolutionary game theory use empirical examples largely as "illustrations" of the theory, the evolutionary economics I will focus on mostly is empirically oriented.

Recent developments in the understanding of the mathematics of nonlinear dynamic systems, and the recognition that many physical systems display properties that such dynamic models can explain and illuminate, have provided an important stimulus to evolutionary theorizing in economics (Prigogene and Stengers 1984, Lane 1993). For some readers, the influence of the new mathematics may be most familiar in the role it has played in evolutionary game theory. But while the economic evolutionary theories considered in this chapter have several things in common with evolutionary game theory, they are different in important ways, and this is reflected in how they have drawn on the new understandings of general nonlinear dynamic systems. First, for the most part (there are exceptions) evolutionary game theory continues an older tradition in game theory of thinking of a given finite set of (basic) strategies, with equilibrium being defined in terms of these or mixes of these. In contrast, in the more general formulation of nonlinear dynamic systems, an equilibrium, if there is any such thing, is seen as emerging out of the dynamic process, and often involves patterns of behavior and activities that were absent early in the process. The number and nature of possible equilibria thus often cannot be specified ex ante. Second, while concerned with certain regularity properties in the time series, writers who identify their work as analyzing complex dynamic systems seem quite ready to believe that the system always will be "out of equilibrium."

Much of the work on complex dynamic systems is carried out through computer simulation. However, the tremendous increase in the power of computers—along with the recent availability of programming languages and techniques that greatly facilitate simulation of complex dynamic systems—should be regarded as a factor in its own right that has stimulated the development of formal evolutionary theorizing in economics. To recall the quote from Marshall at the beginning of this chapter, the complexity of "biological conceptions," in particular evolutionary processes, no longer poses the same analytic obstacles that it did in the time of Marshall—or even twenty years ago.

Earlier I suggested that the appeal of equilibrium formal theorizing in economics was much more than a matter of computational feasibility, but reflected as well notions of aesthetics and elegance. But elegance is in the eye of the beholder. Those working with the new models of dynamic complex systems clearly are developing a sense of aesthetics of their own. And appreciation of a different kind of elegance seems to be spreading among economists.

In any case, the developments described above have contributed to the rise of a body of writing by economists and kindred scholars who are interested in understanding and explaining aspects or sources of long-run economic change, and have developed quite explicit and self-consciously evolutionary models for that purpose. These writings are the focus of this chapter. I will be concerned with evolutionary theorizing that arises out of empirical research, as contrasted with studies that develop evolutionary models or arguments because they are interesting in their own right, and which bring in empirical cases mainly as examples. Much, if not all, of this evolutionary theorizing has been developed by the authors because they have felt that "mechanical analogies" simply would not do for their task, and that "biological conceptions" were more illuminating. And in contrast with most earlier writing, these writers have made their evolutionary theorizing explicit.

Like Marshall, most of these writers, while drawn to biological conceptions or metaphors, have resisted simply transferring evolutionary concepts used in biology to their area of inquiry, but rather have tried to analyze the evolutionary dynamics at work there in their own right. This has not always proved easy. In many cases the processes involved appear to be, when they are looked at closely, quite complex. Also, there still is little experience that can be drawn upon in constructing an evolutionary theory germane to economic change. The studies I will review here are highly varied, reflecting not only their different subject matter but also the authors' particular ways of formulating an "evolutionary" theory. All of the theories considered here are formal theories, in that they have been explicitly put forth by their authors as a theory to explain particular phenomena. Some are expressed mathematically; some in words. The distinction that Winter and I made between formal and appreciative theorizing did not hinge on the media of exposition, although almost invariably theory expressed mathematically is formal theory in our terms. In our terms, the hallmark of a formal theory is the explicit setting out of a causal account, however expressed. A highly relevant question, of course, is the logical coherence of the theoretical statement. Here, the use of mathematics would seem to help, but the history of economic thought displays many coherent verbal theories, and some incoherent mathematical ones.

The remainder of this chapter is organized as follows. In Section 2, I draw out the similarities and differences between the evolutionary economic theories I will be examining and evolutionary theory in biology and sociobiology.

I turn next to the evolutionary theories that are the focus of this chapter. Section 3 is concerned with a group of evolutionary theories about particular phenomena associated with long-run economic change: science, technology, business organization, and law. Sections 4 and 5 deal with evolutionary theories that treat clusters of coevolving variables, the former with models of economic growth driven by technical advance, the latter with the coevolution of technology and industry structure.

In Section 6 I explore the question of whether business firms, and other organizational economic actors, are flexible enough that they can adapt under the winds of change, or whether significant change requires the birth of new organizations and the demise of old ones. The empirical record tells a mixed story.

In the concluding section I reflect on the present state of evolutionary theorizing in economics. I also will attempt to sharpen the discussion of the ways in which evolutionary theorizing is different from neoclassical theorizing, and to propose some criteria that might enable one to evaluate the strengths and weaknesses of the alternatives. Some economists would argue that that issue ought to hinge on the quality of the predictions, but I will suggest that the issue is more complex than that.

2. What Is an Evolutionary Theory?

What are the characteristics of an "evolutionary theory" of economic change, as contrasted with theories of economic change that employ "mechanical analogies"? In what ways are economic evolutionary theories similar to evolutionary theories in biology and sociobiology, and in what ways are they different? These are the questions addressed in this section.

2.1. Evolutionary Theory as a General Theory

One way to define evolutionary theory in general would be to start from biology, where evolutionary theory is best worked out, and explore where one can find close analogies to the variables and concepts of that theory in other areas of inquiry—in this case, economics. However, I believe that following this route would tie the discussion much too closely to biology. After all, as Hodgson (1993) has discussed at some length, the term *evolution* was in wide use long before it took on meaning as the name of a particular theory in biology.

I believe that much of the appeal of evolutionary language in economics is connected with the broader use of the term, as contrasted with its specific use in biology. Further, to start with biology risks getting stuck in notions that, while salient in biological evolution, seem irrelevant or wrong-headed when applied to economics. It seems more fruitful to start with a general notion of evolution and then examine applications in specific areas—like biology or economics—as special cases.

The general concept of evolutionary theory that I propose, and I employ in this chapter, involves the following elements. The focus of attention is on a variable or set of them that is changing over time, and the theoretical quest is for an understanding of the dynamic process behind the observed change; a special case would be a quest for understanding of the current state of a variable or a system in terms of how it got there. The theory proposes that the variable or system in question is subject to somewhat random variation or perturbation, and also that there are mechanisms that systematically winnow on that variation. Much of the predictive or explanatory power of the theory rests with its specification of the systematic selection forces. It is presumed that there are strong inertial tendencies preserving what has survived the selection process. However, in many cases there are also forces that continue to introduce new variety, which is further grist for the selection mill.

This definition of a general evolutionary process certainly is not original to me. It has been put forth by a number of scholars seeking to generalize the concept of evolution beyond the details of the processes involved in Darwinian biology. See, for example, Campbell (1974), Dawkins (1976), Dennett (1995), Plotkin (1994), or Hull (2001).

All of the evolutionary theories of economic change I will discuss have these characteristics. They also are central, of course, in evolutionary theory in biology. However, biology makes heavy use of other concepts that, by and large, are not used in economics. The fact that sexuality and mating play a major role in the evolution of many species is important in biology but seldom used in economics. The concept of generations is used in biology but does not apply easily to analyses of the evolution of technologies, firms, or institutions.

On the other hand, in some of the theories considered here the new "variety" that is created as grist for winnowing is systematically oriented toward new departures that seem appropriate to the context. That is, there is a directionally adaptive aspect to the innovation process. Also, what entities "learn" in such processes may, in some models, be passed on to other entities. That is, some of the economic evolutionary theories are Lamarckian, a version of evolutionary theory that has been discredited in biology. Some emphasize group selection. Other aspects that distinguish economic models from biological ones will be developed along the way.

In any case, the proposed general definition of an evolutionary process certainly rules out certain theories of change, for example those that are wholly deterministic. Thus under this definition, as apparently under Marshall's conception, Kepler's laws of planetary motion, together with Newton's gravitational theory that explains them, would not define an evolutionary theory. Nor would the standard neoclassical theory of economic growth, which basically presumes a moving general equilibrium, be regarded as an evolutionary theory. Neither would the execution of a detailed plan for the construction of a building, or any realization of a prespecified blueprint, be considered an evolutionary process.

The definition I am proposing also rules out theories of change in which all the action is "random," as in certain models in economics that purport that within an industry the growth or decline of particular firms is a random variable, possibly related to the size of the firm at any time, but otherwise not analyzable (see, for example, Simon and Bonini 1958). One can trace through the random processes built into such models and predict the distribution of firm sizes at any time—for example, that under certain specifications it will asymptotically become log normal. But under the definition presented here, these models would not be considered evolutionary models of economic change.

However, let's revise the building construction story as follows. Assume that the original house design is a tentative one, because the builder is not exactly sure how to achieve what he or she wants, and thus the plan initially contains certain elements without any firm commitment to them, indeed that are there partly by chance. As the building is constructed, the builder gets a better idea of what the plans imply and where the original design is inadequate, and, where construction in place permits, revises the plan and the path of construction accordingly. Now, revise the firm growth model. Assume that the firms differ in certain identifiable characteristics, and that growth of those with certain characteristics turns out to be systematically greater than those that lack them. The industry gradually develops a structure in which only firms with those characteristics survive.

Both models now contain both random and systematic elements. Further, the systematic ones act by winnowing the random ones. In the house design case, design elements turn out to please or displease the builder, and are accepted or rejected accordingly. In the industry evolution case, the "market" or something is selecting firms that have certain attributes. A limitation of both stories is that neither is explicit about what it is that seems to give advantage. But both give hope that the analyst might be able to find out. Perhaps it is "cost per square foot" or "nicely shaped spaces" or some combination that explains why the builder revises the design as the information comes in. Perhaps it is production costs or ability to innovate that is determining whether firms thrive or fail. Of course, the theory has limited explanatory power until the question of selection criteria gets answered. But if that question is answered adequately, the theory can explain, and to some extent predict.

The analytic structure of these two examples is reminiscent of that of evolutionary theory in biology, without being a clone of it. The latter case, however, seems closer to theory in biology because it refers to an actual population of things, while the former does not appear to, at least at first glance. In biology the use of the term *evolutionary* nowadays is firmly associated with analysis of actual populations of things. An embryo, or more generally a living creature, usually is described as developing, not evolving. In part, this use of language reflects a predilection discussed earlier—that change "according to a plan" is usually not regarded as evolutionary. However, it is recognized widely that many random occurrences will affect the development of an embryo or a tree. The prejudice against using the term *evolutionary* to describe such biological processes stems from the fact that the term has been preempted for use in describing another class of biological phenomena. However, is it clear that prejudice should carry over outside of biology?

Consider our house builder, or an individual learning to play chess, or a firm trying to find a strategy for survival in a competitive industry. The house builder can be regarded as having a number of plan variants, or perhaps as having one initially in mind but being aware that there are possible changes that might turn out to be desirable. One can similarly regard the novice chess player and the firm. If firms, persons learning to play chess, and house builders learn from experience and winnow or adapt their plans or strategies or behaviors, is it unreasonable to think of these as evolving? In reflecting on this, one might recognize that the learning, or adaptation, can be modeled in terms of a change in the probability distribution of possible actions that an entity might take at any time, coming about as a result of feedback from what has been tried, and the consequences. These "learning" equations have basically the same form as the equations that describe the evolution of populations.

This fact has long been recognized by scholars seeking to extend the concept of evolutionary process beyond its application in Darwinian biology. See, for example, Campbell (1974), Plotkin (1994), or, for a mathematical statement, Holland et al. (1986).

There is no great value in extended intellectual haggling about the precise boundaries that demarcate models of change that can be called evolutionary from those that should not be. As indicated, I choose to use the term *evolutionary* to define a class of theories, or models, or arguments, that have the following characteristics. First, their purpose is to explain the movement of something over time, or to explain why that something is what it is at a moment in time in terms of how it got there; that is, the analysis is expressly dynamic. Second, the explanation involves both random elements that generate or renew some variation in the variables in question, and mechanisms that systematically winnow extant variation. Third, there are inertial forces that provide continuity of what survives the winnowing.

The variation in the theory can be associated with an actual variety that exists at any time—as a distribution of genotypes or phenotypes, or firm policies. Alternately, it may characterize a set of potential values of a variable, only one of which is manifest at any time. Thus I would include theories of individual, organizational, or cultural learning and adaptation under my umbrella, if they fit other characteristics. Indeed, as we shall see, a characteristic of many of the economic evolutionary theories we will examine is that individual learning, organizational adaptation, and environmental selection of organizations all are going on at the same time.

2.2. Evolutionary Theory in Biology

As is the case with any active scientific field, there is far from full agreement on all matters among modern biologists, ethnologists, paleontologists, and other scientists concerned with biological evolution. However, the following sketch captures that part of the generally agreed upon core that is most useful to lay out for our purposes in this chapter, as well as some of the relevant bones of contention. (The following draws from many sources, but especially Lewontin 1974; Sober 1984; Hull 1988, 2001; Mayr 1988; Plotkin 1982, 1994; and Jablonka and Ziman 2000.)

The theory is concerned with two actual populations as contrasted with potential ones. One is the population of genotypes, defined as the genetic inheritance of living creatures. The second is the population of phenotypes, defined in terms of a set of variables that happen to be of interest to the analyst, but which include those that influence the "fitness" of each living creature. These might include physical aspects, like size or sight, behavioral patterns, like song, or responses to particular contingencies, like something that can be eaten and is within reach, or a potential mate, or a member of one's own "group" soliciting help.

Phenotypic characteristics are presumed to be influenced by genotypic ones but not uniquely determined by them. Modern evolutionary theory recognizes that the development of a living creature from its origins to its phenotypic characteristics at any time can be influenced by the environment through which it passes—the health of the mother when it was in embryo, the availability of food in the environment, or the fact that when young it lost an eye in an accident. Modern evolutionary theory also recognizes a variety of learning experiences that shape the behavior of a phenotype, including how it was taught by its mother, whether particular behaviors early in life were rewarded, and so on. However, if we hold off for a moment considering evolutionary theory that recognizes "culture" as something that can be transferred across generations, the hallmark of standard biological evolutionary theory is that only the genes, not any acquired characteristics or behavior, get passed on across the generations.

The notion of "generations" is basic to biological evolutionary theory. The phenotypes get born, live, reproduce (at least some of them do), and die (in most species ultimately all of them do). On the other hand, the genes get carried over to their offspring, who follow the same generational life cycle. Thus the genes provide the continuity of the evolutionary system, with the actual living creatures acting, from one point of view, as their transporters from generation to generation. For species that produce this way, sexuality provides a mechanism for combining genotypes in a manner that may create new ones. Mutations also create new genotypes. On the other hand, selection winnows the genetic variety through differential reproduction by (pairs of) phenotypes, which augments the relative frequency of the genes of the more successful reproducers and diminishes that of the less.

In the generally held interpretation of this theory (there are other or more complex interpretations as well), selection operates directly on the phenotypes. It is they, not their genes per se, that are more or less fit. To repeat what was stressed above, phenotypes are not uniquely determined by genotypes. However, the theory assumes a strong enough relationship between the two that systematic selection on phenotypes results in systematic selection on genotypes.

There are several controversial, or at least open, aspects of this theory that are germane to our discussion here. For economists, perhaps the most interesting question is whether, and if so in what sense, evolution can be understood to "optimize" fitness.

The optimization notion here clearly has roots in Herbert Spencer's notion (1887) of "survival of the fittest," and the implicit context is one in which competition among members of a population is sufficiently fierce that only the "fittest" survive. In recent years theorists have formalized this idea as a game for survival, and developed the concept of an "evolutionarily stable strategy" as the equilibrium solution to that game. (See, for example, Maynard-Smith 1982.) The concept of "strategy" in these models is broad enough to encompass any phenotypic characteristic that matters for survival, and the strategies that survive in equilibrium are those that can best (at least small numbers of) other pre-specified strategies in the survival game.

In what sense is what survives optimal? The semantic correspondence between survival and optimality seems most straightforward if the "game" is about different kinds of strategies passively competing for the same environmental "niche," and one type wins out. The winner might be understood as the most efficient forager, or something like that. However, things get somewhat more complicated if the game isn't simply about passive competition for a niche but includes some strategies that involve attacking competitors of other sorts. Then both efficient foraging and fighting prowess count in defining what is optimal, if that term is to be used to characterize what survives.

Even in such simple contexts, there are some subtleties that qualify the association of what "survives" with "optimal." For one thing, how a strategy fares in a series of plays of a game depends on the mix of strategies with which it competes. Thus what survives depends on what else is competing in the game. More, if the number of individuals associated with any particular strategy is finite, the very process of competition may eliminate along the path to an equilibrium strategies that would be in a stable equilibrium set as calculated ex ante. That is, the equilibrium may be strongly path dependent.

Other complications come into view when one recognizes that "strategies" may have many aspects, and these may interact strongly in determining ability to compete and survive in a given environment. Thus being an effective predator requires one package of attributes, the ability to get at the leaves on tall trees, a different package. But then, whether a "gene" or an aspect of a strategy enhances survival or not may be strongly dependent on the other genes or aspects of strategy. And a "mutation" that may be lethal in one species or strategy may be helpful in another. Thus if strategies themselves evolve, they likely do so in a strongly path dependent way.

There may be important interactions across coexisting phenotypes or strategies. The existence of giraffes provides opportunities for large, strong predators. But the number of the latter that can survive in equilibrium may depend on the number of the former, and vice versa. In turn, the ecological equilibrium depends on the number of trees and the leaves that are available to giraffes. The emergence of an insect whose caterpillars feed on leaves of the tall trees may bring down the whole ecosystem.

Also, a number of students of biological evolution have argued that the selection environment almost never is constant (see Gould 1980, 1985). The insect population may grow large, and then itself collapse after it has diminished the population of live trees. If the selection environment is not a constant, the phenotypes extant today may be strongly shaped by those that survived in a possibly very different environment some time ago (say, giraffes that could eat the leaves of low bushes that the caterpillars do not like), and the offspring they had, as well as recent winnowing of the group extant yesterday. Again, the equilibrium is strongly path dependent, and today's "optimum" may be very local and likely poor stuff compared with what might have been.

Gould, among others, reads the evidence as indicating that the selection environment not only changes but on many occasions is relatively lax. In a loose selection environment, different phenotypes may grow in number more rapidly than others, largely due to a combination of breeding capability and luck, rather than to any special capabilities for "survival" in the environment in question. The same authors argue that the extinction of particular phenotypes usually is the result of catastrophes that happened to hit clusters of them, rather than the result of losing a competition with other phenotypes.

One also can ask what meaning there is to the optimality concept in a context in which mutation continues to go on, and some of the mutations enhance fitness, at least in prevailing environments. Modern evolutionary biology is not simply about selection pressures on extant phenotypes; it is also about changes that appear from time to time in species, and also about the origins of new species. These latter phenomena would seem to require analysis of evolutionary processes that involve not only out-of-equilibrium behavior but also the emergence of novelty. (See, for example, Fontana and Buss 1992, Lane 1993.)

2.3. Sociobiology

As indicated, animal behavior has for a long time been a "phenotypic" characteristic of interest to evolutionary theorists. That behavior often involves, in an essential way, modes of interaction with fellow members of one's species. Over the past thirty years an important subdiscipline has grown up concerned with exactly these kinds of social behavior patterns. Much of this has been concerned with nonprimate animals—insect colonies, bird families and flocks, and so on. A sizable portion of it has, however, been concerned with humans. The part of the sociobiology literature concerned with nonhumans recognizes that learned behavior can be passed down from generation to generation, but in general it has presumed, first, that the particular capabilities to learn and to transmit to offspring are tied to genes, and second, that the "learning" does not progress from generation to generation. To the extent that these behaviors enhance fitness, there is selection on the genes that facilitate them, according to the arguments sketched above. But learned behavior does not follow an independent cross-generational path of its own.

The early work by Edward Wilson (1975) on the biological bases of human social behavior carried over basically this model. However, in subsequent writings by Charles Lumsden and Edward Wilson (1981), and by other scholars interested in extending evolutionary theory in biology so as to be able to treat human culture, prominently Luigi Cavalli-Sforza and Marcus Feldman (1981), Robert Boyd and Peter Richerson (1985), and William Durham (1991), human culture was recognized as something that could be modified, and improved, from generation to generation, and that had its own rules of transmission. These latter models all do presume a basic genetic biological capacity of humans for the development and transmission of culture. But beyond that, they treat the connection between the evolution of human behavior and culture, and genetic evolution as something far more complex than that assumed in the models of insect and bird societies.

There are a number of important differences among these models. Lumsden and Wilson, and Cavalli-Sforza and Feldman, tend to treat elements of culture as directly determining what people do and how effectively they do it, while Boyd and Richerson, and especially Durham, treat culture as prominently involving understandings and values that, like genes, influence behavior or capabilities but do not directly determine them. (We shall see similar differences regarding how different scholars define "institutions" when we consider that subject in Chapter 5.) Perhaps the most important difference among these models is the extent to which biology is seen as constraining and molding culture beyond the preconditions that all of these theories recognize. Put in the terms coined by Wilson, there are disagreements regarding how long the "leash" is, and the extent to which evolution of culture itself has significantly extended the length of that leash. Here Lumsden and Wilson are far closer to the animal sociobiology models than the other authors.

For the purposes of the discussion here, I want to focus on certain commonalities of the theories in this literature, which, I believe, limit their range of applicability. In particular, all of them use as their examples relatively simple practices or artifacts or ideas or norms that can easily be thought of as being transmitted from person to person. Each tries to break down "culture" into small "gene-like" subunits, which are assigned terms like *meme*, or *culturgen*. The simple technology-artifacts and beliefs employed as examples are a far distance from complex technologies like those associated with making semiconductors or aircraft, or scientific theories like that of biological evolution itself, or systems like patent law. While teachers and opinion leaders are admitted as "transmitters" or "influencers," there is nothing in these studies like universities or scientific societies. Various forms of human organization are discussed, but there is no treatment of organizations like industrial R & D laboratories, or business firms more generally, or elections or legislatures or courts.

Most of the analyses clearly recognize that in principle an element of culture can spread for reasons that have little to do with enhancing individual biological fitness in any straightforward manner, and some stress that as a general proposition. Boyd and Richerson even present a model example in which the professional life of, say, a teacher, or a member of the clergy, is assumed to carry attractions of its own, but those who follow the calling actually have a smaller number of offspring than those who do not. Membership in the profession as a whole is sustained intergenerationally by new recruits. However, none of these analyses attempts to come to grips with the paths of cumulative evolution taken by cultural structures like science, technology, the law, standard forms of business organization, and the like, which clearly have been drawn and shaped by particular value systems, and particular mechanisms for inducing and winnowing change.

While important and interesting in its own right, the body of writing on cultural evolution that traces its origins to biological evolutionary theory, and then makes a sharp break, has not as yet tried to come to grips with the dynamics of change in modern industrial societies. To do so requires, it would seem, building into evolutionary analysis much more of the institutional complexity of modern societies than the literature above has hazarded thus far. Boyd and Richerson recognize this explicitly when they remark: "Understanding the institutional complexity of modern societies will require the mating of micro-level theory like the one we have developed here with the more aggregated one of Nelson and Winter" (1985, p. 296).

This is just what the various studies we shall consider in the following sections have tried to do, if with varying levels of success.

3. The Evolution of Particular Aspects of Culture

There are three key differences between the evolutionary theories I consider here and in the following sections, and those in sociobiology. First, there are no ties whatsoever between the cultural selection criteria and processes and biological fitness. Any coevolution in these theories is not between memes and genes, but between various elements of culture. This is not to deny that progress in these areas of culture proceeds in ways that are dependent on certain biological properties of humans. But this kind of linkage is not central in the analysis.

Second, the authors of the theories considered here are interested in explaining how and why a particular aspect of "culture" changed over time the way it did. Because their explanation is in terms of the workings of an evolutionary process, this forces them to identify some particular characteristics of merit and the selection mechanisms enforcing them, which reinforce certain behaviors or inclinations and dampen others. The theorists of biological and cultural coevolution discussed above have coined the term *cultural fitness* but seldom have gotten around to identifying just what that means in particular cases where biological fitness is not an important variable at stake. Third, evolutionary theorists, coming from sociobiology, have by and large assumed selection mechanisms work directly on individuals and transmission mechanisms are person to person, and that memes, like genes, are carried by individuals. Yet these perceptions seem quite inadequate for an analysis of how science or modern technology evolves, or forms of business organization, or law.

This section will be concerned with evolutionary theories of just these elements of culture, all of them major and obviously intertwined aspects of the process of long-run economic change. The theories discussed in this section largely repress the intertwining. Each theory deals with just one of these variables, which is viewed as proceeding on its own, as it were. In the following two sections I shall consider theories in which interdependence and coevolution are recognized.

The collection of theories discussed here are all qualitative, and expressed verbally. All are formal theories in the sense of being put forth as self-conscious abstractions about what is driving the dynamics of the variables in question. However, none is developed mathematically. And some seem much better posed analytically than others, in that their logic seems tighter.

I also want to stress that each of the bodies of evolutionary theorizing discussed in this section is very large. My treatment of each, therefore, must be highly selective. My particular selection is designed not so much to be representative of the literatures involved as to bring out some analytic issues about evolutionary theorizing.

3.1. Science

The proposition that science "evolves" has been around for some time, and there has been and continues to be a lively discussion about just how that evolutionary process works. For the most part, the various theories put forth do satisfy my definition of what qualifies as an evolutionary theory. (For overviews, see Plotkin 1982, 1994; Hull 1988, 2001.)

Of recent writers in this vein, Donald Campbell (1960, 1974) probably is the most cited. Using Campbell's term, the development of new scientific hypotheses, or theories, is to some extent "blind," in that their originators cannot know for sure how they will fare when they are first put forth. Thus new scientific theories are like "mutations" in that some will succeed and be incorporated into the body of science, perhaps replacing older theories or correcting them in some respects or adding to them, and others will not succeed. Campbell relies largely on the ideas of Karl Popper (1968) for his "selection mechanism." Under Popper's argument, scientific theories never can be proved true, but they can be falsified. New theories that solve scientific problems and are not falsified are added to the body of science. That is, employed and "not falsified" is the characterization of fitness in this theory of science. For the most part Campbell treats science as a relatively unified body of doctrine, and his language implies a scientific community together searching after truth, and collective evolutionary learning. On the other hand, his theory is compatible with the notion of individual scientists putting forth their particular theories in hope of winning a Nobel Prize. A good case can be made that both images of science—cooperative and competitive—are partly correct (see Hull 1988, 2001).

In any case the theory leaves open two questions. The first is what determines which theories are to be rigorously tested, and what is the standing of theories that have not been tested. The set of "theories" that have not (as of yet) been subject to rigorous testing do not all necessarily have the same standing. Some may never be brought to a serious test simply because they are regarded as irrelevant, or on their face absurd. Others may fit so well with prevailing understanding that they are absorbed without direct testing. The second question is what falsification means. In many cases the conclusions of a test may be ambiguous, or there may be reason to question the way it was run, or whether it was appropriate. Often a theory that seems to fail a test can be patched up with a well-crafted modification or amendment. These issues open the door to a much more complicated theory of the evolution of science than at least the simple interpretation of Campbell's.

The "social constructionists" recognize and revel in these complications (see, for example, Latour 1986). They propose that very few theories, or scientific arguments more generally, are ever completely falsified or even put to a test that all would regard ex ante as conclusive. Thus scientific opinion is what matters, and in a context in which different individuals and groups have different opinions, what is considered scientific fact and is published in reputed journals, taught to graduate students, and so on, is largely a matter of scientific politics.

Thomas Kuhn (1970) presents a view somewhat between Campbell and the social constructionists. On the one hand, Kuhn proposes that most "normal science" proceeds in almost unthinking acceptance of prevailing theory, and that there is strong built-in disbelief of results that challenge that theory. On the other hand, also central to Kuhn's theory of the evolution of science is that unanswered questions or anomalies tend to accumulate, and as they do, questions increasingly are asked about the adequacy of prevailing theory. A standard response of the scientific community is to propose modest modifications or additions to prevailing theory. However, these may not succeed, or the developing theoretical structure may come to be seen as rococo. The seeds then are planted for a scientific revolution.

Campbell and Kuhn (in their earlier versions) do not address the issue of competing theories. However, such competition is the heart of scientific revolutions. Imre Lakatos (1970) proposes that broad theories should be regarded as defining research programs. These programs can be judged by the community as proceeding effectively—that is, as making good progress—or as more or less stuck. Lakatos proposes that there are almost always competing theories around. The one that defines the more effective research program tends to win out. But again, one can ask what defines "effective." A particular theory almost always points to a number of predicted implications, and exploring these defines a variety of puzzles and problems and tasks. A research program may be good in dealing with some of these, and not so effective with others. What counts?

Several different theories of the evolution of science have been described above. Some are in conflict. In particular the social constructionists would seem to be at odds with scholars, like Campbell, who believe that new scientific hypotheses, or at least those taken seriously, are subject to testing, and that enough of the tests are sufficiently objective and unambiguous to monitor the enterprise. This view also has been expressed strongly by Kitcher (1993) and by Hull. Does science make progress? While social constructionists are skeptical about this, and Thomas Kuhn is of several minds, I think it fair to say that most of the theorists who propose that science evolves, certainly Popper, Campbell, Kitcher, and Hull, believe that the process does generate progress, at least along the lines of research pursued. While occasionally we delude ourselves that we understand something when we do not, and often the going toward better understanding is hard, by and large, through science, we have come to know more and more about nature and how it works. Or at least that is the flavor of this body of theorizing.

3.2. Technology

A number of analysts have proposed that technology evolves. The analyses of Rosenberg (1976, 1982a, 1982b), Constant (1980), Nelson and Winter (1982), Freeman (1982), Dosi (1988), Basalla (1988), Saviotti (1996), Mokyr (1990), Petroski (1992), Ziman (2000), and Vincenti (1990, 1994) are strikingly similar in many respects. To keep the discussion below simple, here I will follow Vincenti. In later chapters I will develop a broader perspective.

In Vincenti's theory, the community of technologists at any time faces a number of problems, challenges, and opportunities. He draws most of his examples from aircraft technology. One of his best worked out cases involves the development of retractable landing gear (Vincenti 1994). Vincenti observes that in the late 1920s and early 1930s, aircraft designers knew well that the standard pattern of hooking wheels to fuselage or wings could be improved upon, given the higher speeds planes were then capable of with the new body and wing designs and more powerful engines that had come into existence. They were aware of several different possibilities for incorporating wheels into a more streamlined design. He argues that trials of these different alternatives were, in the same sense put forth by Campbell, somewhat blind. This is not to say that the engineers thinking about and experimenting with solutions were ignorant either of the technical constraints and possibilities or of what was required of a successful design. Rather, his proposition is that, while professional knowledge and appreciation of the goals greatly focused efforts at solution, there still were a number of different possibilities, and engineers were uncertain about which would prove best, and disagreed among themselves as to where to place bets.

This kind of uncertainty, together with the proposition that uncertainty is resolved only through ex post competition, is the hallmark of evolutionary theories. In this case it turned out that having the wheel be retractable solved the problem better than did the other alternatives explored at that time. Thus, "fitness" here is defined in terms of solving particular technological problems better.

One might propose that identification of this criterion only pushes the analytic problem back a stage. What determines whether one solution is better than another? At times Vincenti writes as if the criterion were innate in the technological problem, or determined by consensus of a technological community who are, like Campbell's community of scientists, cooperatively involved in advancing the art.

However, Vincenti also recognizes that the aircraft designers are largely employed in a number of competing aircraft companies, whose profitability may be affected by the relative quality and cost of the aircraft designs they are using, compared with those employed by their competitors. But then what is better or worse in a problem's solution is determined at least partially by the "market," the properties of an aircraft customers are willing to pay for, the costs associated with different design solutions, and so on. In the case of aircraft, the military is an important customer, as well as the airlines. Thus the evolution of aircraft at least partially reflects military demands and budgets, as well as civilian.

As with the case of science, some authors dispute that the evolution of technology follows a path that might be considered as "progress," or even that there are any objective criteria for technological fitness. The book by Wiebe Bijker, Thomas Hughes, and Trevor Pinch (1987) surveys various theories of "social construction" of technology. Michael Tushman and Lori Rosenkopf (1992) develop a more nuanced view of social determinism, but one which also implicitly denies the importance of economic efficiency, save as a gross screen. On the other hand, evolutionary theorists of the development of technology of the Vincenti camp believe strongly that there is technological progress, and ask the reader who doubts to compare modern aircraft with those of fifty years ago, modern pharmaceuticals with those available before World War II, et cetera.

In subsequent chapters I will analyze the process of technological advance more extensively and in greater depth.

3.3. Business Organization

Alfred Chandler's research (1962, 1990) has been concerned with understanding how the complex structures that characterize modern multiproduct firms came into existence. For our purposes his story is especially interesting, in that it is a story of coevolution. The coevolution is not of genes and memes, but of technology and business organizations. He argues that a variety of technological developments occurred during the mid- and late nineteenth century that opened up the possibility for business firms to be highly productive and profitable if they could organize to operate at large scales of output, and with a relatively wide if connected range of products. He describes various organizational innovations that were tried, and while his central focus is on those that "succeeded," it is clear from his account that not all did.

Chandler's "fitness criterion," argued in a manner similar to Vincenti, is that the new organizational form solved an organizational problem. Presumably the solution to that problem enabled a firm to operate at lower costs, or with greater scale and scope, and in either case, with greater profitability. Like Campbell and Vincenti, Chandler clearly sees a community, in this case of managers. But he also sees companies competing with one another. His argument is that companies that found and adopted efficient managerial styles and structural forms early won out over their competitors who did not, or who lagged in doing so. Oliver Williamson (1985), drawing from Chandler but putting forth a much more explicit formal theory, proposes that a relatively sharp "fitness" criterion determined which organizational forms survived and which ones did not—economic efficiency.

Chandler's and Williamson's accounts of the development of the large multidimensional corporation stress the need of top firm managers concerned with market-defined efficiency somehow to decentralize and yet still control large and diversified bureaucracies. Marxians highlight a different aspect of the organizational forms that evolved—that they sharply reduced the importance of workers with special skills, and hence shifted power toward capital. Neil Fligstein (1990) presents a still different view on corporate fitness that emphasizes responsiveness to changed legal regimes, public policies, and the climate of political opinions more generally toward what corporate action and form ought to be.

As with the case of technology, some recent writing has proposed that the path that has taken us to the modern large hierarchically organized corporation is one we did not have to take, and that in fact better paths existed. I will pick up this theme later.

3.4. Law

The final example I will address in this section is the body of theory that proposes that the law evolves. Donald Elliot (1985) has written a rich survey of the various evolutionary theories about law. I will focus here on only a small portion of that intellectual tradition.

In particular I will be concerned with the body of theorizing, put forth by scholars such as Harold Demsetz (1967) and William Landes and Richard Posner (1987), that the common law evolves in directions that make it economically efficient. While different authors in this tradition have proposed different mechanisms, for all of them, decisions to litigate provide the force that gets the law to change. In some versions it is argued that litigation is more prevalent when the law is "inefficient" than when it is efficient, because in the latter cases conflicts are more likely to be settled out of court without any change in the law, although the reasoning behind that proposition is not clear in all accounts. In some versions judges (juries) are inclined to decide cases that do arise in ways that are consistent with economic efficiency, and those judgments in turn modify the common law in that direction. Other versions assume no such inclination, but rather hold that cases will continue to be litigated until an "efficient" judgment is made, at which time it will become precedent and litigation will diminish. I confess I do not find the logic of these theories persuasive.

Criticizing this simple view of legal evolution, Robert Cooter and

Daniel Rubinfeld (1989) emphasize the complex nature of legal disputes and their settlement, including the actions individuals take that may risk suit, decisions of potential plaintiffs to assert a legal complaint, bargaining regarding out-of-court settlements, and the proceedings of cases that actually get decided in court. They express skepticism about whether there are any strong forces leading to efficiency, and argue that, if there are any such strong forces, they must be due to the inclinations of judges. They are skeptical of this too, citing other legal values—like fairness—and also pointing to the fact that judges may have their own interests.

Ruben and Bailey (1992) have proposed an interesting variant on this theme. They note that lawyers have a strong financial interest in the shape of the law, and in particular benefit when the law forces litigation. They go on to propose that the recent shift of legal precedent toward more favorable reception of consumer suits regarding products that cause them harm is, largely, the self-motivated work of lawyers.

Note that the theories discussed above are similar in certain respects but differ in others. They are similar in that they all are concerned with a particular aspect of culture, and focus on its evolution. They are similar in proposing that the processes that generate new cultural elements or modify old ones are to some extent blind, although the details of these mechanisms differ from case to case, and in some the mutation or innovation mechanisms have strongly directed elements as well as random ones. However, in each of these theories the "selection mechanism" provides a large share of the explanatory power. That is, the power of these theories depends on their ability to specify "fitness" plausibly.

Both neoclassical economists and economists inclined to evolutionary theorizing are prone to look to a market or a market analogue as the mechanism that defines what will "sell," and to "profit" or its analogue as the reward for actors that meet the market test. The theories above clearly differ in the extent to which they can be forced into that mold.

There certainly is no real "market" out there in Campbell's or Kuhn's or Lakatos's theory of science as an evolutionary process, save for the metaphorical "market of scientific judgment." In the cases of technology and the organization of enterprises, a moderately persuasive case can be made that, in many sectors at least, real markets, not metaphorical ones, have a powerful influence on what is "fit" and what is not, and that profit is an important measure of fitness. However, as we have seen there are dissenters, mainly from outside economics. One important issue is the extent to which competition provides a sharp fitness test in sectors where markets are operative. If it does not, there is room for a variety of nonmarket forces to influence what "survives." Also, there are serious questions about the range of sectors—kinds of technologies and organizations—where markets are strongly operative. In the case of military or medical technologies, or military bases or hospitals, it can be argued that market forces are weak, and that the "selection environment" is determined largely by professional judgments, and by political processes that regulate how much professionals in the sector have to spend. The analytic problem, then, is to identify how these forces define fitness.

The dispute about what determines how the law evolves highlights these kinds of questions. Clearly there is no real market out there, but one set of authors argues that market valuation of prevailing law and its alternatives does influence what the law becomes, and strongly. Other authors are not so sure that "efficiency" in an economic sense guides the evolution of the law so much as ideology, or interests, or power. One could take a position that it depends, with sometimes one influence prevailing, and sometimes another. However, in the absence of ability to explain or predict what influence will dominate in particular cases, while evolutionary theory may provide a useful language for historical discussion, the theory has little predictive power, and its explanations are at least partially ad hoc.

This would seem to be a big strike against an evolutionary theory of the law, or at least one that is this complex. On the other hand, one can argue that the illumination of the complex, contingent, dependent process by which the law evolves is a strength of the theory. Such an analysis reveals the apparent strong predictive power of a simpler theory—in this case that the law always adjusts so that it is maximally efficient—to be fool's gold. I take it that this is Gould's argument against the proposition that evolution optimizes biological fitness.

However, this kind of understanding of complexity that a good and well-posed evolutionary theory may yield needs to be distinguished sharply from weaknesses in prediction and explanation that stem from the fact that a theory is not coherent. Thus the argument that the law evolves so as to be efficient, for example, is an assertion that may or may not be empirically correct, but which originally was presented with no coherent evolutionary theory behind it. The proposition that litigation stops if and only if the law is efficient may provide part of an evolutionary theoretic basis for such an analytic argument, but that proposition needs more justification than it often is given, and the general argument almost surely needs some other assumptions as well.

Once one is confident that the theory put forth is logically coherent, the central question remains as to whether one finds the theory plausible, given what one knows about the facts of the matter. But evolutionary theories are no different in this regard than any other kind.

4. Evolutionary Models of Economic Growth
Fueled by Technical Advance

The body of evolutionary theorizing considered in this section differs from that discussed in the preceding one in at least two respects. First, the theorizing is more complex in the sense that it involves a number of different variables, and the focus is on their coevolution. Second, the theory in many cases is expressed mathematically; in some cases the logical connections are developed as theorems, while in others they are explored through simulation methods.

While concerned with economic dynamics, the kind of analysis contained in neoclassical growth theory almost certainly was among the kinds Marshall had in mind when he referred to theories based on mechanical concepts of equilibrium. Within that theory, economic growth is viewed as the moving equilibrium of a market economy, in which technical advance is continuously increasing the productivity of inputs, and the capital stock growing relative to labor inputs. These two phenomena together provide the explanation for the increase in labor productivity and per capita income that are the standard measures of growth.

Technical advance is an essential element of the neoclassical account. As I discussed in Chapter 1, the past few years have seen a number of interesting proposals to amend the simple neoclassical growth model so as to highlight the idea that technical advance is to a considerable degree endogenous. However, as I argued there, the new models do not address the problems with neoclassical growth theory identified by the authors of evolutionary alternatives.

In particular, as I have noted, virtually all serious scholars of technical advance have stressed the uncertainty, the differences of opinion among experts, the surprises that mark the process. Mechanical analogies involving a moving equilibrium in which the actors always behave "as if" they know what they are doing seem quite inappropriate. Most knowledgeable scholars agree with Vincenti that the process must be understood as an evolutionary one. The challenge faced by the authors considered in this section has been to devise a theory of growth in which technical advance and capital formation together drive growth, as in neoclassical growth theory, and that is capable of explaining the observed macroeconomic patterns, but on the basis of an evolutionary theory of technical change rather than one that presumes continuing equilibrium.

Without any exception I know about, the evolutionary theories of economic growth that have been developed all draw inspiration from Joseph Schumpeter's *Capitalism, Socialism, and Democracy* (first published in 1942). In that work, Schumpeter developed a theory of endogenous technological advance resulting from the investments made by business firms to best or stay up with their rivals. The earliest class of formal evolutionary growth models based on these ideas was developed by Winter and myself (1974), and because it has provided much of the base for subsequent work, I shall concentrate on it. However, I also will consider variants or extensions that have been developed by others.

In these models, firms are the key actors, not individual human beings. Of course (implicitly) firms must provide sufficient inducements to attract and hold the individuals that staff them, but within these models individuals are viewed as interchangeable and their actions determined by the firms they are in.

In turn, the firms in these models are, from one point of view, the entities that are more or less fit—or in this case, more or less profitable. But from another point of view, firms can be regarded as merely the incubators and carriers of "technologies" and other practices that determine "what they do" and "how productively" in particular circumstances. Winter and I have used the term *routines* to denote these. The concept of routines is analytically similar to the genes in biological theory, or the memes or culturgens in sociobiology.

The term *routine* connotes, deliberately, behavior that is conducted without much explicit thinking about it, as habits or customs. At the same time, within these models routines can be understood as the behaviors deemed appropriate and effective in the settings in which they are invoked. Indeed, they are the product of processes that involve profit-oriented learning and selection. Metaphorically, the routines employed by a firm at any time can be regarded as the best it "knows and can do." To employ them is rational, in that sense, even though the firms do not go through any attempt to compare their prevailing routines with all alternative ones. Whether that translates into "optimizing" behavior depends on what one means by that term. (For a fine discussion of this issue in biology and in economics, see Schoemaker 1991.)

These models generally involve three different kinds of firm "routines." First, there are those that might be called standard operating procedures, which determine how and how much a firm produces under various circumstances, given its capital stock and other constraints on its actions that are fixed in the short run. Prominent among these are the technologies it commands. Second, there are routines that determine the investment behavior of the firm, the equations that govern its growth or decline (measured in terms of its capital stock) as a function of its profits, and perhaps other variables. Third, the deliberative processes of the firm, those that involve searching for better ways of doing things, also are viewed as guided by routines. While in principle within these models search could be focused on any one of a firm's prevailing routines—its technologies or other standard operating procedures, its investment rule, or even its prevailing search procedures— in practice, in all of them search is assumed oriented to uncover new or improve old production techniques. Winter and I have found it convenient to call such search R & D. Other authors of similar models have invoked the term *learning* to describe analogous "improvement" processes.

Firm search processes provide the source of differential fitness; firms whose R & D turn up better technologies will earn profits and grow, relative to their competitors. But R & D also tends to bind firms together as a community because in these models a firm's R & D partly attends to what its competitors are doing, and profitable innovations are, with a lag, imitated by other firms in the industry.

The firm, or rather the collection of firms in the industry, perhaps involving new firms coming into the industry and old ones exiting, is viewed as operating within an exogenously determined environment. The profitability of any firm is determined by what it is doing, and what its competitors do, given the environment. Generally the environment can be interpreted as a "market" or set of markets.

Note that in the theory that has been sketched above, just as routines are analogous to genes, firms are analogous to phenotypes, or particular organisms, in biological evolutionary theory, but there are profound differences. First, firms do not have a natural life span, and not all ultimately die. Neither can they be regarded as having a natural size. Some may be big, some small. Thus in assessing the relative importance of a particular routine in the industry mix, or analyzing whether it is expanding or contracting in relative use, it is not sufficient to "count" the firms employing it. One must consider their size, or whether they are growing or contracting. Second, unlike phenotypes (living organisms) that are stuck with their genes, firms are not stuck with their routines. Indeed they have built-in mechanisms for changing them.

The logic of these models defines a dynamic stochastic system. It can be modeled as a complex Markov process. A standard iteration can be described as follows. At the existing moment of time, all firms can be characterized by their capital stocks and prevailing routines. Decision rules keyed to market conditions look to those conditions' "last period." Inputs employed and outputs produced by all firms then are determined. The market then determines prices. Given the technology and other routines used by each firm, each firm's profitability then is determined, and the investment rule then determines how much each firm expands or contracts. Search routines focus on one or another aspect of the firm's behavior and capabilities, and (stochastically) come up with proposed modifications that may or may not be adopted. The system is now ready for the next period's iteration.

The theory described above can be evaluated on a number of counts. One is whether the view of behavior it contains, in abstract form, is appealing given what it purports to analyze. The individuals and organizations in these models act, as humans do in the models of sociobiology, on the basis of habits or customs or beliefs; in the Nelson-Winter model all these define routines. While firm routines can be regarded as the result of a learning process, the implicit "rationality" in these models certainly is a "bounded" one, in the sense of Simon (1947) and March and Simon (1958). As we shall see, it is quite possible to build a certain amount of foresight into the actors in an evolutionary theory. However, if one wants a model in which it is presumed that the actors largely understand the details of the context in which they are operating and competing, save for the truly stochastic elements, and are able to choose their best action in the light of this full knowledge, one might as well use a full-blown neoclassical rational-choice model. This of course is what is done in the new neoclassical growth theories.

The theory can be judged by the appeal of the theory of technical progress built into it. The view is certainly "evolutionary," and in that regard it squares well with the accounts given by scholars of technical advance, like Vincenti, at least in abstract form. It must be noted that, within the theory, "evolution" is going on at several different levels. New technological departures are being generated by individual firms, which in effect "select" them, deciding which to introduce and which not to. (For an empirical study of evolution within a firm, see Burgelman 1994.) Firms also, by scanning their competitors' technologies, are deciding which of those technologies to take aboard and which not. In addition, there is market selection on firms that are doing well.

Within this class of models, profitability determines the "fitness" of a technology, and of firms, and firms are the only organizational actors. These observations call attention to the fact that this theory would seem to apply only to economic sectors in which the market provides the (or the dominant) selection mechanism, winnowing both technologies and firms. It is not well suited for dealing with sectors like medical care or defense, where professional judgments or political process determine what is fit and what is not. Selection environments clearly differ from sector to sector, and it would seem that these differences need to be understood and built into sector-level analyses. (For an elaboration of this point, see Nelson and Winter 1977.)

However, the central purpose of the models considered in this section is to explain economic growth at a macroeconomic level. Thus a fundamental question about them is this: Can they generate, hence in a sense explain, the rising output per worker, growing capital intensity, rising real wages, and relatively constant rate of return on capital that have been the standard pattern in advanced industrial nations and what neoclassical growth theory seems to explain? The answer is that they can, and in ways that conform well with underlying appreciative theory.

Within these models a successful technological innovation generates profits for the firm making it, and leads to capital formation and growth of the firm. Firm growth generally is sufficient to outweigh any decline in employment per unit of output associated with productivity growth, and hence results in an increase in the demand for labor, which pulls up the real wage rate. This latter consequence means that capital-using but labor-saving innovations now become more profitable, and when by chance they appear as a result of a "search," they will be adopted, thus pulling up the level of capital intensity in the economy. At the same time that labor productivity, real wages, and capital intensity are rising, the same mechanisms hold down the rate of return on capital. If the profit rate rises, say because of the creation of especially productive new technology, the high profits will induce an investment boom, which will pull up wages and drive capital returns back down.

These deductions of evolutionary growth theory would not surprise an advocate of neoclassical theory. On the surface they appear similar to those of neoclassical growth theory. Indeed for evolutionary theory to have credibility, these predictions had better be similar, because any broad growth theory needs to be consistent with the basic empirically documented broad features of economic growth as we have experienced it.

However, while at first glance the mechanisms explaining these patterns have a certain surface similarity in evolutionary and neoclassical theory, if one looks beneath the surface one can see that the mechanisms in fact are very different. In particular, one theory is based on the assumption of a moving equilibrium, and the other most emphatically is not. And if one takes a closer look, it becomes clear that evolutionary theory enables one to see, to expect, phenomena to which neoclassical theory is blind, or that it denies. At the same time that the model generates "macro" time series that resemble the actual data, beneath the aggregate at any time there is considerable variation among firms in the technologies they are using, their productivity, and their profitability. Within this model, more productive and profitable techniques tend to replace less productive ones, through two mechanisms. Firms using more profitable technologies grow. And more profitable technologies tend to be imitated and adopted by firms that had been using less profitable ones. Thus the theory is consistent with both the large body of empirical work that has documented considerable and persistent intraindustry, interfirm dispersion (for example, Rumelt 1991 and Mueller 1989) and with what is known empirically about the diffusion of new techniques (see Metcalfe 1988). Neoclassical growth theories have trouble being consistent with these elements of economic growth as we have experienced it.

Soete and Turner (1984), Metcalfe (1988, 1992), and Metcalfe and Gibbons (1989) have developed evolutionary growth models focusing on diffusion. These authors repress the stochastic element in the introduction of new technologies that was prominent in the models described above and, in effect, work with a given and fixed set of technologies. However, within these models each of the individual technologies may be improving over time, possibly at different rates. At the same time, firms are tending to allocate their investment portfolios more heavily toward the more profitable technologies than toward the less. As a result, rising productivity in the industry as a whole, and measured aggregate "technical advance," is the consequence of two different kinds of forces. One is the improvement of the individual technologies. The other is the expansion of use of the more productive technologies relative to the less productive ones. Both groups of authors point out that the latter phenomenon is likely to be a more potent source of productivity growth when there is prevailing large variation in the productivity of technologies in wide use, than when the best technology already dominates in use. Thus the aggregate growth performance of the economy is strongly related to the prevailing variation beneath the aggregate.

The model by Silverberg, Dosi, and Orsenigo (1988) develops the basic theoretical notions introduced in this section in another direction. In their model there are only two technologies. One is potentially better than the other, but that potential will not be achieved unless effort is put into improving prevailing practice. Rather than incorporating a separate "search" activity, in Silverberg and colleagues a firm improves its prevailing procedures (technologies) through learning associated with operation. What a firm learns is reflected in its increased productivity in using that technology, but some of the learning "spills over" and enables others using that technology to improve their productivity for free, as it were. In contrast with the other models considered in this section, in which firms do not "look forward" to anticipate future developments, in the model of Silverberg, Dosi, and Orsenigo, firms, or at least some of them, recognize that the technology that initially is behind in productivity is potentially the better technology, and also that they can gain advantage over their competitors if they invest in using and learning with it, if the spillovers are not too great. In contrast with the Nelson-Winter model, a firm may employ some of both technologies, and hence may use some of its profits from using the prevailing best technology to invest in experience with the presently inferior technology that is potentially the best. If no firm does this, then of course the potential of the potentially better technology never will be realized.

An early "innovator" may come out a winner, if it learns rapidly and little of its learning spills over, or its competitors are sluggish in getting into the new technology themselves. On the other hand, it may come out a loser if its learning is slow and hence the cost of operating the new technology remains high, or most of its learning spills over and its competitors get in in a timely manner, taking advantage for free of the spillover.

Several other evolutionary growth models have been developed. Gunnar Eliasson and colleagues have been constructing over the years a very detailed evolutionary model calibrated on the Swedish economy (see Eliasson's chapter in Day and Eliasson 1986). Chiaromonte and Dosi (1993) recently have blended into the Silverberg-Dosi-Orsenigo model elements of the Nelson-Winter assumptions about stochastic search for new techniques. Iwai (1984a, 1984b), Conlisk (1989), Kwasnicki (1996), and Saviotti (1996) also have published models in this class. There clearly is a lot of richness in these "Schumpeterian" models of economic growth, and I believe a lot of potential. It remains to be seen how many economists studying economic growth using the "old" theoretical technology will be attracted to gamble on the new.

5. Path Dependencies, Dynamic Increasing Returns, and the Evolution of Industry Structure

The models considered in Section 4 go a certain distance toward consistency with the appreciative theoretic accounts of long-run economic change, but there still is a lot that is "mechanical" about them. Certain variables grow over time, in particular output per worker and real wages. Others remain more or less constant, like the rate of return on capital and factor shares, or at least show no systematic drift. However, by and large nothing goes on that could be called "development." While industry may become more concentrated over time, there are no major changes in industry structure of the sort often highlighted in economic histories. No radically new technologies emerge, no new institutions.

The evolutionary theories considered in this section have more of a developmental flavor. They involve path dependencies, dynamic increasing returns, and the coevolution of technologies, firm and industry structures, and supporting institutions.

While path dependencies and dynamic increasing returns are built into most of the models we already have considered, this was not the center of attention of the authors. Over the past few years, however, a considerable literature in evolutionary economics has grown up focused on these topics. The works of Brian Arthur (1988a, 1988b) and Paul David (1985, 1992) are particularly interesting. My treatment here will aim to generalize the issues they address.

5.1. Technology Cycles and Dominant Designs

I begin by considering models that focus on competition among technologies. Students of technical advance long have noted that, in the early stages of a technology's history, there usually are a number of competing variants. (For a fine discussion and a number of illustrative case studies, see Utterback 1994.) Thus in the early history of automobiles, some models were powered by gasoline-fueled internal combustion engines, some by steam engines, some by batteries. As we know, gradually gasoline-fueled engines came to dominate and the other two possibilities were abandoned. The standard explanation for this is that gasoline engines were the superior mode, and with experience that was found out. The Silverberg, Dosi, and Orsenigo paper contains a model of this mechanism. In their analysis a potentially superior new alternative requires some development—learning—before its latent superiority becomes manifest. It can take time before that development occurs and, with bad luck, it even is possible that it never occurs. But by and large the potentially better technology will win out.

In the Arthur and David models, one can see a different explanation for why the internal combustion engine won out. It need not have been innately superior. In these models there are dynamic increasing returns, in that the more a particular technology is employed, the greater its attractiveness relative to its competitors. Thus in the case in question, all that was required for the gasoline engine to come to dominate was a run of luck. For some chance reason it gained an initial lead, and this started a "rolling snowball" mechanism.

What might lie behind an increasing-returns rolling snowball? Arthur, David, and other authors suggest several different possibilities. One is that each of the competing technologies involved is what Winter and I have called a cumulative technology. In a cumulative technology, today's technical advances build from and improve upon the technology that was available at the start of the period, and tomorrow's, in turn, builds on today's. The cumulative effect is like the technology-specific learning in the model of Silverberg and colleagues. According to the cumulative technology theory, in the early history of automobiles, gasoline engines, steam engines, and electrical engines might all have been plausible alternative technologies for powering cars. While we now know that gasoline engines became dominant, according to this theory this might have been simply a matter of luck. By chance, inventors tended to concentrate on it, or by chance big advances were made. However, once the gasoline engine had been developed to a point where it was significantly superior to extant steam or electrical engines, investing time and resources to advance those other technologies came to appear a bad bet, because they needed to close such a large gap in performance before they would be competitive.

There are two other dynamic increasing returns stories that have been put forth. One stresses advantages to consumers or users if different individuals buy similar or compatible products—this has been called network externalities—that lend advantage to a variant that just happens to attract a number of customers early. The other stresses complements, for example where a particular product has a specialized complementary product or service, whose development may lend that variant special advantages. Telephone networks, in which each user is strongly interested in having other users have compatible products, is the most commonly employed example of the first case. Videocassette recorders—which run cassettes that need to be specially tailored to their particular design—or computers that require compatible software, are often used as examples of the second. (For a very good general discussion and review of the literature on both of these stories, see Katz and Shapiro 1994.) However, while the stories are different, the mathematics used to formalize them tends to be the same (see, for example, Arthur 1988a, 1988b). Also, the phenomena often are intertwined, and also linked with the processes involved in the development of cumulative technologies, as in David's (1985) example of the QWERTY typewriter keyboard.

To return to our automobile example, people who learned to drive in their parents' or friends' car powered by an internal combustion engine almost certainly were drawn to similar cars when they themselves came to purchase one, in part to avoid the new learning and potential surprises that would be involved if they bought a steam- or battery-powered one. At the same time, the ascendancy of automobiles powered by gas-burning internal combustion engines made it profitable for petroleum companies to locate gasoline stations at convenient places along highways. It also made it profitable for them to search for new sources of petroleum, and to develop technologies that reduced gasoline production costs. In turn, this increased the attractiveness of gasoline-powered cars to car drivers and buyers.

Note that, for those who consider gas-engine automobiles, large petroleum companies, and the dependence of a large share of the nation's transportation on petroleum a complex that lies behind many social ills, the story spun out above indicates that it did not have to be this way. If the roll of the die early in the history of automobiles had come out another way, we might today have steam or electric cars. A similar argument recently has been made about the victory of AC over DC as the system for carrying electricity (for an open-minded discussion, see David 1991). The story also invites consideration of possibly self-interested professional judgments or political factors as major elements in the shaping of long-run economic trends, a subject I will pick up shortly. After all, under these theories all it takes may be just a little push.

Other analysts may see the above account as overblown. Steam- and battery-powered car engines had major limitations then and still do now; gasoline clearly was better. AC had major advantages over DC, and still does. According to this point of view, dynamic increasing returns is an important phenomenon but is unlikely to have greatly influenced which technology won out, in most important cases. I predict that this issue will be a lively topic of empirical research and argument over the coming years.

There also is a more general open question about the range of technologies for which a "dominant design" emerges, for any reason. The various dynamic increasing returns stories seem plausible for some product classes, but not for others. And in some product-class areas, different user needs may tend to prevent a particular product from coming to dominate the market, even if there are dynamic increasing returns. Pharmaceuticals, the value of which are extremely sensitive to both the particular disease and the particular characteristics of the patient, are a good case in point.

5.2. Firm and Industry Structure

I turn now to a different but related body of evolutionary writings— that concerned with the evolution of industry structure as a technology develops. It is tied to the notion that for most technologies, after a period of time a dominant design emerges, but it is not committed to a particular theory of how that happens, whether because the truly better variant is finally found and consensus develops around it or because of dynamic increasing returns phenomena. In any case, within this body of evolutionary theorizing, the establishment of a dominant design has important implications regarding the subsequent nature of R & D, and for industry structure.

The basic argument would appear to have two sources. The first is Mueller and Tilton (1969), based on their speculations about patterns of industry evolution they were observing. The second is Abernathy and Utterback (1975), based on their detailed study of automobiles. Because the Abernathy and Utterback story is closely linked to an interesting theory of what happens to R & D as a dominant design emerges, I will follow it.

The basic proposition is that, prior to the emergence of a dominant design, there is little R & D directed toward improving production processes, because product designs are unstable and the market for any one is small. With the emergence of a dominant design, the profits from developing better ways of producing it become considerable. Often the development of better production processes will involve the exploitation of latent scale economies, and the establishment of capital-intensive modes of production. In turn, the improvement of production processes that are specific to a particular broad design further locks it in, and disadvantages competing designs.

The argument then is that this pattern of technological evolution causes a particular pattern of evolution of firm and industry structure. In the early stages of an industry—say, automobiles—firms tend to be small and entry relatively easy, reflecting the diversity of technologies being employed and their rapid change. The industry consists of a number of smallish firms, but with a lot of entry and exit. As the quality of the products improve, and the market grows, so does the number of firms active in the industry. However, as a dominant design emerges and specialized production processes are developed, barriers to entry begin to rise as the scale and capital needed for competitive production grows. Also, with the basic technology set, learning becomes cumulative, and incumbent firms are advantaged relative to potential entrants for that reason as well. After a shakeout, industry structure settles down to a collection of established, largish firms.

When this theory was first put forth, there were only limited data supporting it. Since that time Gort and Klepper (1982), Klepper and Graddy (1990), Utterback and Suarez (1993), Utterback (1994), and Malerba and Orsenigo (1993, 1994) have provided convincing evidence that this pattern of evolution in fact holds over a wide range of industries.

A recent formal model developed by Klepper (1993) accepts the broad empirical story, but puts forth a different evolutionary theory to explain it. In Klepper's model the investments made by a firm in product innovation are independent of firm size, but investments in process innovation are positively related to firm size. As in the more standard story, in the early days of a technology's history, firms are small, for that reason little process R & D is done, and entry barriers are low. The presence of many firms makes for rapid product innovation. But as profitable extant firms grow and invest more in process innovation, entry barriers rise. Shakeout occurs because of rivalry among the extant firms, increasingly competing on the basis of cost. No dominant design emerges in the Klepper model, but as the number of extant firms dwindles, product innovation slows.

5.3. Supporting Institutions

The writing on the coevolution of technology and industry structure tends to define industry structure rather conventionally. However, there are a number of studies that define industry structure more broadly, or look outside the industry, narrowly defined, and are concerned with the coevolution of a technology and industry with various supporting institutions.

As an industry becomes established, one frequently observes not only the development of technical and product standards but also the emergence of standard patterns of interaction more generally between firms, suppliers, and customers, and across firms in the industry. Economic relations become embedded in social ones, along the lines described by Mark Granovetter (1985), and people become conscious that there is a new industry, and that it has collective interests and needs. Michael Hannan and Glenn Carroll (1992) discuss in some detail these processes of "legitimation" and their consequences. Industry or trade associations form. These give the industry a recognized organization that can lobby on its behalf for regulation to its liking, for protection from competition from outside the group, for public programs to support it, and so on. This is another feature of an industry's evolution that can lock in status quo.

More generally, while the formal evolutionary growth models of Section 4 and the dynamic increasing returns models discussed at the beginning of this section take the basic parameters of the "selection environment" (usually treated as a market) as given, many of the sociologists studying industry evolution stress that the industry itself strongly molds its own selection environment. It does so through the rules of behavior and forms of interaction among firms that evolve spontaneously, through the formation of a variety of industry-related organizations that decide matters like standards, through political action. (See, for example, Tushman and Romanelli 1985, Rosenkopf and Tushman 1994.) In turn, such action may be central in determining what design or system turns out to be dominant. (For such a discussion bearing on electric power systems, see McGuire, Granovetter, and Schwartz 1993.)

If the technology on which the industry is based has novel characteristics, new technical societies and new technical journals tend to spring up. In some cases whole new fields of "science" may come into being (Rosenberg 1982a, chap. 7; Rosenberg and Nelson 1994). Thus the field of metallurgy came into existence because of a demand for better understanding of the factors that determined the properties of steel. Computer science was brought into existence by the advent of the modern computer. Chemical engineering and electrical engineering rose up as fields of teaching and research because of industry demand for them that arose after the key technological advances that launched the industries. Earlier I noted the apparent blindness of much of the writing on how science evolves to the use of science in technology. The technology-oriented sciences directly provide a "market-like" environment stimulating research on various topics and also a stringent test environment for new scientific theories and other published findings.

The emergence and development of these technology-oriented sciences tend to tie industries to universities, which provide both people trained in the relevant fields and research findings that enable the technology to advance. The development of these sciences naturally lends extra strength to prevailing technologies. On the other hand, the presence of university research tends to dilute the extent to which existing firms have knowledge advantages over potential entrants. Also, research at universities just may become the source of radically different technological alternatives.

Recognition of the role of technical societies and universities in the development of modern technologies opens the door to seeing the wide range of institutions that may coevolve with a technology and an industry. Often legal structures need to change. Thus there may be intellectual property rights issues that need to be sorted out—biotechnology is a striking contemporary case in point. There almost always are issues of regulation, as was prominently the case in radio and, in a different manner, biotechnology again. Hughes (1983) has described in great detail the wide range of legal and regulatory matters that had to be decided before electric power could go forward strongly, and how the particular ways they were decided affected the evolution of the technology and the industry. The coevolution of law and technology and industry structure has been only lightly touched on in the writings on how the law evolves.

In many cases new public-sector activities and programs are required. Thus mass use of automobiles required that societies organize themselves to build and maintain a system of public roads. Airplanes required airports. The development of radio, and of commercial television, required mechanisms to allocate the radio spectrum. Peter Murmann (2003) provides us with the most detailed and persuasive account to date of the coevolution of technology, firm and industry structure, and supporting institutions, in his study of the rise of the German dyestuffs industry in the last decades of the nineteenth century.

These examples indicate that the evolution of institutions relevant to a technology or industry may be a very complex process involving not only the actions of private firms competing with each other in a market environment, but also organizations like industry associations, technical societies, universities, courts, government agencies, and legislatures. In turn, the way these other organizations evolve and the things they do may profoundly influence the nature of the firms and the organization of industry. I shall discuss these issues further in the chapters that follow.

6. Responding to the Winds of Change

Evolutionary theory in biology provides a sharp answer to the question of how life responds in situations in which major environmental changes make existing dominant life forms ill adapted. To the extent that better adapted life forms are present in at least small numbers, these and their similar offspring will thrive and multiply, and their now poorly adapted peers will tend to die out. Some new varieties created through mating or mutation that would have had no chance in the old regime may do well in the new one. Others that would have prospered now may have no chance.

How is it in economics? If one considers firms or other organizations as carriers of basic practices—earlier I called them routines—what happens when the market or something else changes? A fundamental difference between organizations and organisms, of course, is that the former are not stuck with their routines but can change them, while the latter cannot change their genes. Thus, unlike the case in biology, it is meaningful in economic evolutionary theory to ask about the extent to which significant adjustment to changed environmental conditions—for example, a sharp change in patterns of consumer demand or factor availabilities and prices, or the advent of radically new technology—is achieved largely by old organizations learning new ways, or requires the death of old organizations and the birth of new ones.

Some of the organizational ecology models developed by sociologists take a position that firms are like biological organisms. Thus Michael Hannan and John Freeman (1989) posit (for the purposes of their formal theorizing) that organizations cannot change their ways at all. Under this view, society's ability to respond to change depends entirely on the presence at any time of a variety of organizations, or the generation of new ones. (For more eclectic surveys of sociological approaches to the evolution of organizations, see Aldrich 1979, Scott 1992, and Baum and Singh 1994.)

While this position may sound bizarre to many economists, a number of careful students of firm behavior have been impressed that the set of things a firm can do well at any time is quite limited, and that, while firms certainly can learn to do new things, these learning capabilities also are limited. Thus Mueller (1989), Cool and Schendel (1988), and Rumelt (1991) have shown that, within an industry, there tend to be persistent differences across firms in profitability or productivity. While "imitation" is an important economic phenomenon, there would appear to be durable firm differences, associated with unique resources or competences. Dosi, Teece, and Winter (1992) have argued that, to be effective, a firm needs a package of routines, including those concerned with learning and innovation, that are "coherent." But that coherency, on the other hand, entails a certain rigidity.

Paul Milgrom and John Roberts (1990), commenting on a wide range of recent literature on firm competences, have stressed that competences tend to come in strongly complementary packages of traits. As Daniel Levinthal (1997) argues, this undoubtedly is an important reason that successful firms often are difficult to imitate effectively, because to do so requires that a competitor adopt a number of different practices at once. It also is an important reason why firms that do well in one context may have great difficulty in adapting to a new one. Recently, Gavetti and Levinthal (2000) have attempted to model firms that both attend to the possibilities of making marginal improvements in their practices, and scan significantly different ways of doing things. Even within their model, being able to do this effectively is not easy.

Winter and I (1977, 1982) and Dosi (1982, 1988) have used the concept of technological regime or paradigm to refer to the set of understandings about a particular broad technology that are shared by experts in a field, including understandings about what a firm needs to be doing to operate effectively in that regime. Tushman and Anderson (1986) have coined the phrase "competence destroying technical advance" to characterize new technologies when the skills and understandings needed to deal with them are significantly different from those relevant to the old. There is now considerable evidence (see Tushman and Anderson 1986, Utterback 1994, Christensen and Rosenbloom 1995, Henderson and Clark 1990, and Henderson 1993) that when such a new technology comes along, the old entry barriers fall, new companies enter, and many old ones fail. Thus organizations may be more like organisms than many economists are wont to believe, and significant economic change, like significant biological change, may involve large elements of creative destruction.

What about the institutions that support a particular industry or technology? Can the old ones change to meet the changed needs, or must a basically new set come into existence? If the latter is the case, does this tend to involve the ascendancy of new regions or nations, and the decline of the old? William Lazonick (1990), among others, has argued that the broad organization of work and institutions for training labor that worked so well for British industry in the late nineteenth century became a handicap in the twentieth. Thorstein Veblen's famous essay (1915) on the rise of Germany as an economic power stresses more generally that British industry was sorely handicapped in adopting the new technologies that were coming into place around the turn of the century by an interlocking set of constraints associated with her institutions and past investments, whereas Germany could work with a relatively clean slate.

These ideas have been revisited by Perez (1983), and by Freeman and Louca (2001), who have developed the concept of a "techno-economic paradigm." Their argument starts along lines developed by Schumpeter many years ago: different eras are dominated by different fundamental technologies. They then propose that, to be effective with those technologies, a nation requires a set of institutions compatible with and supportive of them. The ones suitable for an earlier set of fundamental technologies may be quite inappropriate for the new ones. The authors propose that the period since 1970 has seen the rise of "information technologies" as the new basis of economic effectiveness, and argue that effective accommodation requires a very different set of institutions than those required in the earlier era.

Theorists of this ilk tended, in the 1980s and early 1990s to look to Japan as the country whose economic institutions were appropriate to the new era. As growth in Japan turned sluggish and the U.S. economy surged in the late 1990s, the institutions of the United States again appeared to be the ones that would support economic growth. While in my judgment the broad perspective of this school—that institutions matter, and the ones that are appropriate for economic growth tend to change as the key driving technologies change—is right-headed, we still lack a good theory that enables us to judge just what are the institutions that are appropriate for an era.

7. Reprise

This chapter has aimed to provide an overview of recent writings by economists, and some other social scientists, who have put forth express theoretical arguments that the variables the authors are examining change through evolutionary processes. I have concentrated on works in which empirical subject matter is the focus of attention and an evolutionary theory is invoked to explain the observed or alleged pattern of change, and largely have neglected works in which the formal aspects of an evolutionary theory are central and empirical subject matter is brought in mostly as stylized examples. However, a unifying characteristic of the writings surveyed here is that the evolutionary theorizing is set out explicitly, as contrasted with coming in mostly as a way of talking about the empirical subject matter.

As I argued in the introduction, the latter approach long has been common in economics. It is the express evolutionary theorizing that is relatively new. The theoretical arguments I have surveyed range from quite precise and formal, to storytelling. Virtually all of the them, however, are put forth by their authors to provide a different—and in the author's view, a better—theory than one that uses the conventional assumptions of "equilibrium" theorizing.

This of course raises the question of what one might mean by "better." More accurate prediction? "On the button" prediction never has been a hallmark of economic analysis, and it is unlikely that predictions motivated by an evolutionary theoretic framework are systematically better or worse than those motivated by a neoclassical theory. The heart of quantitative prediction making in economics lies in the details of the prediction equations, and these almost always reflect judgment of the particular context as much as formal theory.

Better explanation? If by "better" one means statistically "better fits" in various senses, again the heart of the exercise is in the details of the equations that are fitted, and those details are as much a matter of art as of broad formal theory. Indeed, formal general theory usually provides only loose constraints on models designed to fit particular bodies of data.

On the other hand, if by "better explanation" one means one that is consistent with informed judgments as to what really is going on, that is exactly the case for evolutionary theory put forth by those that advocate it. In general, those informed judgments reflect inferences drawn from a broad and diversified body of data. Thus evolutionary theories of productivity growth at a macroeconomic level feel right to their advocates, not simply because they can be tuned to fit those particular data pretty well, but also because the evolutionary explanation is consistent with observed differences in productivity and profit among firms, and with the fact that even obviously superior new technology usually diffuses slowly, and like observations, that it takes more strain for neoclassical theory to encompass.

This, I would argue, is an important part of what the "betterness" criterion ought to be. Does the explanation ring right to those who know the details of the field? It would seem that this is the issue Marshall had in mind when he wrote the sentences that began this chapter. Mechanical theories did not ring right with him.

But he also raised the issue of complexity. If there is value in formal theory in economics, it lies in the ability to work through complex causal arguments, but if the complexity is too great, one may lose the ability either to understand what the theory is doing—what assumptions lead to what conclusions—or to check the logic for accuracy, or both. For the reasons discussed in the introduction, economists now are far better able to deal with complexity in general, and the complexity of evolutionary models in particular, than we were twenty years ago, much less in Marshall's time. There is no doubt, however, that evolutionary theories still tend to be complex.

Thus those who are attracted to developing and employing them to address the phenomena in which they are interested are making an intellectual bet that the price of added complexity is worth paying to buy the better ability to devise and work with a theory that rings right. The bet is that evolutionary theory opens up a productive research program, to use Lakatos's idea, that is foreclosed or more difficult if one stays with mechanical analogies.

The use of formal evolutionary theory in economics is still new, and the proponents of evolutionary theory are struggling with both techniques and standards. It is clear that a number of the evolutionary theories put forth by economists in recent years are difficult to follow in terms of their cause-effect logic, and some may be logically incoherent. Merely adopting evolutionary theoretic language does not automatically lead to a logical model. But a number of the new evolutionary theories do seem coherent, and analytically powerful. The coherence and power of evolutionary theorizing obviously depends on the skill and diligence of the theorist. There would appear to be nothing different here between neoclassical and evolutionary theorizing.

This said, it is clear that one of the appeals of evolutionary theorizing about economic change is that that mode of theorizing does seem to better correspond to the actual complexity of the processes, as these are described by the scholars who have studied them in detail. There is no question that, in taking aboard this complexity, one often ends up with a theory in which precise predictions are impossible or highly dependent on particular contingencies, as is the case if the theory implies multiple or rapidly shifting equilibria, or if under the theory the system is likely to be far away from any equilibrium, except under very special circumstances. Thus an evolutionary theory not only may be more complex than an equilibrium theory; it may also be less decisive in its predictions and explanations. To such a complaint, the advocate of an evolutionary theory might reply that the apparent power of the simpler theory in fact is an illusion.

A good case can be made that the topics and sectors where evolutionary theories that have been developed to date are notably weak regarding prediction, and somewhat ad hoc on explanation, are those where standard neoclassical theories have great difficulties also. They are areas where there is no real market, or where market selection is strongly mixed with political or professional influences. The problem in theorizing here clearly lies not in the evolutionary art form but in the complexity of the subject matter.

Many years ago Veblen (1898) asked, "Why is economics not an evolutionary science?" In my view, economics would be a stronger field if its theoretical framework were expressly evolutionary. Such a framework helps us see and understand better the complexity of the economic reality. That, I think, is its greatest advantage. But it does not make the complexity go away.

CHAPTER 4

On the Nature and Evolution
of Human Know-how

1. Introduction

Modern humans possess an astounding amount of effective "know-how": technique and knowledge that allow us to do things that early humans—much less nonhuman animals—could not dream of doing. This chapter is concerned with the cognitive and cultural conditions that make these achievements possible.

The techniques or goal-directed practices of nonhuman animals are bound by a relatively tight biological leash, to use the terminology of E. O. Wilson (1975). Although animals such as rats, or our primate relatives, clearly learn with experience, and may pass on learning to other animals with whom they are in contact, from everything we know, it seems there is a vanishingly small amount of intergenerational cumulative learning that results in the improvement of practice over time even among the primates. As generations proceed, the biological leash does not get longer. Major changes in practice are dependent on changes in the biological base itself; that is, on biological evolutionary changes in gene frequencies and associated developmental processes.

The contrast presented by progressive advances in know-how in many arenas of human activity is staggering. Humans today cannot run much faster or shout much louder than humans of a century—or fifty centuries—ago, nor are our eyes any better. But we can get where we are go-

* Based on Katherine Nelson and Richard R. Nelson, "On the Nature and Evolution of Human Know-how," *Research Policy* 31 (2002): 719–733.

ing far faster by bike, by car, or by airplane. We can communicate over long distances by flags, telegraph, wireless, and now e-mail. We can see the galaxies an incredible distance away, and also the smallest molecules, through the technologies we have progressively developed over time. The biological leash has become longer and longer, so that today our species knowledge capabilities in many arenas appear very loosely attached to our biological makeup.

Human know-how of these kinds is carried not in our individual genotypes but in our minds, and thus explaining these advances must at some level involve understanding the human mind. Yet it is a mistake to think that this process involves a simple substitute of individual brains for individual genomes. Rather, the minds of individual human actors are extended through the collective memories of the community as well as through the artifacts and symbols—especially spoken and written language—of their social worlds. The know-how that lies behind the achievements noted here is part of human culture, in the sense that their core aspects are shared among those within a society who have the credentials to know, and who have gone through the appropriate cultural learning processes.

These advanced and complex sets of human know-how are typically called "technologies." These same characteristics—of being carried in the mind, not the genes, and being part of human social and material culture—obtain for such more mundane, individually learned techniques as frying an egg, ordering a meal at a restaurant, diapering a baby, and tying one's shoelaces. But what is remarkable about the kinds of know-how that are called technologies is how powerful they have become over the years.

This chapter explores some connections between two bodies of empirical research and theorizing that bear on technological know-how and its advance. Cognitive science is concerned with the nature and mechanisms of human knowing. The focus of cognitive science has not been on the knowledge involved in complex technologies, nor on the processes by which human know-how is expanded over time. However, some of the debates in cognitive science resonate with debates among scholars of the advance of technological know-how in an interesting way, and the developing view among a number of scholars of cognitive science, that human knowledge must be understood as a "hybrid" of ability to do, to reflect, to symbolize, and to communicate with other humans, can be helpful, we believe, in orienting some of the theorizing about technological advance. We review selective aspects of this literature in Section 2.

Empirical research and theorizing about the advance of technological know-how has proceeded with almost no interaction with cognitive science. We find it interesting, therefore, that one of the sharp debates in early cognitive science—between those who stressed the understanding and command of logic used in human problem solving and those who played down those elements and stressed the trial and feedback nature of human learning and knowing—also has played out among scholars of technological advance. And one can see in recent theorizing about technological advance as an "evolutionary process" something akin to the hybrid theory of human knowledge taking shape in cognitive science. These conceptions seem highly relevant to sorting out how the processes by which technology evolves differ from evolutionary processes in biology, and in illuminating evolutionary epistemology more generally. This is the subject matter of Section 3.

While in both of these sections we will discuss a wide range of writings, this chapter should not be regarded as a literature review in any standard sense of that term. Instead of trying to cover a representative range of writings, we focus our presentation rather tightly on particular strands in the two literatures that we think mesh together well, and we largely ignore writings, even important and well-known ones, that we do not see as making up part of the consistent analytic framework that we propose is coming into view.

2. The Construction of Knowledge in the Individual and Species

There are at least four different kinds of questions relating to human know-how: how it is acquired, how it is retained in memory, how it is invoked or used in relevant circumstances, and how it is communicated to others. Studies vary in the extent to which they focus on these different questions. And while human knowledge is often considered and studied as a single kind (that is, as information), clearly different subtypes of knowledge exist and involve different kinds of learning, memory, mobilization, and communication. A standard distinction often recognized by cognitive scientists is between "knowing how" and "knowing that," with the former referred to as procedural knowledge and the latter as declarative knowledge, but these distinctions may be somewhat crude.

For example, there is the kind of know-how involved in riding a bike and the kind involved in recognizing a face. Many writers refer to both of these types as procedural, in that they are in some sense automatic skills carried out more or less unconsciously. However, there would appear to be important differences between the nature of the salient know-how in these two cases. In particular, the latter involves centrally the ability to recognize and discriminate among complex patterns. Reflect on the kind of knowledge required to play chess competently. This kind of knowledge may share something with face recognition, because in both cases identification of complex patterns is required, but competent chess playing clearly involves additional elements as well. Thus a competent chess player needs to know the rules of chess and also what moves within the rules are appropriate in what contexts. This latter form of knowledge often is called declarative, a term meant to connote both that the kind of knowledge is conscious and that it can be articulated. However, the distinction here with procedural knowledge, which is assumed to be unconscious and not capable of articulation, may be a matter of degree, not kind. And the ability to use a map to figure out the best way to drive from Washington to Boston, while also called procedural, and which clearly shares something with the ability to play chess, would appear to involve different elements as well.

In any case, it is clear that humans invoke and simultaneously call on a variety of different types of knowledge in many different kinds of real-world settings. How this knowledge is represented in memory is one of the major issues that cognitive science has addressed, and that we will attempt to sort out in the rest of this section. As we do so, we will generally follow the rule that *knowledge* is a general term referring to the content of all the long-term memory/representations humans possess, while *know-how* refers to those bits of knowledge related to the use of technology, even in its simplest forms, for example in tying shoelaces or beating an egg.

2.1. Competing Models, or Different Domains of Applicability?

The broad field of cognitive science has, from its modern inception, been intimately intertwined with research in the field of artificial intelligence (AI). As the name suggests, the founding fathers of AI were deeply interested in the proposal that the workings of the digital computer, with its linear von Neumann architecture, could serve as a plausible model for the workings of the human mind. Classic AI was not concerned with learning processes, but rather with how information was processed and represented; it focused on the nature of the processes involved when humans engaged in activities like playing chess, solving puzzles, or proving theorems.

The content and structure of the human mind was assumed to be analogous to the content of a computer, with symbols readable by the mind stored in various locations standing for data, or particular relationships, or more complex mental representations and programs. Thinking and problem solving were assumed to involve working with these symbols. Under the notion that the human mind worked like a computer, the key concepts were information storage and processing, and computation. Logical computations are carried out on representations. As will become clear in the discussion to follow, the content, structure, and function of mental representations has now become a central issue, one that is relevant to the topic of this chapter.

The formulation of Newell and Simon (1972), probably the most influential of the cognitive scientists working on this theory, assumed that human problem solving involved the use of a set of built-in, or learned, heuristics, which were constrained by the rules of logic. Humans solved complex problems, such as chess, in the same ways that computers were used as problem-solving aids by engineers trying to design complex pieces of apparatus, through logical computation.

Other AI-oriented cognitive scientists focused on the organization and use of complex structures of human knowledge, as contrasted with logical calculation. This branch of AI came to be known as "expert systems." Here the orientation was toward the range of knowledge, in the form of symbolic representation of features of a complex reality, that an expert such as a doctor needed to have in his or her head in order to be able to solve a problem (diagnose a disease). But while the orientation of this group was more toward what was stored in memory and how, and less toward the processes of complex calculation, the underlying assumptions about the human mind were the same, namely that the human mind worked in a way much like the way modern digital computers worked.

This theory about the nature of human cognition, and human know-how, had some strong challenges. In particular, Dreyfus and Dreyfus (1986) argued powerfully, and scathingly, that much of human knowledge was very different from that articulated by artificial intelligence theory, and that the modern electronic computer, with von Neumann architecture, was not a good model of human problem solving and action taking. However, for a long time AI models continued to be the "only major game in town." In a review volume written as recently as 1990, AI models dominate the exposition (Posner 1990). The notion that human thinking is information processing, calculation in a quite literal sense, is the central argument and organizing principle of most of its chapters.

However, by 1990 another paradigm of human knowing and problem solving that stressed parallel distributed processing (PDP), as contrasted with linear processing, and that has come to be called "connectionist" theory, was beginning to provide a challenge to "good old-fashioned artificial intelligence" (GOAI—the term was coined by Dreyfus) in a number of important areas. The challenge was especially focused on contexts where the heart of the problem was pattern recognition rather than complex problem solving of the sort involved in playing chess, although connectionist theory also provided a challenge to the latter, in that a key characteristic of an expert chess player is the ability to recognize configurations on the board in order to choose the appropriate play. Also, connectionist theory differed from GOAI in having built into it a theory of learning. Connectionist models, like GOAI, use computers as a research paradigm. In this research a computer is "trained" and "learns" to recognize a pattern, in effect, by trial-and-error and adjustment learning. Such models are explicitly designed to be analogous to neural networks of the brain, with many sources of information contributing simultaneously to the representations of patterns to be recognized by the network.

In contrast with traditional AI, where the various bits of information relevant to a problem are seen as stored in symbolic form in particular assigned places, and assembled in logical operations controlled by a central processor, in connectionist theory the brain's representation of the world is distributed across a variety of different locations and assembled where appropriate as a "pattern," the elements of which may be quite dispersed within the system (neural or electronic). Various patterns that are stored or can be temporarily assembled, are, as it were, tried out against an external stimulus. The pattern that fits best is invoked. In connectionist theory, the logic-constrained information processing that is central in artificial intelligence is played down. The basic operations involve computations, but computations of a different kind—not reasoning but pattern matching. In a very real sense, much of human knowledge, for example the ability to recognize a face, or a printed or hand-written letter, is tacit, very much in the sense of Polanyi (1958). Indeed, several of the connectionist writers have recognized, even stressed, the compatibility of the theory they are espousing with that of Polanyi.

This brings out an important difference in the modeling goals of the two types of models. AI of the Newell and Simon type assumes the existence of structured knowledge; conscious deployment of the knowledge through calculated reasoning is the goal of the model. In contrast, PDP models go deeper into the system, focusing on how knowledge is built up, basically at an unconscious, automatic, pattern-recognizing level. How the knowledge is used is of less immediate interest. Note here that representations are central to both, but in GOAI these have a built-in logic of the symbolic system, whereas in PDP the operative representations emerge from the process of assembling information.

This approach to models of human cognitive processing has had an increasing influence over the past fifteen to twenty years, in part because the capacity of modern computers for parallel processing analogous to operations of the neural system of humans and other animals has made more complex models possible. Moreover, it has had some impressive successes, including models of language acquisition that challenge the dominant innate theory models. However, the work is still in the early stages of theory building, and it remains to be seen how successful it will be at tasks other than pattern matching—problem solving, for example.

For some time, some of the limitations of connectionism, as well as its promise, have been evident. In particular, in their efforts to get away from the "human as logical problem-solver" view of Newell and Simon, connectionists have ignored the kind of human know-how involved in solving mathematics problems, or thinking through the best route between Indianapolis and Buffalo. This is not to deny that recognizing complex patterns may be an important part of these kinds of problem-solving endeavors, but the solutions also almost certainly involve some logical operations of the sort that the older AI theory had focused on. Thus Johnson-Laird (1983) has been arguing for some time that much of human reasoning involves both the generation of "mental models" and their mental manipulation in problem solving. In addition, philosophers like Dreyfus have observed that connectionist theory, like the older AI, implicitly or explicitly assumes a recognizing or calculating mind that is separate and distanced from those parts of the body that are actually acting and experiencing—sending signals, as it were—to a separate mind. And the things that are being experienced remain farther away still.

Since the early 1990s, another major new strand of cognitive science has developed in which the mind is seen as very much in a body, and the body is seen as very much in its environment. Some key writers in this group include Clark (1997); Hendriks-Jansen (1996); Hutchins (1996); and Varela, Thompson, and Rosch (1991). Several aspects of these new works in cognitive science are especially relevant to the topics of this chapter. First, traditional AI and connectionism tend to see human knowledge as somehow residing in a mind that contemplates a context that calls for action, or at least for recognition and identification of some kind, but that stands outside of that context. In contrast, the authors in this group emphasize that knowledge, learning, and application all take place in an action context. All stress the biological evolutionary origins of the human mind, and its workings in an environment, and they argue that the mind must have evolved to enable humans to cope better with real problems. A human mind is very much a part of human action, designed to keep the organism alive and well in a real environment. The title of Andy Clark's book, *Being There*, captures this flavor.

Both classical AI and connectionist theory have focused on particular kinds of problems faced by humans that require (or seem to) particular kinds of structures or operations in the mind: problem solving that involves a certain degree of conscious logical manipulation, on the one hand, and recognition of complex patterns, which seem to require a certain amount of mental imaging, on the other. These new treatments, however, are much more open regarding the range of contexts and problems that human beings must learn to solve. Indeed, several of these authors emphasize problem contexts that are simple and structured enough so that there is no need to invoke mental representations, or logical manipulation, as necessary requirements for appropriate response.

The empirical research focused on in Clark's book involves the design of robots that learn to move about in a room without crashing into walls to find the robot equivalent of food, through trial-and-error actions associated with particular sensory feedback. Such a pattern of action, and interaction with their environment, in effect "keeps them alive." The authors propose that much of human knowledge is gained in analogous ways, simply by "being there" in the environment. This is obviously a very basic kind of human knowledge, and it arguably underlies our ability to carry on our daily lives without in effect crashing. On the other hand, Clark and others do not deny, but indeed stress, that certain kinds of problems and challenges faced by humans, and effective human responses to those problems, do require the learning of complex contexts and patterns, and logical manipulation. This theme of multiple kinds of knowledge is developed in elegant and elaborate form by Merlin Donald, whose work we will consider shortly.

With respect to human know-how and problem solving in complex contexts, each of these authors highlights the role of human language, and argues two points that are highly relevant, given our orientation (although they differ in the extent to which they emphasize these). First, human language is seen not only as a vehicle of communication between persons but also as a tool used by individual humans for thinking through complex problems—that is, as a vehicle for abstraction and cognitive manipulation, and for internal dialogue. Second, they stress the cultural nature of much of human knowledge, in the sense that what humans know and what they do in various contexts are, to a large degree, learned from other humans. They all see language as a central vehicle of cultural knowledge-storing and transmission.

Merlin Donald (1991) develops a perspective on human knowing that is at once differently oriented from the authors we have just considered, and strongly complementary. Donald is explicitly concerned with different kinds and levels of human knowing, and the associated mechanisms of learning, memory, and representation. His theoretical method for investigating these matters is to view them in the light of the biological evolutionary roots and processes that define the "origins of the modern mind," as his book is titled (Donald 1991).

Donald's basic proposition is that the modern human mind is a hybrid mix of four different kinds of knowledge and learning processes that evolved sequentially, the first two in phylogenetic evolution, the third partly in phylogenetic and partly in cultural evolution, and the fourth strictly in cultural evolution. The first level of knowledge and learning can be characterized as individual knowing derived from direct experiential interactions with the environment (as a lab rat learns by interacting with the constraints of a maze, or a robot "learns" by exploring a room). This is the level humans share with their mammalian ancestors, including their close relatives, the primates. The basic framework of representing knowledge at this level is in terms of episodes of events, or event representations. Such representations are called up in context and can be used to guide action and interaction with others, and to anticipate next moves, supporting short-term planning. However, they do not lend themselves to out-of-context thinking and planning. In essence, this is a step up from the robot's action-mapping of the contours of a room; but it is limited with respect to deliberation, and it is strictly an individual knowledge of the world, from a very limited perspective.

In Donald's theory, a major transition took place in hominid evolution with the move to the second level of knowledge representation, which is based on learning from and with others through mimesis. Under Donald's conception, human mimesis is based on imitation of the activities of others, but involves much more than learning through imitation and the ability to invoke what is learned in the appropriate circumstances, which is a capability possessed by many other animals. It involves the internalization and representation of the imitated actions, which enables deliberate recall and manipulation of the action out of context. It also in humans may involve manipulation and regeneration of imitated actions mentally to form new ways of doing things. Here, what humans can do can be recognized as an advanced form of what some of the great apes can do, and a very advanced form beyond those of other mammals. Mimetic skills are the basis for many human capabilities, such as tool making, games, and sport, as well as the capacities for acting together, as in hunting or dancing. Donald's conception of mimesis clearly is akin to Johnson-Laird's (1983) conception that humans think by manipulating mental models, with the difference that, for Donald, in mimesis this manipulation does not employ language or other abstract mental tokens.

It is apparent that Donald's first two levels of human knowing have been largely neglected by classic cognitive science in its AI forms, although anticipated to some extent by the "embodied and situated cognition" group discussed just previously. The importance of mimesis for human cultural life, social knowledge sharing, and as a basis for further evolutionary change in cognitive potential is one of Donald's most creative contributions to the theory of human knowledge, in our opinion. Mimesis does not require language.

The next transition in this scheme is that toward shared knowledge gained through oral symbolic language, especially narrative. The unique competence in language possessed by all human beings but not other creatures (although most other complex animals have communication systems of other, simpler kinds) is asserted by all cognitivists, although not always given separate consideration. Narrative, as Donald stresses, is the natural product of language and is the basis for explanatory structures, such as religion and the myths that hold a community together. Complex language representations make possible complex cultural systems of organization, and the cultural sharing of much complex world knowledge, such as navigation systems (Hutchins 1996). External symbolic representations also become internalized in mental representations that enable a new cognitive level of knowledge manipulation.

The fourth layer of knowledge representation was developed in cultural evolution as externalized memory—knowledge constructed through and made into enduring forms through written symbols and graphic forms. This level of knowledge clearly is limited without language, and is greatly facilitated by the existence of a spoken language, but goes far beyond what is achievable with oral language alone, enabling the acquisition of cultural knowledge systems that are shared across communities widely separated in both time and space. Externalized written forms of memory have made possible, Donald claims, the development of logic, formal theoretical systems, and science, none of which could be developed on the basis of oral language alone. Nor could they be developed by individual minds operating independently.

Formal knowledge systems of this kind depend on symbolic forms and communities that share knowledge of the symbolic systems. Donald observes that technological advance, and cultural change more generally, seemed to speed up significantly as cultures invented and adopted written language forms.

The resulting layered, hybrid modern mind is capable of experiencing, learning, knowing, and problem solving, at all levels, sometimes employed at the same time, but in different ways. For example, playing a musical instrument such as the piano may involve learning by picking out tunes, mimetic skill acquisition, practice, and generation of new forms, oral instruction in the interpretation of musical pieces, learning and following musical notation, and finally the study of music theory, all of which provide different experiences of the playing itself.

The advantage of Donald's proposal is twofold. It recognizes the necessity of setting human knowledge into the biological evolutionary framework congruent with that of other animals, where the point is to learn about and adapt within the world. But at the same time, it recognizes the necessity of the framework that takes account of the special human capacities for symbolic communication and collective problem solving. Further, his work emphasizes that a critical factor in human cultural evolution is that humans have constantly and radically changed the environment itself, thus changing the nature of the adaptation problem in significant ways.

A very different approach to evolutionary epistemology has been taken by "evolutionary psychologists" (Barkow, Cosmides, and Tooby 1992), who also emphasize the problems that humans have had to solve in evolutionary time. Their proposals, however, involve genetically determined brain modules designed to solve specific problems, similar to the innate language modules of Pinker (1994) and Chomsky (1988). The solutions proposed by people like Clark and Donald rest on more general principles that reject the necessity for specific modular solutions to most human problems, in fact implying that plasticity of behavior and cognition is essential to the advances in collective cultural knowledge made over evolutionary and historical time. We do not discuss the proposals of the evolutionary psychology group further in this chapter, therefore.

With the broadening and deepening evident in Donald's model, as we have described, the emerging picture of the nature of human knowledge presented by a major group of researchers and writers in cognitive science now meshes very well with the analyses of human know-how put forth by scholars of modern technology and its implementation. Edwin Hutchins's (1996) study, *Cognition in the Wild,* provides an explicit bridge. Hutchins, an anthropologist by training and a professor in the University of California, San Diego, department of cognitive science, offers his study of navigation as a contribution to cognitive science. However, the arena of employment of human know-how focused on in Hutchins's study is far away from those that have been the focus of attention in the more traditional writings in cognitive science.

Hutchins's study is concerned with the know-how involved in navigating a large ship. The endeavor he analyzes is, first of all, a cooperative and collective one. A number of different people with different knowledge, skills, and tasks are involved in deciding the appropriate direction and in steering the ship. The endeavor is also a cultural one, in that most of the skills employed by the various actors are well defined in the culture, and were learned by individuals who play connected and mutually dependent roles in ship navigation. The use of a variety of artifacts, such as maps and radar, is an essential part of the Hutchins story.

It is striking that Hutchins's perspective of the know-how involved in ship navigation is virtually the same as the characterization of the relevant "organizational capabilities" in a new cellular phone network company, presented in a study by Narduzzo, Rocco, and Warglien in the recent book *The Nature and Dynamics of Organizational Capabilities* (Dosi, Nelson, and Winter 2000). However, these scholars are engaged not in a study in the tradition of cognitive science, but rather are working within the tradition of scholarship concerned with analyzing the nature of the modern know-how possessed by the key organizations that employ it, such as business firms. And Hutchins's analysis also meshes virtually perfectly with the analysis of engineering design presented by Walter Vincenti (1990) in his classic book, *What Engineers Know and How They Know It.*

3. The Evolution of Human "Technology"

It is apparent that modern technologies are "known" simultaneously at several of the different levels we have distinguished above. The skills needed to operate a modern technology are acquired in part through individual experience with the tasks involved, and through mimesis. This is as true for a computer programmer as it is for a piano player or a bicycle rider. The jobs associated with using technologies also are describable, at least to some degree, in words, and the apprentice may learn partly through verbal instructions from the master as well as through mimesis. In addition, instruction manuals and the like generally are available, which take the form of externalized scripts and may also include drawings and plans that supplement words for explanation and instruction. Both the learning and the using of extant technologies is cultural. Most jobs have associated training programs, which may be quite formal. The task of employing most modern technologies involves considerable division of labor and coordination.

Thus a skilled operator of a modern technology possesses at once an ability to do, a mental conception of what the task is and how to do it, at least rudimentary knowledge of how his or her particular actions are supposed to fit in with the actions of others, and some ability to articulate that knowledge in words and other symbols. And a striking feature of modern technology is that, as with science, much of the knowledge is externalized in texts, blueprints, and the like that are accessible to those who have been trained in the art, Donald's most advanced level of human knowing.

The other striking feature of modern technologies, of course, is how powerful they have become, how much our know-how has advanced over the years, and the centuries. However, the study of problem solving involved in advancing the frontiers of science or technology has not been what mainstream cognitive science has been about. In particular, it is clear that the advance of modern science and technology is largely the result of cumulative cultural learning, a process referred to by Donald but not really analyzed by cognitive scientists.

At first thought, the body of recent writings by biologists and anthropologists concerned with cultural evolution as a human add-on to biological evolution (see, for example, Cavalli-Sforza and Feldman 1981, Boyd and Richerson 1985) would appear to link nicely with Donald's perception of the different kinds of human knowing, and the central importance of cumulative cultural evolution as a factor influencing the capabilities of modern humans. But in fact most of this body of writing has been concerned with human behaviors and belief systems that are closely linked to human biological survival, and has not probed at the processes that have led to the most striking human accomplishments, for example the development of modern science and technology.

The study of these topics has proceeded in an arena all its own. It is very interesting, therefore, that while there has been very little intellectual interchange between scholars of the advance of science and the evolution of modern technologies, and cognitive scientists, the former seem to be coming to the same hybrid characterization of human knowledge and problem solving that is emerging in cognitive science.

One common view about technological advance, at least in the modern world, is that it proceeds through an activity—research and development—in which scientific knowledge and technique are applied to the solution of practical design problems, a point of view on "invention" that clearly has much in common with the theory of human problem solving in traditional AI. Another point of view plays down the power of science to guide inventing and stresses the trial-and-feedback tinkering of inventors knowledgeable about the particular technology and drawing from that very specific applied know-how, a perspective that fits aspects of connectionist theory. But there seems to be a growing consensus among empirical scholars that technological advance generally involves both cogitation and planning, drawing on abstract and general knowledge and logic, and trial-and-feedback learning based on hands-on familiarity with the technology. The proposition that the relevant knowledge is largely common property, part of the culture, also is part of the emerging consensus. This "hybrid" point of view is evident in the now considerable number of scholars who assert that technological advance should be understood as an evolutionary process, for example Constant (1980), Nelson and Winter (1982), Mokyr (1990), Vincenti (1990), Petroski (1992), Basalla (1988), and Ziman (2000).

On first reflection, the use of that term would seem to connote a strong connectionist theory of knowledge and problem solving in this arena, with little room for a major role for science or logical calculation. Certainly the scholars who use the term mean it to attack the notion that significant technological advance can be completely thought through in advance or planned in any detail. However, most of the scholars who propose that technology evolves do have an important place in their theory for theoretical knowledge and logic that guides problem solving and inventing.

3.1. Evolutionary Epistemology and the Advance of Technology

Evolutionary theories of technological advance need to be understood as part of the broader body of theorizing that has come to be called evolutionary epistemology. The particular term seems to be due to Donald Campbell (1965, 1974), although Campbell credits Karl Popper (1959) with the basic working out of the concept. As Campbell points out, the broad idea seems almost inevitable when one recognizes the cumulative aspects of human knowledge, and that that knowledge has been developed over many years, with many false steps mixed among the successful ones. Once Charles Darwin had articulated his theory of biological evolution, it was natural to propose that human knowledge and know-how "evolve," at least in a metaphorical sense, and many scholars prior to Popper and Campbell proposed just that. The challenge was to make a useful theory out of an interesting metaphor.

Campbell himself was a unique bridge between cognitive science and scholarship on the development of human knowledge. His training was as a psychologist, and as a young scholar his central interest was in understanding how humans know. This led him into theorizing about the growth of human knowledge, especially about the growth of scientific knowledge. Virtually all contemporary scholars of the development of science, be they philosophers or historians, recognize their indebtedness to Campbell. On the other hand, Campbell was less interested in technology and wrote little about that subject explicitly. It is not surprising, therefore, that while some of the scholars who propose that technology evolves refer to Campbell's work, many seem to be unaware of it.

As noted in the preceding chapter, Campbell used the term *blind* to highlight his proposition that all efforts to gain new knowledge involve an element of groping in the dark. However, neither Campbell nor the theorists who propose that technology evolves ever argued that these efforts are strictly random. Clearly scientists are strongly directed by prevailing scientific knowledge in their attempts to "think through" the best way to proceed on their research. While arguing with the emphasis Herbert Simon placed on human rationality in guiding problem solving, Campbell does not take issue with Simon's argument that such efforts often are sharply directed by prior knowledge and logic related to that knowledge. However, Campbell chooses to emphasize that the very fact that there is a "problem" requires the problem solver to grope beyond the grasp of that knowledge and logic, and that groping is "blind," at least to some degree.

Walter Vincenti's (1990) use of the term *blind*, to characterize the way engineers grope for a satisfactory design, also discussed in the preceding chapter, is similar to Campbell's. At the same time as he highlights the groping nature of design, Vincenti also points out the elaborate and powerful body of knowledge used by engineers in their groping. The core of that knowledge is a set of conceptions regarding the "operational (or design) principles" of the devices or processes in question. (As Vincenti notes, the term comes from Michael Polanyi.) That core knowledge is supported by an often considerable amount of empirical knowledge about the properties and capacities of the various materials and components that might be used in design, and about the characteristics of a design that are valued, disliked, or forbidden. Vincenti also points to the ability of engineers to use mathematics, simulations, and other logical tools in the design process. A lot of knowledge, and logic, as well as trial-and-feedback groping, goes into the conception and development of a new design.

Relatedly, the process by which one competing design solution is chosen over another often involves a significant analytic element, as well as pragmatic judgments regarding what is better than what. That is, for a new technological departure to be accepted, it often is important that there be answers, acceptable to the relevant communities, to the questions of just how and why it works, and of what its operating characteristics are likely to be in circumstances in which, as of yet, there is no actual experience. The "social constructionists" (for example, Bijker 1995) writing about technological advance stress, in addition, that assessments of what is desirable and what is not about a technology tend to be forged by the culture along with experience with that technology, and generally do not exist in strong form prior to that experience.

Medical treatments are a fascinating case in point. On the one hand, it is clear that, even in the present, many medical treatments that doctors deem to be effective are so regarded almost totally on the basis of empirical evidence, some in the form of reports of controlled experiments published in medical journals, and some on the basis of a doctor's own experience. Often there is little solid understanding of why a treatment works. On the other hand, it also is clear that doctors distrust empirical evidence that a particular treatment works if there is no plausible mechanism consistent with their broad theories that can explain efficacy, or if the theory used to explain the results runs strongly counter to what they believe. Reflect on the heated rejection by the orthodox medical community of what has been called "alternative" medicine.

Clearly, the processes through which technology evolves are different in important respects from those of biological evolution. Of particular importance, the distinctions among the ex ante conception of a promising new design, its practical manifestation in a piece of hardware and tests in actual practice, and selective retention or rejection are much less sharp than the distinctions in biological theory between new genotype, the phenotype that comes from it and its encounter with the environment, and inclusive fitness of the genotype. In the process of technological evolution, there is considerable selection of alternatives prior to actual full-scale trial. We have noted the use of theory, empirical knowledge, and logical calculation to focus problem solving. Small-scale models may be built and tested; new chemical plant technology is often tested out in pilot plants before a final design is determined and full-scale plant construction undertaken. Wind tunnel tests of small models of planes and plane parts long have assisted aircraft designers. Recently, simulation models have come to play a role in many areas of R & D.

The intertwining of specific technique, artifact, or practice with a body of belief or understanding has been recognized by almost all scholars of technological advance. Nonetheless, different writers have tended to stress one aspect or the other as the fundamental unit that "evolves." Thus Petroski (1992) and Basalla (1988) argue that the artifact is the fundamental unit. Vincenti (1990), Constant (1980), and Mokyr (1990) tend to see the design or operating principle or concept as the fundamental unit. In part the difference can be explained by the technologies being studied or used as the fundamental examples, artifacts like paper clips and premodern waterwheels in the former cases, and broad technologies like those involved in modern aircraft and turbojet engines in the latter cases. These examples indicate clearly that the understanding that surrounds and supports particular artifacts and practices differs greatly in scope and strength from case to case. However, both particular technique and broader understandings or beliefs clearly are always bound together in human technologies, just as they seem to be in many simpler areas of human action. We believe it is a mistake to treat one or the other as primary. They are tightly intertwined levels of knowing, to use Donald's imagery.

3.2. Cultural Evolution

Another key difference between technological evolution and evolution in biology is that the process of technological advance clearly is inherently "cultural." Those involved in trying to improve technology almost always make use of technique and knowledge that, to a considerable degree, is "common property" among an often sizable community. Members of the community sooner or later learn from each other's successes and failures, just as they have learned from the accomplishments and failures of predecessors. And because of this, while particular advances may be associated with the successful efforts of particular people or groups, much of what is achieved soon becomes community property. It does so because professionals in a field have a common base of training, share a common language, and have a similar base of knowledge that sets in context particular new technological developments. And the news of new developments spreads rapidly. The phenomenon of "multiple invention," of the appearance of several quite similar solutions to the same problem made by different people at the same time, demonstrates clearly the shared aspects of technological knowledge. However, what is more usual is that different human problem solvers will take somewhat different paths toward solution, and some will turn out, ex post, to be better than others.

This cultural-community aspect of technological evolution has been absolutely essential to technological advance as it has been experienced. Significant sustained technological advance almost never is the result of the work of only one or a small number of individuals, but rather powerful technologies always are the result of the cumulative efforts of many participants, often made over a long period of time. Gilfillan (1935) has described the interactive process that used to be involved in the evolution of sailing-ship design. One important part of that process was feedback to ship designers from those who purchased their last round of ships, regarding weak and strong points of the design, which led to design modifications. Another part involved diffusion of knowledge about effective design elements among ship designers, with ship purchasers playing a central role in this process. But there also was considerable exchange of information within the guild. In another technological arena, Allen (1987) provides a detailed description of the way in which a community of steel plant owners and operators learned from the successes and failures of new designs built by their colleagues, and modified their own designs accordingly.

These examples highlight the cumulative development of technologies through a sequence of often relatively small steps made by different people. Rosenberg (1996) has emphasized another aspect of technological advance, that an important invention often finds a variety of quite different uses, and these varied paths of development almost always are explored by different individuals and organizations. The history of the widening use of the laser is a good example.

Thus the fact that technologies are widely known, at least within the relevant technological communities, seems essential to the process of progressive advancement of those technologies. Donald has noted that there is evidence of sustained if gradual technological progress in tool design among pre–*Homo sapiens* hominids, who still lacked the capacity for language, and has proposed that significant cumulative advances in such technologies as the making of pottery can proceed simply through mimesis, if there is a cross-generational community of practitioners. However, Donald highlights that a significant acceleration of technological progress occurred after the emergence of language with *Homo sapiens*.

In the modern world, special languages develop around technologies. In turn, the use of written language and other ways of describing a technology, such as graphics, enables externalization of knowledge about it that can be tapped by all those who share the language. Thus the "news" about new technological departures made in one part of the world now moves rapidly to other parts. As the extent to which technologies can be described in words and other symbols has increased, and as the speed with which externalized, symbol-coded information can be communicated has increased, so has the size of the professional community that can stay in touch with new developments, wherever they may occur. Pollard (1981) has described the slow pace at which the basic inventions of the Industrial Revolution were picked up in continental Europe, usually through the movement of British technologists to Europe. The contrast with the speed with which knowledge about new electrical lighting systems and particular developments in those systems moved between the United States and Europe, mostly carried through "externalized" knowledge systems, is remarkable. The news and much of the knowledge about new developments in superconductivity spread almost instantly among members of the technological community throughout the world.

3.3. Technology and Science, Technique and Theory

What we have been calling technology and what has come to be called science clearly have much in common. Both are systems of knowledge. Both employ somewhat specialized languages, and in the modern world both involve extensive externalization of memory. Both bodies of knowledge are largely public. John Ziman (1968, 1978) has stressed the importance of clear linguistic descriptions, and external symbolic representations, as a requirement for science to be widely public, and the same certainly is so of technology. And the publicness of the knowledge is an essential factor permitting its cumulative progress.

However, as Ziman, Popper, Campbell, Kitcher (1993), and other evolutionary epistemologists have argued, science is largely a system of ideas, of abstract knowledge. There clearly is know-how in the body of scientific knowledge, in particular the know-how needed to do science. And scientific knowledge, in recent years at least, has illuminated technology and often opened the door to technological advance. But from the perspective of Ziman and most other philosophers of science, the latter is a valuable by-product of science but not its direct purpose. The central test for scientific knowledge is, "Is it valid?"

Popper and his followers have argued that there can be no firm positive answer to that question about scientific knowledge. The ability to stand up under attempts at refutation may be the best humans can hope for. But in any case, the quest in science is for understanding in its own right. The "usefulness" of a scientific proposition is not, as the pragmatists have proposed, the basic criterion for acceptance or rejection of that proposition, at least as a part of science.

On the other hand, as Vincenti and others who have reflected on the similarities and differences between technological knowledge and scientific knowledge have argued, the central test for technological knowledge is, "Is it useful?" Technological knowledge is part of a cultural system that is basically concerned with accomplishing practical ends, rather than with knowledge for its own sake. The objective is to get to something that works, or works better, according to the standards of the culture, and "understanding" is only important insofar as it helps in that effort. Here pragmatism does help define the relevant criteria.

However, the distinction between selection criteria for new science and new technology may be less sharp than the above argument would seem to indicate. In the first place, technologies, and the areas of human needs and wants that technologies serve, tend to induce scientific research to gain better understanding. Second, an important and stringent testing ground for science often is provided by those who think they see how it might be applied.

While often overlooked, a large share of research funding, even research funding at universities, goes into sciences with names like metallurgy (now materials science), chemical engineering, computer science, pathology. Nor is research in fields like these, or more generally research motivated to solve practical problems or to enable technologies to be understood better, constrained to yield findings of only practical relevance. It is well known that Sadi Carnot's research, which resulted in the laws of thermodynamics, was motivated by his curiosity about steam engines. William Shockley's work *Holes and Electrons in Semiconductors* (1950), which greatly advanced understanding in solid-state physics, was motivated by his need to understand the workings of the transistor that he and his colleagues at Bell Laboratories had stumbled upon. Louis Pasteur's research, which opened up several areas of modern biology, involved his attempt to get a deep enough understanding of a practical problem that a solution could be found.

Donald Stokes (1996) has stressed that much of science is in "Pasteur's Quadrant," both motivated by the desire to solve practical problems, and deeply probing in its search for understanding. A number of historians of science have made the same point, without using Stokes's evocative term. For research results of such science, the questions, is it valid? and is it useful? are intertwined. Further, in some cases the major reason a new scientific finding is tested in the particular way it is, is that someone has thought of a way to put it to practical, maybe even profitable, use. To return to the case of the transistor, the design of the original transistor experiments at Bell Laboratories was motivated by a belief of the scientists involved that prevailing theory in solid-state physics suggested a particular way of making an amplifier out of a semiconductor. One of the results of this research was a significant change in the way semiconductors were understood. The attempts to build an atomic bomb generated a host of tests of elements of theory in nuclear physics.

In the modern era, science and technology have become tightly intertwined, at least in some areas. As we noted earlier, much of modern medicine still consists of knowledge, or belief, that something works, often with only weak understanding of just how and why. As Vincenti has documented in detail, much of the knowledge possessed by aircraft designers remains closely related to experience. But much of the knowledge of modern doctors, and engineers, is certainly science-like. And medicine and engineering are active fields of scientific research.

The distinction between technique or practice, and understanding or theory, has sometimes led to a division of labor regarding the efforts to advance a technology. This is especially so as the understanding aspects of technology have taken on science-like form, and have found their place in universities. Vincenti describes the research at Stanford that led to greatly enhanced knowledge relevant to aircraft propeller design. The researchers who did that work were not themselves about to design propellers. Many researchers at medical schools do not practice medicine or themselves find new pharmaceuticals. However, to a considerable extent their work is judged in terms of its expected value to those who do.

Even in fields where the underlying science is strong, technological advance remains somewhat blind, because the reach of those who are trying to improve it virtually always exceeds what the understanding about the technology clearly illuminates. Thus while radio communication clearly would have been impossible without Maxwell's theorizing and Hertz's critical experiments and demonstrations, the development of an effective means of radio communication required a great deal of trial-and-feedback effort by inventors and engineers.

And even in technologies that have strong science support, it is a mistake to believe that the process generally has been for the science to advance first, and then the technology to follow the science. As we have noted, in many cases technological advances have been achieved through efforts largely involving pragmatic trial-and-feedback processes. After a significant technological advance has been achieved through those processes, efforts then are made to "understand" the nature of the achievement and the general principles that may lie behind it. If the scientific effort to understand technology theoretically is success-ful, as it certainly was in the case of Carnot and Shockley, this will set the stage for further efforts to improve the technology. Thus, in fields where technological advance is very rapid, it would appear that tech-nique and scientific understanding "coevolve."

The notion that technology evolves, or that technique and under-standing coevolve, that we have been mapping out here is surely a complex one, and one that is very different from evolution in biology. It is interesting, we would argue, that the processes of evolutionary epistemology we have described above are broadly compatible with the theory of human know-how and learning that is emerging in at least certain parts of cognitive science, that stresses different levels of hu-man knowing and their interaction.

CHAPTER 5

Making Sense of Institutions as a Factor Shaping Economic Performance

1. Introduction

There clearly is a renaissance of interest in institutions as a factor shaping economic performance. The particular focus of this chapter will be on the role of institutions and institutional change in economic growth, a topic that lately has attracted a lot of discussion (see, for example, Matthews 1986, North 1990). However, the issues, and for the most part the range of relevant writings, are those that are central to consideration of the role of institutions in economic life more generally.

The surge of new interest by economists in how institutions affect economic performance can be regarded as a return to old ground. Institutions of course were a central concern of Adam Smith and his great classical followers. However, given the recent history of the field, the renewed interest in institutions on the part of many economists can be recognized as a growing conviction that satisfactory understanding of economic performance requires going beyond the lean logic of at least stripped-down neoclassical theory.

However, our perusal of the new (and old) literature on institutions in economics and in social science more broadly has convinced us that there is a difficult road ahead before institutions can be woven into a

---

* Based on Richard R. Nelson and Bhaven Sampat, "Making Sense of Institutions as a Factor Shaping Economic Performance," *Journal of Economic Behavior and Organization* 44 (2001): 31–54.

coherent theory of the determinants of economic performance. The term apparently means significantly different things to different authors. The notion of institutions itself is not yet a coherent concept, at least not across the various users of the term.

On the other hand, we think we have come to understand some of the reasons behind this diversity. And that understanding, we believe, helps to clear the way to developing a concept of institutions that can be integrated into a coherent theory of economic activity.

We proceed as follows. First, in Section 2, we "box the compass," discussing various strands of institutional analysis in economics and in the other social sciences. Then, in Sections 3 and 4, we develop a concept of institutions that, we think, may be useful for analysis of economic performance, and economic growth in particular. In Section 5 we provide some examples of the theory at work. In Section 6 we pull strands together.

2. Writings on Institutions and Economic Activity: Boxing the Compass

2.1. Motivations behind the New Writings

There have been several wide-ranging and thoughtful reviews of institutional ideas in economics. We have benefited in particular from those by Geoffrey Hodgson (1988, 1994, 1998), Thrainn Eggertsson (1990), Malcolm Rutherford (1994), and Richard Langlois (1986, 1989, 1999). In addition, Hall and Taylor (1994) recently have surveyed the varied meanings of institutions in political science, and Powell and DiMaggio (1991) have compared the concepts of institutions in economics with those in sociology. These reviews obviate any need for us to provide an extensive review of our own. By and large below we follow along the lines they have charted, although our stress will be different in various places.

All of these reviewers identify the new institutional writings in economics with attempts by economists to enrich, or to get away from, the austere assumptions about human behavior contained in at least the standard versions of neoclassical theory. Those writers that might be called "neoclassical institutionalists" (this is the group on which Eggertsson focuses) are sympathetic with the dual presumptions about human and organizational behavior contained in neoclassical theory: that human actors understand reasonably well the contexts in which they are operating, and choose actions that in fact are appropriate, given their objectives and the opportunities and constraints they face. Their concern is that the theory, in its simple version, does not adequately recognize certain very important variables that define the structure for human action.

But there also is another group of institutionalists who take what for most modern neoclassical economists is a more radical theoretical stance, arguing that the belief systems and preferences taken as a given by that theory, with the former at least presumed to match the actual reality, need to be explained, not assumed. More generally, this branch of the stream of institutional analysis posits that human rationality needs to be understood as a social and cultural phenomenon. Among the above-cited authors, Hodgson is particularly interested in this line of theorizing.

We note a similar divide in political science between what Hall and Taylor (1994) call "rational choice" institutionalism and what they call "historical" institutionalism. On the other hand, in sociology the dominant position clearly is that beliefs and values are socially constructed, at least to some degree. We will propose later that there therefore is a natural affinity between the more unorthodox strand of institutional theorizing in economics and institutional theorizing in sociology.

We want to flag right away, since the fact is highly relevant to our current inquiry, that the authors of a number of the works now included under the collection called "the new institutional economics" did not originally call what they were analyzing an "institution." This is so, for example, of the early writings on property rights. The term *institutions* generally is invoked by those using it to denote a broad concept under which are included a number of specific instances. But if, as we suggested above, the term is used by various authors to denote what they think is missing from neoclassical theory, given the diversity of authors it would be strange if all the things called institutions were of the same ilk. We believe they are not.

To tip our hand somewhat, the basic question we will be asking is not, What is the right general definition of institutions? because we do not think there is a general answer to that question. Somewhat different particular definitions (generalizations) may be useful for different kinds of analysis. Our quest here is for a concept of institutions that is useful for analysis of factors molding economic performance, and long-run economic growth in particular.

2.2. Strands of Institutional Analysis

All of the above reviews recognize the writings concerned with property rights (Demsetz 1967, Alchian and Demsetz 1973), and more broadly the general law and economics program that developed in the 1960s and 1970s (see Goldberg 1976) as one of the major strands of the new institutional analysis in economics. Much of this body of analysis focuses on formal law (for example, Posner 1981, 1992), but some of it identifies norms of behavior that are enforced through social sanction as contrasted with the force of government. Some of the writing even reflects on norms enforced largely by an individual's sense of what is right and wrong (see, for example, Sugden 1989 and Axelrod 1997).

Many of the writers in this camp, and several of the broad surveyors of institutional writing in economics, propose that all of these elements define the "rules of the game." The rules of the game are proposed to be important for two reasons. First, well-understood rules establish baseline conditions for human interaction, and give a certain predictability to what other parties will do in a particular context that permits individual decision making, and multiparty negotiation, to proceed with some degree of certainty, the actions of different individuals to be coordinated, and efficient transactional agreements to be achieved. (This is, in effect, the Coase theorem.) Second, rules can constrain and mold economic behavior in ways that rule out actions that, if widely practiced, would be economically costly.

Most of the articles of this genre cite Coase's (1960) article "The Problem of Social Cost" as providing the intellectual starting place for their work. And like Coase, the writings here mostly focus explicitly or implicitly on transactions among different economic parties, and transaction costs.

Coase's earlier (1937) article "The Nature of the Firm" clearly is the source of another broad strand of economic institutional analysis. The body of writing on firm organization and governance now is vast, and is concerned with a variety of topics, from what determines the boundaries of firms, to what explains the ownership pattern of a firm (that is, who works for whom), to internal problems of agency and their management, to corporate culture (Kreps 1990). Some of the writers here, Williamson (1975, 1985) in particular, have been strongly influenced by the writings of business historians like Alfred Chandler (1962, 1977). However, most of the writing of this genre is focused on the present situation and not on how it has evolved.

The natural generalizing language here would seem to be that of "governing structures," which is not quite the same as "the rules of the game." On the other hand, Williamson in particular stresses that governance refers to transactions, which he proposes as the basic unit of economic activity. This establishes a certain affinity between the rules-of-the-game conception of institutions and the governing-structures view.

While Williamson's focal governing structures relate to firms, that concept of what institutions are would seem quite compatible with the designation of other kinds of governing structures as institutions. Thus many economists have written about prevailing "labor market institutions" in a way that suggests they have in mind the governing structures, perhaps including but transcending the rules of the game, that define how labor markets work and the structure of employer-employee relations. Economists have written in the same vein about "financial institutions." Some have called the Bank of England an institution, and the American Federal Reserve System.

Still another strand of the new institutional writing in economics, and the center of the new institutional analyses in political science (Hall and Taylor 1994), is concerned with the structures that induce and govern collective decision making. The prisoner's dilemma problem and the potential tragedy of the commons have attracted a lot of attention. Here the orienting question often is: Can humans devise a system of rules, or a governing structure, to deal with problems of this sort, which would exist in certain contexts absent some kind of institution to prevent them? Thus Elinor Ostrom (1991) has been concerned with how institutional structures get formed that deal with, or prevent, overuse and careless use of common resources.

Axelrod's work (1997) on the forces generating and sustaining cooperation is another good example. In his analysis of how a large group enforces cooperative behavior on the part of its members, he places stress on the norms supporting cooperation, and on the norm of punishing those who violate the cooperative norm.

As the Ostrom work on protecting the commons and Axelrod's on cooperative behavior in large groups indicate, the new institutional writings by political scientists, as that by economists, aim to identify and analyze the influence of forces and structures that, in the eyes of the analyst, are ignored or underestimated by earlier analyses. Thus Jon Elster (1989a, 1989b) has proposed that to explain certain kinds of human action and interaction, it almost surely is necessary to recognize the role of internalized norms, even though these are difficult to square with rational actor theory of the conventional sort, a position also taken by Ostrom (1998) and Axelrod (1997). Other political scientists stick with rather austere assumptions about informed human rationality, but bring in various constraints and structures to explain behavior that simpler analyses cannot. An important example is the work of scholars such as Shepsle and Weingast (1982), who explain why majority voting tends to lead to more predictable and stable outcomes than earlier analyses, influenced by Arrow's impossibility theorem, had deemed likely. The explanation is posed in terms of procedural rules of voting.

But to return to analysis of governing structures in economics, Williamson proposes that his focus on transactions links his modern institutional analysis with that of the older American institutionalists, in particular the perspective of John Commons (1934). Indeed, it would appear that the desire to make such a connection across the generations is a good part of Williamson's motivation for calling his analysis, which at that time was largely concerned with the modern capitalist firm, "institutional."

However, as Rutherford (1994), Hodgson (1988, 1994), and Langlois (1989) document in detail, there were a variety of different earlier traditions of institutional analysis in economics, not just one. The American institutional economics tradition includes not just Commons, who did focus on transactions, but also Thorstein Veblen, who defined institutions in terms of widely common and predictable patterns of behavior in a society, including generally shared "habits of thought" as well as of action (see, for example, Veblen 1899). In his review, Langlois (1989) focuses attention on the long-standing German and Austrian tradition of institutional analysis, which seems closer to Veblen than to Commons but contains special elements of its own.

Langlois is especially interested in the development by Friedrich Hayek of a body of thought that has spawned a group of present generation economists who say they are institutionalists in the "Austrian" tradition. For Hayek and the modern Austrians, institutions are defined as widespread and widely recognized practices in a society that commonly are deemed appropriate in the circumstances (see, for example, Hayek 1967, 1973).

As Langlois has noted in several places (Langlois 1995, 1999), the notion that institutions define rules for behavior can mean either that rules set constraints or that behavior itself follows a set of rules (see also Crawford and Ostrom 1995, Jepperson 1991, Scott 1991). While most of the neoclassical institutionalists have the former in mind, even within these ranks there are some who lean toward the latter, being inclined to define institutions in terms of prevailing Nash equilibrium behavior (see Schotter 1981). For Hayek and Veblen, the notion of institutions clearly carries the latter connotation. The position is that behavior itself follows a regular pattern that needs to be explained on the basis of additional, or deeper, or other, arguments than simply informed rationality.

Hodgson, in particular, highlights the embedding of economic activity and behavior in the broader cultural context that is central in Veblen (and also in Hayek). That theory of behavior certainly is a far distance from that of the group of modern neoclassical economic institutionalists, treated by Eggertsson in his 1990 volume, for whom institutions are seen as influencing human behavior that is basically "cold turkey" rational. Recently Eggertsson himself (1999) has moved a significant distance from his earlier articulation, and has focused on the role of culture in influencing human behavior. Given the way the disciplines have developed in the time since Veblen wrote, these views today ring much truer in sociology than in economics.

The lines between what some analysts call institutions, and what might be called culture are very blurry in modern institutional analysis in sociology. Thus Walter Powell and Paul DiMaggio (1991) argue, as would many sociologists, that the patterns of organization and behavior one sees in firms generally are those deemed "appropriate" within the relevant business culture. For the most part firms do not engage in any wide-ranging scan of alternatives, but rather simply do the standard thing. Scott (1991) includes symbol systems under his concept of institutions. And in anthropological analysis, institutions tend to be seen as an aspect of culture, or at least something that is determined by culture. Mary Douglas (1986) has written a book with the title *How Institutions Think*.

There clearly is an important difference between Veblen, Hayek, and the modern Austrians, on the one hand, and many of the modern neoclassical institutionalists, on the other, that all of our reviewers have noted. The former do not believe that the strong rationality assumptions of neoclassical theory provide the right explanation for the relatively effective human behavior that one apparently observes in contexts where there is considerable common experience. (Hodgson clearly associates himself with this point of view, if not with all of the "fellow travelers.") For the Austrians, institutions define, mold, and support "rational behavior" in such contexts. Individual persons and economic units do not "think out" good practice for themselves but rather do well by doing what is conventional in the context.

There is a related contrast between, on the one hand, the old American institutionalists in the school of Commons and many of the new neoclassical institutionalists, and, on the other hand, institutionalists of the Austrian tradition, regarding how they see institutions as arising and changing. Hayek saw institutions largely as the unplanned consequences of human action, with the actual structures that developed, and their effects, not well predicted by the individuals who influenced their development (see Powell and DiMaggio 1991 for a general discussion). While Commons (1924, 1934) does recognize that customs, norms, and rules can arise spontaneously, his writings emphasize the role of conscious collective governmental action—through the legislatures and the courts—in working out conflicts between such institutions and deciding which should become law or supported by policy, and thus made more precise and durable.

The difference between a theory that posits that institutions involve conscious coordinated planning, and a theory that posits they are the result of a largely uncoordinated evolutionary process, does not map immediately onto a difference about whether prevailing institutions are "efficient" or not. Much of the early "neoclassical" institutional writing following Demsetz on property rights, and the law and economics tradition in general, presumed that the law was efficient, and that changes in the law reflected changes in the "rules" that are socially optimal. Similarly, much of the writing on business organization assumes that organizational forms are chosen rationally and are optimal, given the context. (See also Ruttan and Hayami 1984.) But on the other hand, Hayek, who was an evolutionist on the first count, saw prevailing institutions as largely efficient.

Recently there has been a noticeable breaking away from this position. The intellectual movement of Douglass North from an early position that institutions evolved in a way that assured they always were close to efficient (for example, Davis and North 1971, North 1981), to his present belief that societies that possess relatively efficient institutions are very lucky (for example, North 1990), may well reflect a general trend in theorizing about these matters. Earlier we noted that Eggertsson has made a similar shift in point of view.

The position that institutions need not be and often are not efficient opens the door to seeing prevailing institutions as a hindrance and a trap, and to explaining cross-country differences in economic performance as being caused by differences in institutions. North (1990) takes this road, in a way that is reminiscent of Adam Smith's arguments more than 200 years ago.

For a long time, economists and other social scientists have been asking the kinds of questions for which "institutions" often is the name given to the answers. The use in institutional analysis of the terms, concepts, and modes of analysis of modern game theory is something of a Johnny-come-lately. However, recently formal game theory, or at least the language of formal game theory, clearly has played a prominent role in various parts of the new institutional analysis, in political science and in sociology, as well as in economics. Thus while earlier institutionalists often defined institutions in terms of widely accepted and enforced rules, the specific language concerning "rules of the game" clearly is drawn from formal game theory.

Martin Shubik (1975) was among the earliest of the formal game theorists to associate "institutions" with the often complex rules of the game. Later, of course, this became quite common. Game theorists like Andrew Schotter (1981) have pioneered in proposing that the rules of the game themselves are a matter of choice, and thus that institutions are consciously chosen rules of the game, a point of view quite consistent with some of the authors discussed earlier. On the other hand, more recently many game theorists have proposed that the rules of the game tend to "evolve," an argument along the lines of the Austrian tradition.

In recent years the notion of multiple possible equilibria, again a notion sharpened up by formal game theory, has become prominent in the new writings about institutions. Again, Schotter was among the earlier analysts to note this, and to propose that institutions therefore needed to be defined in terms of "the way the game is played" as contrasted with simply "the rules of the game," which admits a range of possible equilibrium patterns of actual play (see also Sugden 1989).

Indeed "path dependence" has become an increasingly popular idea in theorizing about the evolution of institutions. The notion that repeated games can have a wide variety of equilibria, each supported by a given set of beliefs and expectations, is now well understood by social scientists theorizing about institutions. And this conception has pulled a number of institutional theorists, who earlier had conceptualized institutions somewhat differently, to stress the expectational aspects involved.

Formal game theory obviously is a highly stripped-down and stylized model of reality. It is interesting, therefore, that the concepts of institutions that come out of analyses using formal game theory reveal the same varied bestiary as do the concepts associated with less formal analyses. Some authors identify institutions with the rules of the game, or with the governing structures controlling the players, others with the way the game is played, others with systems of beliefs and expectations. What about the proposition that institutions should be defined to include "all of the above"?

We believe there is a real inclination to do just that. However, it also is clear that many writers working in the field are arguing that this is something to be avoided.

North (1990), in his recent analysis of institutions and economic growth, takes pains to state that, under his conception, institutions define the environment within which organizations can grow up and within which they operate, but that organizations are not institutions. And a variety of particular organizational forms are compatible with a given broad institutional regime. Mark Granovetter (1985) has taken a similar stance, proposing that social scientists not "overinstitutionalize" human behavior, but rather admit that there can be a variety of behavior patterns (that need to be explained on other grounds) compatible with a given set of institutions. North's interests recently have turned to the role of ideology, and ideas, in influencing human behavior, but he has tried hard to keep his institutions concept separable from his concept of ideology.

On the other hand, for Williamson, standard organizational forms are among the most important of an economy's institutions. Institutional economists from Veblen to Hayek to Schotter have defined institutions in terms of standard and expected patterns of behavior. And Veblen includes under his concept of institutions "habits of thought common to the generality of men."

2.3. What Is Common and What Is Different across the Concepts?

Despite the obvious diversity, there are certain common perceptions, or themes, that run at least through significant subsets of what we have described above. These seem to promise that a broad but coherent conceptualization of institutions is possible.

In particular, virtually all the analysts who call themselves institutionalists, or who are called that by surveyors of the field, have their attention focused on human interaction, in contexts where the interests of one party, and the efficacy of the actions of that party, are strongly influenced by what other parties do. Many focus on the uncertainty, indeed the chaos, that would exist in such contexts absent reliable expectations regarding what others will do, and the rules and norms that mold that behavior and lend predictability to it.

Many of the analyses are concerned explicitly with transactions between economic parties, and transaction costs. In some cases the focus is on transactions between economic units; the property rights literature is a good example. Other analyses focus on interpersonal transactions within economic units, as in the principal-agent literature. A number are focused on the problem of achieving coordination, a form of "transaction," in contexts where there is a collective interest in channeling and controlling self-interested behavior, and achieving a pattern of action that is in the collective interest. Political processes, more broadly, are widely regarded as being strongly institutionalized.

But while these shared and overlapping elements lend a certain commonality to different notions about institutions, it is clear that there is very considerable diversity as well. Why?

Many of the authors who have tried to define institutions have had their central interest in a particular phenomenon or factor that they thought important and neglected in standard theory—property rights, and standard modes of organizing business, are good examples—but they or others wanted to consider that instance as an example of a broader set of things that would be called institutions. This path has led to different broad definitions of institutions for two reasons. First, different authors have started with different focal instances. Thus property rights and modes of organizing business have some attributes in common but differ in important ways, and tend to induce different generalizations. Second, the natural generalization of any particular instance is not obvious. Is the appropriate generalization of property rights the rules of the game, or something else? Governance structures seems a better generalization of modes of organizing business, but one can think of others.

Other authors have been attracted to define institutions as a variable or aspect of a general theory of human behavior they espouse, with particular institutions as "for instances." However, the theories of behavior, and the focal examples used to illustrate those theories, generally are not the same. Thus writers who have tried to define institutions in terms of the theory of behavior contained in modern game theory have a different view of human rationality than the old institutionalists, like Veblen, and the old and new Austrian institutionalists. And even when theorists hold roughly the same theory of behavior, they may identify "institutions" with different aspects of that theory. While many economists having game theory in mind associate institutions with the rules of the game, others define institutions in terms of a particular set of equilibrium expectations and behavior associated with how the game actually is played.

Thus either a "bottom up" or a "top down" approach to the definition of institutions can lead to a wide range of different definitions, and flavors. Because of the common elements in conception mentioned above, there is a tendency to ignore these differences.

Part of the difference here, but not all of it, relates to the level of the analysis. Some authors use the term *institutions* to characterize what economic agents do in certain settings, some to characterize the particular norms and rules that lie behind and mold what they do, some to describe the broader cultural and social context within which particular norms and rules take shape. While one can see a semantic chain linking the various definitions, at the poles at least the conceptions of how to define institutions are very different. Indeed, they may involve quite different theories about human behavior.

2.4. Is There a Problem?

We think the analysis above highlights and explains the syndrome. Is there a problem here, and if so, what is the problem?

One basic question would seem to be whether the term *institutions* is needed at all. We think that, regardless of how one might answer that question, we are stuck with the term. While it might be better if we could expunge it from our vocabulary, that doesn't seem to be in the cards. And if we, the economists and other social scientists using the term, understand the issue, and define institutions coherently and clearly in a particular analysis, there is no reason why diverse use should be a major problem.

However, it does strike us as something of a problem, or at least a matter that calls for readers to take special care, when all of these meanings are lumped together. To call the legal regime, the standard modes of organizing business, constitutional democracy and the party system usually associated with that form of government, and a belief in individual liberties and the appropriateness of capitalism, all "institutions" that support economic growth is a recipe that makes coherent analysis very difficult. This is so even if all these factors are associated with economic growth.

More generally, it is our belief that it is a mistake to try to get the word *institutions* to cover too much conceptual ground. We are persuaded that the term *institutions* in any particular use needs to be carefully tailored to the questions under consideration, and to the broad theory being employed to probe at those questions. This means that the concept of institutions will not be, and probably should not be, exactly the same in all arenas.

Put another way, our argument is that a useful concept of institutions can be developed for analysis aimed at particular phenomena only in the context of a broader theory bearing on those phenomena that naturally invokes, as it were, a relatively coherent concept of institutions. In any case, this is how we proceed in our attempt to "make sense of institutions" as a factor in economic growth.

3. Building Institutions into Economic Growth Theory

3.1. The Challenge

Scholars studying economic growth are in considerable agreement regarding the "immediate" or "proximate" factors behind the cumulatively vast increases in output per worker and living standards that many economies have achieved over the past two centuries. Here almost all economists would list as key elements technological advance, investments in physical capital, and the growth of human capital. When pressed, many economists would recognize, as well, factors relating to the efficiency with which firms operate, and the effectiveness of the processes that allocate and reallocate resources.

Economists also are in broad agreement that institutions are an important factor molding and involved in economic growth. But there is far less coherence across the analyses.

There would seem to be widely shared agreement on two matters. One is that one ought to bring in institutions to deepen the analysis and try to explain some of the variables treated as proximate factors behind growth. Thus this strand of growth theorizing tends to involve reflections on the institutions supporting technological advance, physical capital formation, education, and the efficiency of the economy and the resource allocation process.

The second broadly shared conception, and one that we will use as the basis for our subsequent analysis, is that institutions influence, or define, the ways in which economic actors get things done, in contexts involving human interaction. They do this by making certain kinds of transactions attractive or easy and others difficult or costly. Thus, while very parsimoniously modeled, markets, and the prices generated by markets, are part of the growth theory espoused by virtually all economists. So too firms. Security of property and clarity and enforceability of contracts enter many accounts of the factors that support economic growth. Many economists recognize the importance of mechanisms for collective action. Economists tend to call all of these things, or the things that shape them, "institutions."

Beyond this, consensus breaks down. Indeed, as we suggested above, there is not much agreement among economists working in this arena even regarding exactly how to define institutions.

3.2. A Proposal

At its broadest level, our proposal is to fasten onto the concept of institutions as structures that define or mold the way economic agents interact to get things done. We have noted that much of the general writing by economists about institutions has been concerned with just that. However, the implicit or explicit strategy has been to get at the subject indirectly, by defining institutions in a manner that is in some ways broader and in other ways more restricted, than the rules of the game, or general cultural beliefs and values, and then considering how these mold and constrain patterns of human interaction in economic life. Our proposal is to start with and focus on the latter, and to bring in deeper shaping factors as needed to provide an explanation for the observed interaction patterns.

A major advantage of this analytic strategy, in our view, is that the modes of economic interaction that the analyst believes to be important in determining economic performance immediately become the objects of description and analysis. This seems a promising way of defining an empirical, as well as a theoretical, research program.

More specifically, we propose to elaborate on the concept of an "economic activity" (a key building block of at least one sophisticated version of the "production function" idea) so as to recognize the multiparty interaction involved in the operation of most productive economic activities—interaction that sometimes goes on inside economic units, and sometimes between them. In the activity analysis formulation, an activity is associated with a vector of inputs and outputs but also implicitly with a process. An important advantage of the activity formulation, from our point of view, is that it invites natural discussion of how the activity is done. While that notion generally is presumed to involve a description of the "physical" technology involved, like the open-hearth process for making steel, here we propose also to include a characterization of the "social" technologies involved: the division of labor, the way the work is coordinated and managed, and so on. (The notion of "social technologies" that in some ways are similar to "physical technologies," but that involve patterned human interaction rather than physical engineering, also has been put forth in North and Wallis 1994.)

We believe that the notion of routinized social technologies encompasses much of what the varied discussion of institutions is about, or at least that part concerned with economic performance. It includes, easily and naturally, intraorganizational interactions, market transactions, mechanisms for invoking and determining collective action, and other relevant modes of human interaction to get things done. The concept of institutions advanced here is more focused and specialized than the rules of the game, but such rules certainly comprise a large part of our institutions concept. The conception of institutions as governing structures is closer to the one we propose, particularly if that concept is blended with "the way things customarily are done." However, we believe that the concept of routinized social technologies serves to focus this orientation in a useful way. Behind the scenes certainly are broad social and cultural values, norms, beliefs, and expectations, but they definitely are behind the scenes in our formulation.

It may be useful to couch our proposal in the language of transaction costs. One way of thinking about institutions is to see them as defining low-transaction-cost ways of doing things that involve human interaction. Note that, under this conception, institutions are constraints, on the one hand. They in effect define the particular ways things must be done if they are to be done parsimoniously. But on the other hand, effective institutions, like effective physical technologies, define productive pathways for doing things. Absent an effective social technology for doing something, it may be very costly to do that thing, or doing it may be impossible. We develop these notions in the following section.

We have slipped into the position of seeing routinized social technologies as institutions in themselves, and this is the language we will use in the following discussion. However, we have no intention of fighting about words. If the reader wishes, our routinized social technologies can be viewed not as institutions in themselves but rather as institutionalized behaviors shaped by prevailing institutions, more broadly defined.

4. Routines, and Physical and Social Technologies

We propose that the language of routines, as developed in Nelson and Winter (1982), is a convenient language for characterizing social technologies. A routine involves a collection of procedures that, taken together, result in a predictable and specifiable outcome. We focus here on routines that are commonly employed by individuals and organizations to achieve particular ends.

Complex routines almost always can be analytically broken down into a collection of subroutines. Thus the routine for making a cake involves such subroutines as pouring, mixing, and baking. These operations generally will require particular inputs, like flour and sugar, and an oven. In turn, virtually all complex routines are nested and linked with other routines that must be effected to make them possible, or to enable them to yield value. Thus a cake-making routine presupposes that the necessary ingredients and equipment are at hand, and the provision of these at some prior date required their own "shopping" routines. And before these artifacts could get to the store, they had to be designed and produced, activities involving their own complex structure of routines.

As the example suggests, the productive operation of any particular routine generally is keyed to and made effective by the embodiment of the operation of other routines in materials and equipment. (See Langlois 1999 for an elaboration on the theme that routines can be embodied in machines.) The cook "turns on" the oven and sets its temperature gauge to 350 degrees. The oven then carries out its routine.

We noted above that our concept of a routine admits, indeed highlights, that choices are made in the course of performing a routine. On the other hand, the term connotes that the flow of action in the activity proceeds more or less automatically. Routines do not eliminate choice, but they do sharply channel it. Choices need to be made about what broad routine to invoke in the first place, and a whole series of choices need to be made along the way in operation of the routine. However, under the theory put forth here, given a particular objective and the context for its pursuit, these choices are highly focused and, to a considerable extent, are made routinely, that is, without much conscious thinking about it.

Thus, to return to our cake making example, a given cake recipe—a routine for making a cake—generally allows the mixing to be done by hand or with an electric mixer. Margarine may generally be substituted for butter. An individual cook may use a little bit less of this, and add some of that, without breaking very far from the recipe. Making a chocolate cake involves basically the same recipe as making a vanilla cake, except for a few inputs and steps. Thus there is room within a routine for variation, perhaps motivated by particular tastes, or the kind of cake the cook deems appropriate under the circumstances (it is a birthday cake, and the birthday child likes vanilla), or the skill and experience of the cook, or input availabilities (there is margarine but not butter in the refrigerator), or perhaps by input prices (butter is very costly these days). Many cake makers have their own particular secrets that they regard as contributing to superior products.

However, one important aspect of productive routines we want to highlight here is that, while the particular operation of a routine by a competent individual or organization generally involves certain idiosyncratic elements, at its core almost always are elements that are broadly similar to what other competent parties would do in the same context. By and large the ingredients and the equipment used by reasonably skilled cooks are basically the same as those used by other skilled cake makers. And the broad outline of the steps generally can be recognized by someone skilled in the art as being roughly those described in *The Joy of Cooking*, or some comparable reference.

As the example suggests, the latter aspect of a routine, the part that is broadly familiar to all those skilled in the art, tends to be associated with a title or name, and with written or otherwise codified descriptions and explanations of how it is done. It may also be associated with a theory purporting to explain why the routine works. The ability to explain what one is doing in a reasonably articulate way, and to provide reasons for it, is a principal difference between skilled human behavior and skilled behavior of nonhuman animals.

We do not play down that, almost always, a nontrivial part of what is involved in performing routines may not be explainable in a way that completely permits someone who is not already familiar with the practice to "do it" without a lot of learning by doing. Michael Polanyi's point about the tacitness of much of human knowledge is highly relevant. Further, while some routines (such as the use of rDNA techniques in doing genetic research) are backed by a sophisticated scientific understanding, in many cases the "explanation" for why something works may be more folklore than science (consider the rationales for certain steps in a cake recipe). In fact, routines differ enormously both in the extent to which they are articulated and the extent to which they are understood in a scientific sense.

However, in any case, a key characteristic of most routines that are used extensively in an economy is that, in their broad outlines at least, they are widely known and employed by those skilled in the art. And it is not just happenstance, or the result of separate individual learning experiences that leads to the same learned actions. The standard elements of widely used routines are standard because they are culturally shared.

Particular individual and organizational actors need to have mastery over these culturally shared aspects in order to operate effectively, for two reasons. First, great cake recipes, or effective ways of organizing bakeries or producing steel or semiconductors, tend to be the result of the cumulative contributions of many parties, often operating over many generations. This is a central reason why they are as effective as they are.

The other reason why individual persons and organizations wanting to operate effectively in a particular arena need to tap into the public aspects of the relevant routines is that, as we noted, particular routines tend to be part of systems of routines. The inputs needed for them tend to be available routinely. If help is needed, it generally is easy to get help from someone who already knows a lot of what is needed and can explain the particulars in common language, and so on.

4.1. Physical and Social Technologies as Constraints and as Productive Pathways

We now would like to propose that the program built into a routine generally involves two different aspects: a recipe that is anonymous regarding any division of labor, and a division of labor plus a mode of coordination. We propose that the former is what scholars often have in mind when they think of technology in the conventional sense; we will call this aspect of a routine the "physical" technology involved. And we will call the latter aspect, that which involves the coordination of human action, the "social" technology involved.

From one point of view, prevailing physical and social technologies limit choices regarding how to do things. By "limit" here we mean a soft set of constraints, not a hard one. Earlier we noted that different practitioners will use physical or hard technologies, like cake recipes, in different ways. Different contexts will induce different variants. However, to use a physical technology that is completely different from what professionals in the field are familiar with and have developed over the years involves not taking advantage of that social learning. Available inputs—machinery and materials—generally are tailored for use in prevailing routines, and to try to do something significantly different may require hand-crafting the inputs, perhaps at considerable cost and risk of failure.

On the other hand, as Schumpeter argued years ago (1934), breaking from prevailing routines is exactly what innovation is all about. Continuing economic progress is impossible without it. But innovation is risky for exactly the reasons just put forth.

We propose that the situation is similar regarding the aspects of a routine that involve division of labor and coordination mechanisms. Individual organizations operating a particular routine inevitably will differ in how labor is divided and work coordinated, both within the particular organization in question and across the borders of the organization, just as they will differ in the details of the physical technology employed. These differences may reflect variations in opportunities and contexts. As circumstances change, a particular organization may modify its ways of doing things in ways that are responsive to those changes. However, there are a lot of advantages in abiding by at least the broad outlines of prevailing and generally accepted social "rules," "modes of organizing work," and "appropriate practice," and not taking a route that is deemed strange or inappropriate to those who have to be involved.

At the same time, prevailing social technologies—institutions (or institutionalized behaviors, if one wants to define institutions as the rules of the game behind the scenes)—may be highly inefficient compared with other ways of organizing transactions, should these be effectively implemented. In particular, prevailing institutions may not work well with new physical technologies, or when faced with new conditions of demand and scarcity. But institutional innovation, like innovation in physical technologies, is risky.

There is widespread recognition that powerful physical technologies generally are involved centrally in productive routines. Under neoclassical theory at least, there has been less explicit and systematic reflection on the roles of effective social technologies in productive activity, although as we have noted this is what much of the new discussion of institutions seems to be mostly about. This is our focus here.

We begin with the simple observation that the routines associated with most complex production operations are not and cannot be accomplished by one person working in isolation. One person certainly can make a cake, if that person has access to the necessary flour, sugar, implements to stir, an oven to bake it in, and so on. But even the routine for cake making involves operations linked to other people or organizations, if one expands the description of that routine to include steps to gain control over the necessary inputs. How does one get the necessary flour and sugar? What if the oven is on the blink? How does one arrange to get it fixed?

We propose that "knowing" prevailing social technologies, and what they allow and deny, is just as important as "knowing" available physical technologies in determining the available range of "choice" facing a particular actor. Thus in the cake-making example, in this society at least, sugar and flour tend to be available at one kind of store, which may or may not also sell mixing devices, but almost never ovens. Ovens are available at a different kind of store. What goods different kinds of stores provide, and how one gets to obtain merchandise from them, define a good part of the institutional context for cake making. To be an effective cake maker, one needs to know not only the recipes but also how to get the right ingredients.

That knowledge, and the prevailing social technology in this context, of course involves much more than who sells what, but also matters of law and law enforcement, and customary practice. To take merchandise from a store without paying for it is a crime. Cash is legal tender for purchase, but the custom may be for particular kinds of stores also to accept personal checks, or credit cards. These institutional elements define the social technologies available for shopping.

In the example above, prevailing institutions are defined in terms of how they affect ways to get things done where the doing involves coordinating the actions of independent individuals or organizations. In stripped-down neoclassical economics, these mechanisms are often subsumed under the concept of "markets." The discussion above aims to unpack the market concept and make it something that can be modeled as a set of processes or routines. A well worked out routines model of a market would incorporate how prices are set, and how prices affect the details of what is done by actors buying and selling in that market. But it would involve a considerable amount of other "institutional" detail as well.

Institutions, as we are developing the term, also constrain effective routines within organizations. Thus in any era in any country (or at least within particular subcultures) there are some widely held notions about how a bakery should be run that, if violated, might make it difficult to get regulatory clearance, or bank credit, and notions about appropriate job classifications and payment that, if violated, could cause labor trouble.

Broad organizational forms define institutions, to the extent that they are thought of as the appropriate ways to organize economic activity. Thus Ford's organization of mass production provided a model followed by many companies engaged in producing assembled products that was for many years considered the norm. Presently, Toyota-style "lean production" now is the vogue. In both cases, at least the broad outlines of the organizational format became well known, if not always easy to carry out in practice. In both cases a broad "theory" about why the mode was efficient came to be widely articulated and accepted. That is, these forms were institutions, or generally available social technologies.

While our focus here is on economic institutions, or more generally institutions that mold economic performance, not political ones per se, it is clear that political institutions play an important role in economic performance. The way management and labor negotiate, or fight, about wages and work rules, is a good example. These procedures tend to be highly patterned, that is, institutionalized, if with a significant stochastic element. In turn, these patterns of interaction are molded by a body of formal law, which in turn is the result of how a nation's political institutions grind out legal resolutions to the demands of competing interests. Does the labor union have to vote on a contract negotiated by its representatives and management? Will a passionate minority accept the decision of a majority? In many cases prevailing social technologies need to be understood as reflecting a kind of truce between different interests.

As the examples indicate, social technologics—institutions—differ in the extent to which they are supported by norms and values. Some, like the institutions of collective bargaining, may be powerfully supported by interests that argue that what is is right and proper. Others, like whether a grocery store sells hardware, may carry very little moral load.

Institutions, both those that define what in a simpler conception would be called markets, and those that mold intraorganizational activity, can be very complex and intertwined. Consider what is involved in the design and development of modern aircraft. One observes that the activities tend to proceed in quite similar ways, regardless of the company in which they are undertaken. The nature of the division of labor and the modes of coordination that have in the past proved effective are widely known in the trade. In turn, that division of labor is molded, and constrained, by the nature of prevailing scientific and engineering disciplines. Engineering schools reflect and enforce this division. While there is overlap, electrical engineers are trained in one set of subjects and aeronautical engineers in another.

Because of this, firms know "the kind of engineer to hire" when they need someone to do a particular kind of job, and they know how to locate that new employee within the prevailing framework of work. The nature of the job market is molded, as well, by such institutions as the meetings of professional societies, which serve as a meeting ground for employers looking for people and engineers looking for jobs, and also by broadly accepted rules regarding when it is and is not legitimate to jump from one employer to another, the mechanisms by which salaries are bargained out, and the like.

We are not arguing, of course, that all companies organize to design planes in exactly the same way, or that every person with a degree in electrical engineering knows the same thing, or that all engineering schools divide the turf the same way. There clearly are nontrivial differences across societies, between firms in a given society, and even among projects within a firm. And there is change, often significant change, over time. But at a given time within a particular society there tends to be certain reasonably well established practices in these arenas. Major deviation from them is, at the least, cause for notice and surprise, and likely will lead to inadequate outcomes. That is, the design of aircraft, the structure of technical professions, the division of fields in engineering schools, and the structure of the job market for engineers are all institutionalized.

In the language of transaction costs, institutions define and provide ways of doing things that require coordinated interaction with other parties where the transaction costs are low. This is not to say that one cannot organize the division of labor and interparty coordination through means that are not institutionalized. But the transaction costs of doing so may be much higher. An institution is like a paved road across a swamp. To say that the location of the prevailing road is a "constraint" on getting across is, basically, to miss the point. Without a road, getting across would be impossible, or at least much harder. Developing an institutionalized way of doing something may be the only way to achieve a low-transaction-cost way of doing it.

5. Institutions in a Theory of Economic Growth

The question of how institutions fit into a theory of economic growth of course depends not only on what one means by institutions but also on the other aspects of that theory. While in Section 3 we stressed the common elements of the theory of economic growth employed by most knowledgeable scholars of the subject, we also noted that there were some differences. We believe that the concept of institutions as defining or shaping social technologies fits well with most variants. However, not surprisingly, the formulation we have given fits extremely well, like a glove on a hand, our particular view. Below we articulate that view, first at a quite general level, and then as a way of interpreting two important historical episodes.

5.1. Technological Advance as the Driving Force

Earlier we noted the widespread agreement among scholars of economic growth regarding the key "proximate" sources, in particular the advance of physical technologies, and rising amounts of physical and human capital per worker. These days any theory of economic growth that does not assign to technological advance a major share of the credit for growth would be regarded as odd by most scholars of the field. However, our own views on this matter are more extreme than most.

At least for countries operating at the technological frontier, we would argue that, without the creation of new technology, very little productivity growth from existing levels can be achieved simply through increases in physical and human capital per worker. For economists who find the standard production function concept useful in their thinking, our argument is that the relevant elasticities of substitution are very small, if the production function concept is defined in terms of given technology.

Put more positively, our argument is that the economic growth we have experienced needs to be understood as the result of the progressive introduction of new technologies that were associated with increasingly higher levels of worker productivity, and the ability to produce new or improved goods and services. As a broad trend, they also used progressively more capital. (The varied reasons for the capital-using nature of technological change has been developed in Chapter 1.) Rising human capital intensity also has been a handmaiden to that process, being associated both with the changing inputs that have generated technological advance and with the changing skill requirements of new technologies.

Within this formulation, new "institutions" and social technologies come into the picture as changes in the modes of interaction—new modes of organizing work, new kinds of markets, new laws, new forms of collective action—that are called for as the new technologies are brought into economic use. In turn, the institutional structure at any time has a profound effect on, and reflects, the technologies that are in use, which ones can be easily adopted if the conditions are right, and which are being developed.

We noted earlier that there is a long tradition in economics of ascribing to prevailing institutions the failure of certain economies to adopt available productive technologies. North (1990) among others recently has rearticulated the "institutional obstructions" theory of economic backwardness. And Christopher Freeman and Carlotta Perez (1988) have proposed that the changing of the national locus of industrial leadership that has occurred several times over the past two centuries has been the consequence of the ability of some nations, but not others, to put in place institutions suited to the new technologies. In so arguing, they are of course echoing a theme voiced long ago by Veblen (1899, 1915).

The conception and language of "routines" is well suited to this theory of growth. As noted, the notion of operating with a particular routine connotes that, while there may be a range of input mixes and output characteristics compatible with a basic "recipe," that range is quite constrained. Thus, so long as old routines continue to be used, there is only limited room for increasing worker productivity by increasing inputs per worker. Significant productivity increase requires the introduction of new routines, which in general will involve new recipes or physical technologies. And, in turn, these new physical technologies often will require new social technologies if they are to be employed productively.

We believe that the concept of institutions as social technologies, the routines language for describing them, and the theory we have sketched of how institutions and institutional change are bound up with the advance of physical technologies in the process of economic growth, become more powerful the closer the analysis gets to describing actual social technologies in action. We turn now to two important particular developments in the history of experienced modern economic growth: the rise of mass-production industry in the United States in the late nineteenth century, and the rise of the first science-based industry—synthetic dyestuffs—in Germany at about the same time. Given space constraints, our discussion must be very sketchy, but we hope we provide enough detail that one can see our proposed conceptualization in action.

5.2. The Rise of Mass Production

During the last part of the nineteenth century and the first half of the twentieth, manufacturing industry, particularly in the United States, experienced rapid productivity growth, associated with the emergence of a number of new physical technologies that together set the stage for mass production. The new railroad technologies and the development of the telegraph enabled firms producing transportable goods to reach distant markets much more quickly and reliably than before, thus opening the potential for large-scale production and marketing.

The advance of machine tool technology, and improvements in metals, allowed the design and development of machinery that was very productive at high, sustained rates of production.

The bringing into place of these new technologies was accompanied by the growing scale of plants and firms, rising capital intensity of production, and the development of professional management, often with education beyond the secondary level. However, these latter increases in physical and human capital per worker, and in the scale of output, should not be considered as independent sources of growth, in the sense of growth accounting; they were productive only because they were needed by the new technologies.

At the same time, it would be a conceptual mistake to try to calculate how much productivity increase the new technologies would have allowed had physical and human capital per worker, and the scale of output, remained constant. The new production routines involved new physical technologies that incorporated higher levels of physical and human capital per worker than the older routines they replaced. To operate the new routines efficiently required much larger scales of output than previously.

And they also involved new social technologies. Chandler's great studies are largely about the new modes of organizing business that were required to take advantage of the new opportunities for "scale and scope." The scale of the new firms exceeded that which owner-managers and their relatives and close friends could deal with, either in terms of governance or finance. The growing importance of hired professional management, and the diminished willingness of the original family owners to provide all the financial capital, called for the development of new financial institutions and associated markets. The need for professional managers also pulled business schools into being. More generally, the new industrial organization profoundly reshaped shared beliefs of how the economy worked, and came to define the concept of modern capitalism.

The development of mass production proceeded especially rapidly in the United States, in part, at least, because of the large size of the American market, but also because the associated new institutions grew up rapidly in the new world. In general Europe lagged. On the other hand, the rise of new institutions to support science-based industry occurred first in Europe.

5.3. Synthetic Dyestuffs

We turn now to consider our second example: the rise of the first science-based industry, in Germany, that occurred over roughly the same time period as did the rise of mass production in the United States.

Our formulation of this second case is somewhat more elaborate, and also somewhat more stylized. We propose to present a nearly formal account of the rise of the organic chemical products industry toward the end of the nineteenth century, and of the ascendancy of German firms over their British rivals. The basic story has been told by several scholars, but the account we draw most from here is that contained in the recent book by Peter Murmann (2003). Murmann's account is presented in standard language. The account we present here is "semiformal" in the sense that it makes explicit use of the concept of routines, and the physical and social technologies involved in routines.

Several new packages of routines play the key roles in our story. The first is a new physical technology for creating new dyestuffs, with university-trained chemists as the key inputs, which came into existence in the late 1860s and early 1870s as a result of improved scientific understanding of the structure of organic compounds. However, this development would not have had the economic impact that it did without the invention of a new social technology for organizing chemists to work in a coordinated way for their employer—the modern industrial research laboratory. A third element in our story is another social technology, the system of training young chemists in the relevant physical technology, that is, in the understandings and research methods of organic chemistry. This social technology was university based and funded by national governments.

Several different kinds of "institutionalized" organizations play key roles in our theoretical story. First, there are chemical products firms, of two types. The old type does not possess an industrial research laboratory, and achieves new dyestuffs slowly through processes that involve only small levels of investment. The other kind of firm, the new type, invests in industrial research laboratories, and because of those investments achieves new dyestuffs at a much faster rate than do old firms. There are two other kinds of organizations in this story as well.

One is national universities that train young chemists. The other is national chemical products industry associations, which lobby government for support of university training. National political processes and government funding agencies also are part of our story, but they will be treated implicitly rather than explicitly.

Our "model" involves specification of certain institutionalized national markets, one for chemists who work in industry, and the other for the dyestuffs that firms produce. Chemists have a national identity, and the firms do also. German chemists (we will assume that they all are trained in German universities) require a significantly higher salary to work in a British firm than in a German one, and British-trained scientists require more to work in Germany than in Britain. (Alternatively, the best of the national graduates would rather work in a national firm.) This means that, other things being equal, it advantages national firms if their national universities are training as many chemists as they want to hire.

There also are national markets for dyestuffs. The British market is significantly larger than the German market throughout the period under analysis. Other things being equal, British firms have an advantage selling in the British market, and German firms in the German market. However, the advantage of national firms can be offset if a foreign firm is offering a richer menu of dyestuffs. Under our specification, if a foreign firm does more R & D than a national firm, it can take away the latter's market, at least partially.

There are several key dynamic processes, and factors influencing them, in our story. To a first approximation, the profits of a firm, gross of its R & D spending, are an increasing function of the level of its technology, defined in terms of the quality of the dyestuffs it offers and the volume of its sales. This first approximation, however, needs to be modified by two factors. One is that the profits of a firm that does R & D depend on whether the chemists it hires are national or not. The other is that, for a given level of the other variables, British firms earn somewhat more, reflecting their advantaged location regarding the market.

Research and development is funded out of profits, but not all firms invest in R & D. Firms can spend nothing on R & D (as do "old-style" firms), or they can invest a fraction of their profits in R & D (as do "new-style" firms). Initially, all firms are "profitable enough" to be able to afford a small-scale R & D facility. Some (the new-style firms) choose to invest in one, and others don't. If the profits of a new-style firm grow, they spend more on R & D.

Given the availability of the new R & D technology, it is profitable to invest in R & D, and given the competition from new-style firms, firms that do not do R & D lose money. This is so in both Germany and the United Kingdom. In both countries a certain fraction of firms start to invest in R & D when the new technology arrives. These profitable firms expand, and the unprofitable ones contract. As firms that do R & D expand, their demand for trained chemists grows too. National firms hire nationally trained chemists first, and then (at higher cost) foreign-trained chemists.

The supply of chemists provided to industry by universities is a function of the funding those universities receive from government. For a variety of reasons, the supply of German chemists initially is much greater than the supply of British chemists. This initial cost advantage to German firms that do R & D is sufficient to compensate for the disadvantage regarding the location of the product market. And over time, the political strength of the national industry association, and the amount of money it can induce government to provide national universities, is proportional to the size of that part of the national industry that undertakes organized research.

Start the dynamics just before the advent of the scientific understanding that creates a new technique for creating dyestuffs. There are more (and bigger) British firms than German firms in this initial condition, reflecting their closeness to the larger part of the market. No firm has an industrial research laboratory. The supply of chemists being trained at German universities is more than sufficient to meet the limited demands of German firms, and British firms, for chemists.

Now, along comes the new scientific technique for creating dyestuffs. Some British firms and some German firms start doing industrial R & D on a small scale. They do well, and grow. The demand for university-trained chemists grows. Since most of the existing supply of chemists, and the augmentations to that supply, are German-trained, German firms are able to hire them at a lower price than can British firms. The German firms that invest in R & D do well, on average, relative to British firms and their German competitors who have not invested in R & D. They grow, and as they do, their R & D grows. The effectiveness of German universities' lobbying for government support of training of chemists increases as the German industry grows. The reader can run out the rest of the scenario.

6. A Brief Summing Up

We believe that the conception of institutions as defining or shaping social technologies is coherent, broad enough to be useful in analysis of economic growth, and well tailored to fit with other aspects of the understanding of economic growth shared by empirical scholars of the subject. In our view at least, the advance of physical technologies continues to play the leading role in the story of economic growth. Social technologies enter the story largely in terms of how they enable the implementation or development of physical technologies.

Given space constraints, we cannot discuss in any detail here our evolving theory of how institutions change. Subsequent chapters will expand the present discussion significantly. We have proposed that institutional change is to a considerable extent induced by other changes in the ways that economic activities proceed. Other writers on institutions have stressed changes in prices and in the pattern of demand and scarcity more generally. We have focused on changes in the physical technologies that are used, or that are available and deemed promising if social technologies could be adjusted to exploit them effectively. But in turn, prevailing social technologies strongly influence the way physical technologies evolve. Thus it probably is useful to think of physical and social technologies as coevolving.

The use of the term *evolves* seems appropriate. This is not to deny that the processes by which institutions evolve involve thinking, planning, purposive actions, on the part of individuals, organizations, collective bodies. However, if these two cases, and others with which we are familiar, be a guide, the process of institutional change involves lots of trial, failure, trying again, learning from mistakes. And it is very much a cultural evolutionary process.

We have not taken a hard stance regarding the basic theory of human behavior that fits with our conception of the role of institutions.

Our own view involves a strong belief in the importance of shared culture in molding what people think is appropriate to do, but at the same time a belief that in many cases, at least, individual and group learning processes winnow out grossly inferior or self-destructive practices, and when new challenges or opportunities arise, there can be major changes in institutions that allow significant economic progress. We are impressed, on the one hand, by the hold of the broad aspects of culture on what people do, and, on the other hand, by how rapidly particular cultural doctrine can change when there are strong pressures for change and clear signals regarding better things people could be doing. We would propose that, where one does see very rapid adaptive institutional change, the institutions involved do not carry a heavy normative load.

However, the reader does not need to pick up that package along with our proposed perspective on institutions. We think the latter can stand in its own right as a useful way of thinking about institutions as a factor shaping economic performance.

PART III

In the preceding chapters I laid out the proposition that economic growth should be understood as an evolutionary process. Chapter 5 argued in particular that the key driving force is the coevolution of physical technologies and social technologies such as organizational forms, and institutions more broadly.

The chapters in Part III highlight and begin to address the factors behind the fact that the economic progress that has been made over the past two centuries is highly uneven. It is highly uneven across countries. Chapter 2 was concerned with countries that lag behind the frontier, and with how some of them have caught up. But economic progress also is highly uneven across different areas of human need. Uneven progress shows up in the very great differences across industries in their rates of measured productivity growth. It shows up even more strikingly in the unevenness across fields in our ability to deal with particular problems or do various tasks. Thus humans today can travel from one side of the country to the other side in half a dozen hours, something that would have taken months 150 years ago. Many diseases that used to be killers, for which there was no defense or cure, have been tamed. On the other hand, we have made little progress in coping with certain kinds of cancers. And it is not clear that the way we educate our children today is much advanced over, or even very different from, the way we did it a century ago.

Chapter 6 is concerned exactly with the question of why there has been so little progress in education. The analysis is focused on the nature of the evolutionary processes through which advances in various activities occur, if they are to occur. It is proposed that the factors that make for evolutionary, fast progress in certain fields—for example, coping with infectious diseases—do not obtain in education and like fields. An important reason is that the "technologies" involved are to a considerable extent social technologies.

Chapter 7 develops that argument more widely. Several case studies are presented to support the proposition that progress in technologies that are largely physical tends to proceed more smoothly and rapidly than progress in technologies that are largely social. For this reason, institutional evolution tends to be much more sluggish than the evolution of physical technologies. This asymmetry lies at the root of many of the problems faced by modern societies today.

CHAPTER 6

On the Uneven Evolution
of Human Know-how

1. Introduction

Economists long have recognized the advance of human know-how as
the central driving force behind the remarkable increases in living
standards that have been achieved over the past two centuries. However, less attention has been paid to the fact that the advance of effective know-how has been extremely uneven across different economic
sectors and classes of human needs. Some areas of human know-how
today are extraordinarily powerful; consider modern information and
computation technologies, or certain fields of modern medicine. At
the same time, certain human illnesses have defied continuing efforts to deal with them better. Breast cancers remain a major scourge.
And many broad areas of human activity have seen little progress in
know-how. It is not clear that our ability to educate children has advanced much over the past century. Despite a lot of huffing in business
schools and in books on management, there does not seem to have
been much improvement over the years in management know-how.
Why not?

I offer here a very preliminary exploration of this important puzzle, which will be divided into three parts. First, it seems important

* Based on Richard R. Nelson, "On the Uneven Evolution of Human Know-how,"
Research Policy 32 (2003): 909–922.

I am indebted to Dr. Annetine Gelijns and Dr. Alan Moskowitz for checking what I
say about heart surgery in this chapter. I also have consulted the splendid paper by
Edmondson, Bohmer, and Pisano (2001) on an aspect of heart surgery.

to try to get a grip on the nature of modern human know-how. What are its aspects, and how is it organized? Where is it "located," and how is it applied? I shall argue that human know-how is multifaceted and variegated, and stored in different places and forms. Some of it is of the form often thought of as engineering product or process design, relatively well articulated "how it is done" knowledge. However, much is embodied in particular human skills, as contrasted with "blueprint-like" know-how. Some involves sophisticated understanding of why practice works; some simply understanding from experience that a practice does work. And an important part of know-how is knowing how to tap into, and coordinate, the various capabilities and efforts that need to be brought together to do a job.

Second, there is the basic question of how humans achieved the tremendously broad and effective body of know-how that we have achieved. I (in accord with many other scholars of technological advance) will propose that cumulative advance of know-how must be understood as a process of "cultural" learning or evolution. That cultural evolutionary process, in turn, involves the coevolution of technique and understanding. In recent times a good part of that understanding has been associated with a field of science or an engineering discipline.

Third, once one recognizes the extremely unbalanced nature of what we have achieved, it is apparent that our cultural learning or evolution system works much better in certain arenas than in others. In Section 4 I explore the factors that might explain this. Section 5 is concerned with education as a special case. In the concluding section I reflect on some of the consequences, if I am correct about the key reasons why certain areas of know-how are very difficult to advance.

2. The Nature of Human Know-how

Many of the important characteristics of human know-how, characteristics that are important to have in mind in reflecting on how know-how advances, and what makes the advance of know-how difficult in certain areas, can be brought into view by considering a particular example of modern, advanced know-how: the performance of a surgery on a human heart. In the first place, it is important to recognize the variety of particular skills involved, and that effective performance is a group achievement.

Thus the surgeon, who generally is thought of as the key actor, has command over a certain body of practice. So does the anesthesiologist. To a considerable extent these bodies of practice are different. On the other hand, each actor knows "about" the skills of the other. Also, in the performance of an operation there will be a number of assistants involved who have command over certain skills. Some, but not all, of what they do could be done by the surgeon or the anesthesiologist, but it is far less costly to delegate relatively simple tasks to less highly trained and highly paid people. In general the surgeon serves as orchestra conductor, as well as key player in the operation. However, all the players know at least the broad outlines of the overall operation and the details of their own roles in it. A successful operation requires that all of the roles be performed effectively, and in effective tune with one another.

In the case of heart surgery, as in most modern technologies, much of the technique is embodied in specialized apparatus, substances, and other artifacts. The anesthesiologist works with various substances that have been found to be effective, with pieces of apparatus that deliver those substances, and with a variety of dials and other measuring instruments that enable him or her to monitor what is going on. And the surgeon, of course, also works with a complex of materials and instruments. The embodiment of key aspects of the techniques involved in specialized artifacts should be understood as an extension of the team nature of know-how. Clearly much of that know-how is "upstream" from the locus of immediate action.

Another central characteristic of effective know-how is that it involves both a body of practice or technique, and a body of understanding. Behind the surgeon's command of skilled practice, and the anesthesiologist's, lies a broader body of understanding of the human body, of what is involved in the procedures being employed and the conditions of success and failure, and of the various substances and instruments being used. When things are going routinely, that broader body of understanding may never be invoked consciously. But it may play a very important role in holding skilled performance in place, being invoked unconsciously to prevent deviations that could undermine effectiveness or court trouble. And from time to time, in particular when something is seen or occurs that is not quite what is expected, conscious thinking tapping that body of understanding may be essential to effective performance.

Ever since Polanyi (1958) pointed it out, scholars have recognized that some of human know-how is "articulated," in the sense that it can be described and communicated in some form of language, or other symbolic system, while other aspects are "tacit." Thus a good portion of the specialized know-how of the surgeon and the anesthesiologist can control the work of their fingers, but may not be easily explainable in words or other symbols to others—even to other physicians—who, however, perhaps can learn by watching and trying to imitate. But other parts of their relevant know-how can be expressed in a way that can be understood, at least by other professionals with the same background of tacit knowledge.

These articulated parts of know-how often are written up in texts and treatises. Studying these may be an essential, if not sufficient, part of the way that pre-med students become doctors. And experienced doctors will go to the journals, or the Internet, to find out what is new, and sometimes to refresh their own knowledge. Like extant equipment and materials, texts and libraries provide storage for know-how outside of individual human minds.

While it seems natural to associate "tacit" with the practice or technique aspect of know-how, and "articulated" with the understanding aspect, I do not think the mapping is all that neat. Although it is clear that much of technique is tacit, a cake recipe or a blueprint is all technique, but to a considerable extent is laid out and articulated on paper. Also, a considerable amount of technique is embodied in the artifacts used, and while the anesthesiologist may not be able to explain just how his apparatus works, he almost certainly can identify it by name and explain its use in a way that would enable another doctor to obtain and use it. On the other hand, the surgeon may see and understand that something is not going quite right with the operation and yet not be able to explain in words just what he or she sees, or why it seems to signal trouble.

But language, and the ability to lay out know-how in language, clearly is very important in making know-how broadly available—an element of culture, as it were. The know-how of the surgeon and the anesthesiologist is cultural in the sense that much of what they know also is known by other surgeons and physicians, who have gone through similar training programs, use the same equipment, read the same journals, attend the same conferences. There are various mechanisms that facilitate, or even force, sharing of information among anesthesiologists. I do not mean to play down here the tacit aspects of learned skills, which may lie behind very great differences in effective performance, or the efforts of some professionals to keep certain aspects of their technique and understanding privy. But a striking aspect of most broadly important bodies of technique and understanding is that they are broadly shared.

All the same, it is clear that the overall know-how needed to perform complex tasks often is very divided. I have highlighted the separate bodies of practice and understanding possessed by the surgeon and the anesthesiologist. In turn the anesthesiologist may know how to make his equipment work, but little about how to produce or design that equipment. People at the company that sold the machine may know those things, but no one at that company may know all of it. Reflect on whether anybody, or any small group, at Boeing "knows how" to produce, or design, a modern aircraft, including the essential details.

Because overall know-how is divided and widely distributed among different individuals and groups, to be effective, know-how needs to be brought together and coordinated. For that reason, an extremely important part of know-how is knowledge of the elements that are needed, and of how to coordinate and manage their combined operation. Much of the know-how possessed by the chief engineer at Boeing is of this sort.

In another paper (the basis for Chapter 5 of this book), Sampat and I used the term *social technologies* to describe this latter kind of know-how, and differentiated social technologies from *physical technologies,* a term we used to denote what engineers generally mean by technology (Nelson and Sampat 2001). Under the standard conception, physical technologies are recipe- or blueprint-like, characterizing what is to be done, including designation of the particular operations involved (which may require highly developed skills) and the materials required (which may be quite specialized), but they do not speak to how the work is to be divided and coordinated. In contrast, what we call social technologies are associated with effective structures for division of labor, and procedures for task coordination and management.

As with practice and understanding, and tacit and articulated know-how, the physical and social aspects of technologies often are intimately intertwined. Consider the famous Ford mass-production line for Model T cars, or the Toyota method of "lean manufacture." These involve both a set of sequenced physical actions taken by the parties to the process, and a division of labor and a coordinating mechanism so that the actions taken by the particular parties ultimately add up to a finished automobile. Or reflect on the heart surgery example that I gave at the start of this section. Again, one sees a complex mix of physical technologies, employed by a team in which each member must do assigned tasks in harmony with what others are doing.

I propose that the human know-how involved in getting complex things done generally involves this mixture of understanding and practice, of articulated and tacit knowledge, of physical and social technologies, that I have described in the particular case of heart surgery. The analysis by Womack, Jones, and Roos (1990) of how automobiles are produced involves a similar mix of ingredients. Hutchins (1996) describes what is involved in navigating a ship in much the same way that I have described heart surgery, and uses that example as a vehicle for illuminating collective "cognition." Bucciarelli (1994) has arrived at a similar conception in his analysis of what it means to know "how your telephone works."

These kinds of know-how systems have been brought into place, and develop further, through the cumulative actions of many individuals and organizations who have particular objectives in mind. However, the overall system cannot be regarded meaningfully as having been planned. Rather, our know-how systems need to be understood as having evolved, in the sense discussed in preceding chapters.

3. The Key Role of Scientific Understanding

In preceding chapters I laid out the argument that the advance of technologies must be understood as an evolutionary process. At the same time, efforts to advance technology are not completely blind, but are guided by the understandings of those in the field regarding how the technology works, the sources of its strengths and limitations, and promising avenues toward improvement. In the contemporary world, much of this understanding is provided by science, particularly the applied sciences and engineering disciplines whose basic objective is to facilitate technological advance.

For me at least, a striking characteristic of fields in which technological advance has been rapid is that they all seem to be closely connected to a powerful applied science or engineering discipline (see Rosenberg 1974, Klevorick et al. 1995, Nelson and Wolff 1997, Rosenberg 2001). These bodies of scientific knowledge serve, first, to enlarge and extend the area beyond existing practice that an inventor or problem solver can see relatively clearly, and hence go into without being completely "blind." That is, strong science provides guidance regarding which particular paths are likely to lead to solutions or improvements, and which are likely to be dead ends. In technologies illuminated by strong science, an inventor often can see a good distance beyond current best practice.

Second, the sciences and the engineering disciplines provide powerful ways of experimenting and testing new departures, so that a person who commands these can see relatively quickly and cheaply if new ideas work, or are promising or problematic. Thus pilot plants play a key role in efforts to develop new chemical-process technology. Wind tunnels used to play a similar role in aircraft design. Where scientific and engineering knowledge is strong, these days one can explore and test by building computer models. More generally, strong scientific knowledge enables inventors not only to see promising paths but also to reliably assess the promise of the paths in a timely fashion, and without having to build and test a full-scale version in the actual operating environment.

I note, I stress, that these advantages lent by a strong body of understanding do not diminish the importance of learning by doing and using in the advance of a technology. As Vincenti has argued, in the end whether a new design or process is satisfactory, or better than what it aims to replace, can be determined only in "on-line" experience. I shall argue in the next section that the capability to recognize, generate, evaluate, and duplicate on-line variation is absolutely essential. If these capabilities are strong, cumulative technological advance can proceed even if the body of understanding, the underlying science, is weak.

However, for reasons I have put forth above, a strong science base greatly augments the power and efficiency of efforts to advance a technology. I also note, or propose, that when there is a strong body of underlying scientific knowledge, a good share of the work of advancing a technology tends to go on "off-line," in facilities like industrial R & D laboratories. The power of the underlying science means that people who have mastered that body of specialized knowledge are needed to do effective R & D. In general the skills here are very different from those who work on-line. And the activities involved in doing R & D tend to be different from those involved in on-line experimentation. The work of advancing the technology thus tends to be specialized both in terms of what is done, and in terms of the personnel involved. A considerable degree of such specialization is a hallmark of modern industries where technological advance is rapid.

However, as Vincenti has argued, there is no escaping the need for on-line evaluation, and tinkering. In general, in fields where technological advance is rapid there is an interactive mix of learning by doing and using, and off-line R & D. I shall argue in the next section that the ability to experiment, and to learn from experiments, is key to both aspects of the process.

4. Why Has Achievement Been So Unbalanced?

I want to focus now on the puzzle of why the advance of human know-how has been so uneven: spectacular in areas like information and communications, and in dealing with certain kinds of human illness, but very limited in other areas, for example education, or the rehabilitation of criminals.

One obvious reason why know-how has advanced so much more rapidly in some fields than in others is that more resources have been applied to the effort. Business firms have seen certain kinds of advances as being profitable but not others. Governments have been willing to put public funds into R & D on certain classes of problems, but there has been little effective political support for public R & D money in other areas. If one considers human illness, a major reason why little progress has been made on certain tropical diseases is that drug companies do not see the market in poor tropical countries as promising much profit, and publicly funded efforts have been limited.

But while "demand-side" limitations clearly have been important in some cases where the advance of know-how has been very small, as Mowery and Rosenberg (1979) have pointed out, many important human wants remain unmet, even though significant profit could be earned by a person or firm that figured out how to remove the road-blocks to meeting those wants more effectively. There clearly are major differences across sectors and areas of human activity in the ability of society to advance effective know-how. Within medicine, cures have been found for Hodgkin's lymphoma and testicular cancers, but not for prostate and breast cancers. These differences are puzzling and disturbing, and will be my focus in the remainder of this essay.

At one level, signaled above, my basic argument is that the key factor is the strength of the understanding bearing on practice in a field. In an earlier paper (Nelson and Wolff 1997) evidence was provided that the rate of technological advance in an industry is strongly correlated with the strength and vigor of the sciences on which R & D in that industry draws. However, this explanation of course only pushes the question back a level. Why are the sciences that underlie certain technologies so much more powerful than others?

As I have hinted earlier, my tentative answer to the puzzle at this deeper level involves looking at the causal arrow between strength of understanding and ability to experiment fruitfully with a technology the other way around. I want to propose that the ability to conceive and carry out well-defined experimental probes of possible ways to improve technological performance, and to get sharp and reliable feedback on the results, contributes importantly to the human ability to develop an applied science that effectively illuminates that technology.

Of course I recognize that some technologies in effect are born out of prior scientific discovery that was the result of research not particularly oriented toward making new technology possible. The rise of radio technology is a good example. But after a new technology emerges, it begins to pose particular scientific problems and puzzles. Rosenberg (1982a) has argued that a significant portion of the puzzles that science addresses have been revealed or created by the operation of technologies. In turn, the further advance of a technology depends to a considerable extent on how effectively science is marshaled to illuminate the roadblocks to progress.

I have been proposing that the successful development of an applied science or field of engineering research often is the key to the rapid and continuing advance of know-how in a field of activity. Electrical and chemical engineering are fields of research as well as teaching that came into existence as the industries using the technologies on which they are focused grew in importance. The invention and development of the transistor and integrated circuits provided strong intellectual stimulation (and a reason for financial support) for the new field of material science.

These new technology-oriented scientific and engineering fields rapidly enriched and improved their theoretical bases. But from their beginnings they have been very experiment oriented. And much of the experimenting has involved aspects of the technologies that provide the reason for the field's support. In turn, advances in the technologies have provided puzzles and challenges for the sciences. Rosenberg's discussion (2001) of the nature of engineering research and knowledge and its relationship to the advance of practice is particularly apt.

When progress is rapid, there seems to be a strong symbiosis between the particular structure of the technologies and the focus of the sciences underlying them. On the one hand, the technology itself tends to move toward where the understanding is strong. On the other hand, with technology linked to science, the science is able to progress by manipulating aspects of the technology experimentally.

Do I overstate the role of experimentation in the development of science? I do recognize that astronomy, now cosmology, is not strictly an experimental science. However, given its intellectual base in physics, it has been possible to both draw on and focus experimental physical research that probes the fundamental theoretical conceptions of astronomy and cosmology. And the ability to make precise empirical observations of the sort needed to rigorously test evolving cosmological theory has enabled that science to proceed almost as if it were experimental. In some cases nonexperimental data can provide the basis for a strong science. But most of the strong fields of empirical science that have been developed have involved experimentation in an essential way. And I believe that this is especially the case with sciences that illuminate technologies. Those sciences cannot progress effectively, at least not in a way that is useful to advancing the technology, unless the technology itself is suitable for experimentation.

Above I noted that, in fields where technological progress has been rapid, problem solving and inventing is done to a considerable degree off-line, in specialized facilities separated from where the technology actually is being employed. While many of the problems and opportunities are recognized on-line, much of the problem solving is done off-line. For this specialization and separation to work effectively, it must be possible to isolate the technology from much of its operating surroundings, and to work with it in a controlled environment. And performance in that controlled environment must provide reliable information about likely performance on-line. For this to be so, it almost always is necessary that the design that has been developed and tested in a controlled environment off-line be robust to or protectable from different factors that can vary in actual practice, and that cannot be controlled.

This latter requirement also is important if the variations being explored are to be replicable. Replicability of course is essential if what is learned or created off-line in R & D is to be usable in practice, or at least transferable to an on-line setting so that its efficacy can be evaluated. In many fields of technology one sees progress being achieved through an iterative process, with the locus of analysis going back and forth between the lab and actual practice. But replicability also is needed so that over the long run many parties can be involved in efforts to advance the technology, building on one another's work, a condition that, I argued earlier, seems to be essential if progress is to be cumulative.

This latter argument would be valid even if experimentation were nearly completely blind and off-line R & D had little power. However, I have been arguing that not only are these characteristics conducive, probably necessary, if a technology is to be advanced cumulatively and rapidly through experimental trial and feedback, but also they may be necessary, and certainly are conducive, for a body of reliable scientific knowledge, in the sense of Ziman (1978), to grow up that supports efforts to advance know-how in an area. For an applied science or engineering discipline to develop a powerful body of knowledge and technique that illuminates a body of practice and aids in its improvement, that body of practice must lend itself to rigorous study and experimentation, with a capability to evaluate reliably the results of variation. Vincenti's study (1990) of aeronautical engineering knowledge and its development provides strong evidence for this argument.

Am I underplaying the role of the basic sciences, like physics, mathematics, various areas of biology, whose orientation is not defined in terms of a particular technology or solving a set of practical problems?

I do not want to underplay their role. I would propose, however, that advances in basic science mostly have their impact on technological advance by informing and strengthening the applied sciences and engineering disciplines that do have a practical focus. Thus I am proposing that fields of technology that advance rapidly and cumulatively have under them strong applied sciences that in turn are able to draw from strong basic science.

This is not an endorsement of the "linear model." Rather it is a proposition about the structure of a knowledge system that exists in areas where the advance of know-how is strong. I am calling attention to the critical role of what has been called the "bridge" sciences, and proposing that to be effective they need to be, at once, closely oriented to the technologies they are designed to illuminate, and close enough to the basic sciences that they can draw power from them. A large gap, on either side, limits their effectiveness.

Consider some of the implications, if this argument is broadly correct. First, as advocates of support of science long have argued, it is a poor bet, and a likely waste of money, to pour resources into advancing practice in a field if understanding there is weak. There is little, then, to guide efforts to develop technology that will perform significantly better than prevailing practice. And information as to whether or not the new departures are effective may be slow in coming and inconclusive. For this reason, a necessary first step to solving the practical problem or meeting the pressing need is to support the scientific research that enables the problem to be understood. This argument of course is an old one, and it is often made in a self-serving way by scientists.

But second, my argument points to the major difficulties that may need to be overcome, and the long time period that may be required, for a strategy of trying to develop a useful underlying science to be successful. The scientific understanding, to be useful, must link up with the available technologies for operating in the area, or point relatively clearly to practical new ones. Understanding far removed from possible practice does not provide sharp guidance as to how practice can be improved. On the other hand, an attempt to build an applied science that is far removed from strong fields of basic science may yield knowledge of limited power. One implication of this is that the achievement of a science that illuminates a technology may depend on transforming the technology so that it becomes more amenable to scientific inquiry. As I shall argue shortly, there may be strong constraints that make this difficult.

5. The Case of Education

Consider a highly relevant case that illustrates, I believe, several of the points I have just made: the efforts to develop more effective school educational practice. (See Murnane and Nelson 1984, Hagarty 2000.) I think it apparent that neither of the two attributes that I have argued make R & D in a field powerful are strong in the case of education. It is very difficult in education to predict with any precision just how a proposed change in teaching method actually will work out in practice. General understanding of the education process and schooling may provide a broad prediction, but the devil is in the details. And it is difficult, perhaps impossible, to get reliable information on this from simple, inexpensive pilot experiments.

These limitations are closely related, I would argue, to the following problem. The fact that a particular practice seems to work well in a particular context does not mean that it can easily be transferred to another context or, if this is tried, that it will work well there. Partly the problem is that it is difficult to specify in any detail, or to know, the essential aspects that determine its performance; thus replication is chancy. Another problem is that what works well in one context may not work so well in another, and it is hard to control for the relevant variables. Still a third problem, related to the above but of central importance in its own right, is that evaluation is extremely difficult. It may take many years before the lasting effects of a new mode of instruction can be learned. And there may be many different kinds of impact to be considered.

The difficulties here clearly reside in the education process itself. Education as currently practiced largely involves a set of strategies and practices that are generally understood as appropriate in particular contexts, but with a lot of variation across individual classrooms and teachers. There are indeed canons of good practice. But not many educationists are ready to propose that there is a set of foolproof "recipes" that define best practice in teaching. And while novice teachers may learn a lot from observing able, experienced teachers, all teachers have their own particular strengths and weaknesses, and style of operating.

A certain amount of classroom equipment is used: textbooks; perhaps film and video; recently, at least, computers. But while some students of education hold out hope for the Internet and the computer, at present there are no powerful devices used in education comparable, for example, to the apparatus that dispenses and monitors the anesthesia used in heart surgery. Some years ago, Cuban (1986) reviewed experience with using computers and other forms of teaching equipment in classrooms, and concluded that their impact had not been dramatic. In a recent paper, Murnane, Sharkey, and Levy (2002) review a particular educational program that centrally involves use of the Internet, and also a considerable amount of programmed instruction, and which has been implemented in a number of schools. They highlight the apparent broad effectiveness of the program, but also argue that the standardized instruction package and the use of the Internet should be understood as a complement to, not a substitute for, an effective teacher working with students.

It is well known that how an individual child learns in a classroom is strongly affected by the behavior and attitudes of other children in that classroom, and is not independent of what is going on in the child's life outside of school. A major portion of the challenge for a teacher is to organize and manage classroom interaction, as well as to deal with the particular problems or challenges of individual students.

In Section 2 I proposed that all bodies of human know-how bearing on complex activities, like a heart operation, or designing and building an aircraft, or education, involve a mix of articulated and tacit knowledge, and physical and social technologies. It is apparent that the mix in education is heavily weighted toward the tacit and social.

This characteristic is reflected in the limited ability to conduct educational experiments, the results of which could provide reliable guides to how to improve educational practice in real-world settings. For many years such experimentation has been high on the agenda of scientifically oriented schools of education. But consistently the record has been that what is reported to work in a lab school or in another chosen testing arena has been hard to duplicate outside of the locus of the original research. As noted, part of the problem clearly has been that it is impossible to describe what the experimental treatment was with sufficient precision and detail so that one could know whether one was replicating the key elements of it or not. Part is that the context conditions that enabled a particular treatment to work were not fully known, and not necessarily in existence in other places. And part surely is that evaluation takes time and in many cases does not yield unambiguous results.

These basic characteristics of education also limit what can be learned from large-scale statistical studies that collect and analyze data from a number of different schools or classes or modes of teaching. It is not that statistical studies do not identify important correlates of good educational performance. One important correlate is the education and income of a student's parents. Another is the training and experience of a student's teacher. But the former provides no information as to how to improve the performance of schools, given the backgrounds of the students. And while the latter does provide guidance to schools regarding the kind of teachers they ought to hire and about the importance of encouraging promising teachers to stay in the system, it tells very little directly about the educational practices that work best.

The fields of research that one would hope would illuminate the educational process and guide efforts at improvement in fact provide only a dim light. In the first place, research that is focused on subject matter that arguably is closely related to the education process at best seems to yield course-grained and often unreliable conclusions. In the second place, scientific research that limits itself to subject matter where relatively fine-grained and reliable knowledge can be attained tends to generate findings that are a far distance from anything useful in the education process.

Thus a recent (U.S.) National Research Council report, *How People Learn: Bridging Research and Practice* (1999), gives the following as an example of the first kind of research finding, and how such knowledge is useful in education: "Students come to the classroom with preconceptions about how the world works. If their initial understanding is not engaged, they may fail to grasp the new concepts and information that are taught, or they may learn them for purposes of a test but revert to their preconceptions outside the classroom" (p. 10). The contrast of this bit of knowledge, useful as it is, with, say, the discovery that scurvy among seamen was caused by the absence of a class of foodstuffs in their diet, is striking. The latter led relatively directly to dealing with the problem by assuring the availability of those foodstuffs. The understanding highlighted in the NRC report points, but only very broadly, to good teaching practice.

I note that the original discovery about scurvy was not associated with a theory to explain it. Theoretical understanding was achieved only much later, with the discovery of vitamins and their association with body function. But the initial finding regarding the causes of scurvy was sharp and precise enough to identify a treatment that worked. The NRC publication, from which the above quote is drawn, seems blind to the difference between the nature of the findings of educational research and the knowledge base under medical practice, or at least is mute about it.

The same NRC report mentions that more fundamental research has been going on in brain science and cognitive science. Considerable progress has been made toward understanding areas and mechanisms in the brain associated with various kinds of perception and thinking. However, the detailed hard findings at this level are many layers away from providing useful input to guide teaching. The NRC report acknowledges this, and points to the intellectual gap as a real problem: "The concern of researchers for the validity and robustness of their work . . . often differ[s] from the focus of educators on the applicability of these constructs in real classroom settings" (p. 6). But the report does not draw the obvious conclusion that the fine-grained and reliable knowledge coming out of fields like brain science are that way because the subject of research is carefully controlled and far removed from the hurly-burly of the educational process. Again, the contrast with medical care, where biological understanding often is very close to what one needs to know to cope with a disease, is striking.

Since both education and medical care are activities focused on helping individuals, and the recipient of the treatment is a vital element of the process of teaching or healing, I believe the contrast here is well worth exploring further. Most of the significant advances in medical care have occurred over the past 150 years, and have been associated with a tremendous increase in scientific understanding of human illness of various kinds, and of the effects of various treatments. The basic mechanisms in question are biological, and often the biological mechanisms can be understood in terms of the chemistry and (occasionally) physics involved, all strong fields of science. Animals, in many cases, provide convenient models of humans, in circumstances where in vitro chemistry does not illuminate what is going on.

In general the improvements in performance of medical care have occurred in areas where understanding has become strong, but this is not always true. In many cases we have learned that certain treatments work (like limes for scurvy and aspirin for headaches) but initially, at least, have had little understanding of just why. But we were able to learn that lime juice prevents scurvy, and that aspirin relieves headaches and seems to reduce the risk of certain heart ailments, and make use of that knowledge in the practice of medicine, because limes and aspirin are well-defined substances. Thus "swallowing lime juice" or "taking aspirin" are routines that can be well enough described so that people instructed to do it can, with only a small chance of getting it badly wrong.

As these examples indicate, the medical treatments that we have learned work well have tended to be well specified; indeed most of them are substances or other artifacts (eyeglasses) that we have learned (often scientifically) to characterize precisely. And by and large their effects are not greatly influenced by factors from which they cannot be shielded (but consider the warnings on medicines regarding what not to take at the same time). Thus we are able to control and calibrate the treatment, and we are able to learn from variation, either accidental or deliberate.

And of particular importance for the current discussion, these characteristics, where they exist, permit both controlled experimentation regarding new medical practice—new drug regimes, surgical procedures, and the like—and the development of a relatively strong body of biomedical scientific knowledge. While biomedical scientists have a tendency to underplay the importance of what is learned in on-line actual practice, off-line R & D and controlled tests play a very powerful role in facilitating the evolution of medical know-how. (For a careful, balanced discussion rich with empirical examples, see Gelijns 1991.)

Some scholars deeply committed to research to advance educational practice have taken as an insult my argument that the findings of research in those fields simply do not have the power of the findings of biomedical research to illuminate and facilitate the improvement of practice. My argument has nothing to do with the quality of the researchers in the field of education, but rather with the innate limitations on the ability of research to contribute to the advancement of technologies that are largely tacit and social.

Earlier I put forth business management as another field in which, like education, advance scarcely has been dramatic. I propose that the reasons are very similar.

There probably has been less off-line research aimed to develop better management practice than there has been off-line experimental research in the field of education. Most of the research in this area has proceeded by trying to identify firms or cases in which a particular practice is or has been employed, and to compare performance in these instances with cases in which the practice has not been employed. But as with the case of cross-sectional studies of the efficacy of education practice, such efforts have been bedeviled by the great difficulty, on the one hand, of pinning down the essentials of the practice being studied and hence being able to determine when it was actually employed, and, on the other hand, of distinguishing the effects on firm performance of use of the practice from the effects of other variables. These two basic problems are, of course, not unrelated. The various studies of the value of employing "quality circles" offer a good illustration of these problems. (See Cole and Scott 2000; Nelson, Peterhansl, and Sampat 2005.)

My mother discipline is economics. The science of economics has many of the same weaknesses as the science of education, and of business management practice, and, I would argue, for the same basic reasons. The limitations of all three fields largely reflect, under my argument, that the basic human activities in these arenas are highly tacit and social, and difficult to specify with precision. In each of these fields the motivation for study is largely to enable policy to be more effective, and in these fields there is strong awareness that the prevailing science provides at best only general and hedged guidance to policy. In economics, as in education, there is strong faith that "if we only had better scientific understanding" we could develop more effective and reliable policies. But if I am right, the fact that economics as a science provides only broad and uncertain guidance to policy is in good part the result of the fact that the objects of interest are impossible to define and measure with precision. The science of economics can be made precise only by shifting the study to an arena far simpler than that in which we really are interested. And this, many would argue, is exactly what has happened in much of economics. While the results may make for some nice economic theoretical arguments, they do little to illuminate real policy issues.

But to return to the medicine-education comparison, it is interesting to note that, where medical treatment cannot be specified in terms of pills or other physical substances, or a clear-cut procedure like splinting a bone break, or where the effects of treatment cannot be isolated from those of other variables and actions (as in treatment of obesity), or where understanding is weak and animal tests do not provide much information (as in study of the effects of environmental factors on the incidence of cancer) medical R & D does not demonstrate much power. Here the situation is not very different, it seems to me, than in education and business management.

6. Social Technologies and the Evolution of Know-how

Are technologies that are strongly social and tacit important exceptions that fall outside of the remarkable abilities human societies have developed to advance their practical know-how? The discussion above has been concerned only with education in any detail; the discussion of management and economics was at best cryptic. But the elements that seem to make progress difficult in these areas seem quite similar, and to hold as well for areas like the prevention of crime, or teenage pregnancies, or managing the medical care system, or the Internet. Interestingly, the two last examples are of cases in which the underlying physical technologies have become very powerful, but the social technologies needed to manage them are not very effective.

Kline (1995) argues that human behavior in a social context is intrinsically more complex than the operation of a physical machine or other artifact, according to the particular measure of complexity that he lays out. He proposes, persuasively in my view, that fields of science that deal with very complex subjects cannot be expected to come up with the precise laws and relationships that have come out of physics. Are the sciences underlying social technologies relatively weak simply because these kinds of technologies are very complex?

This is one way of looking at it. However, I have put forth a particular set of arguments regarding just why these kinds of technologies are difficult to advance that involves their tacit and social nature in an essential way. I want to stand by my argument that the heart of the problem is the difficulty in these technologies of doing precise and replicable experimentation, and gaining reliable and generalizable knowledge from variation.

This formulation has, among other things, the advantage of leading to the question of whether these characteristics are innate, or whether they can be modified. I am not alone in pointing to these characteristics as an important part of the problem in advancing education.

Indeed there has been a long-standing argument between educators who have advocated bringing more tightly controlled and explicit routine to the education process and those who have resisted this strongly, saying that it hinders tailoring education to the particular needs and capabilities of individual students and the characteristics of particular groups of students assembled in a class (see, for example, Murnane and Nelson 1984). This debate has ranged from argument about whether or not there is one particular way that reading is best taught, to the appropriate use of computers in education. A common strand, however, is the pluses and minuses of developing and using standardized methods.

Recently several economists (see Arora and Gambardella 1994, Dasgupta and David 1994, Cowan and Foray 1997) have argued that the extent to which a technique is tacit or articulated and codified depends to a good extent on the magnitude and skill of the efforts to codify it. While it is not plausible that even a major effort could fully codify the skills of an expert surgeon, or an effective teacher, surely there is something of a common core of good practice that, to some extent, can be codified. There certainly are relatively programmed teaching methods, including those built into computers, that have had some amount of effectiveness. The question is how far this can be pushed without running into the problem raised by those skeptical of routinization. One size of shoe does not fit all feet. But will a reasonable number of well-defined shoe sizes mostly do the job? That turns out to be the case, mostly, with shoes. How about education?

Much of the tacitness of educational practice is bound up, I would argue, with the innately social aspects of teaching and learning. There needs to be effective interaction between teacher and student, and to a considerable extent that interaction is influenced by the larger group in a classroom. The problem with advancing social technologies is that there are strong constraints associated with the capabilities and wills and beliefs of the people whose actions somehow must be enlisted, coordinated, or managed. In turn, these individual and idiosyncratic constraints make it difficult or impossible to standardize a technique, or even to describe with precision what is being done, and make reliable experimentation, or generalizable feedback from operating experience, very difficult as well. Perhaps the course to greater effectiveness is to get rid of these constraints, by substituting physical for social technologies.

In many arenas, exactly this has been done. Taylorism routinized and made explicit the jobs that workers did in manufacturing technology, and machinery and, later, more general automation transformed much of what had been a social technology of management and control into physical technology. Once this was done, it was possible to experiment with new designs for machines and automated coordination mechanisms and make real progress on the management and coordination problem. In turn, routinization and mechanization greatly facilitated the development of strong engineering knowledge.

To some extent computer-programmed instruction does this in education. But it is highly uncertain how far mechanized instruction can be pushed. And there remains the nagging problem that in this society, at least, individual differences are valued, not seen as something to be strongly repressed.

Improving the way we educate children surely is an extraordinarily important goal. Research that will help to guide experimentation and evaluation is of top priority. But perhaps we need to recognize that advancing knowledge and practice here is innately more difficult than advancing know-how in many areas of medicine, or agriculture, or telecommunications. And it is not at all clear that the strategies and organizational structures that have worked well to advance know-how in areas where it has been possible to routinize practice, to make knowledge of best practice well articulated to a considerable degree, and to control or mechanize the processes closely, are the ones that will work well in education.

To some extent the constraints here are of our own making, and we can relax them if we choose. We now use drugs to help control certain individual behaviors that are judged likely to be destructive to self and others, but thus far society has shown reluctance to heavily drug all individuals who are judged likely to commit crimes. Can we require that children deemed likely to be disruptive in class go on drugs? Are we willing to jail parents whose children skip school? We can, if we wish, control at least some of the variables that make it so difficult to routinize and standardize education. And that probably would make it easier to learn from educational experimentation. However, most of us don't want to go very far down this road.

In education, and in other areas, there clearly are limits on our willingness to routinize and mechanize for the sake of better control and the ability to make faster progress. *A Brave New World* is not all that attractive.

CHAPTER 7

Physical and Social Technologies and Their Evolution

1. Introduction

In Chapter 5 I put forward the proposition that economic growth has been largely driven by the coevolution of physical technologies and widely used social technologies, or institutions. The notion that physical and social technologies coevolve is not a new one. Adam Smith was keenly aware that the development and utilization of new "physical technologies" in the above sense often interacted strongly with changing modes of division of labor and new ways of organizing and governing work, what I have called "social technologies." Recall his famous discussion at the start of *The Wealth of Nations* in which the development of machinery for pin making is linked to the increasing division of labor, both of which in turn are connected to the growing extent of the market.

As discussed in Chapter 5, Bhaven Sampat and I propose that much of the discussion about institutions in economics, and social science more generally, is about social technologies, implicitly or explicitly. Thus it is apparent that Veblen's "general habits of action and thought" (1898), Commons's "working rules" (1924), North's "rules of the game" (1990), Schotter's "how the game is played" (1981), Williamson's "governing structures" (1985), and other conceptions of institutions put forth by distinguished economists and social scientists,

---

* Based on Richard R. Nelson, "Physical and Social Technologies and Their Evolution," *Economie Appliquée* 61 (2003): 13–31.

all have a family resemblance. Specifically, virtually all scholars writing about institutions have aimed to call attention to standardized modes of transacting, and interacting more generally, employed by human and organizational actors to get things done in contexts where effective performance requires coordinated action. In several places Geoffrey Hodgson (1988, 1998, 2001, 2004) has discussed the history of institutional economics, old and new, in great detail. Under most conceptions of the term, institutions are generally employed, relatively standardized social technologies (the way the game is played), or the forces that strongly mold and support that action pattern (the rules of the game).

Sampat and I (2001) have opted for the "standard ways of doing things" view on institutions, as contrasted with the factors that mold these, while at the same time pointing out that there is no clean line between these two views. Thus if one considers physical technologies, as differentiated from social technologies, one often can observe that a particular technology is inextricably connected with particular machinery and other specialized inputs that are employed. This often is reflected in nomenclature, as in the "open-hearth method" of making steel. Similarly, the M form of business organization is inextricably connected with a particular kind of division of labor and responsibility among different layers of management. Thus if one refers to the M form as a social technology, one is denoting both a way of making decisions and governing the firm, and an organizational structure which supports this way.

From this point of view, institutions are an important subclass of social technologies more generally—those that are in general and expected use across an area of application, as contrasted with those that vary significantly, depending on the particular individuals and organizations involved. However, the lines here clearly are blurry. Many writers talk about, say, Harvard, or IBM, as particular institutions, clearly having in mind "institutionalized" patterns of doing things that are special to those organizations. Also, I think that many writers on institutions would argue that a central attribute is not simply the presence of relatively durable standard patterns of behavior, but also a system of formal or informal norms and beliefs that these are the "right" ways to do things. I would agree that institutions almost always have such normative support, but that the matter here may be one of degree, not kind.

In any case, the argument and the evidence I present for it here is basically about the differences in evolutionary processes working on physical technologies and social technologies generally, although the social technologies I will use as examples are in widespread use, and are almost expected in the context, and thus they might be regarded as institutions. My argument will be that society's ability to develop effective social technologies is more limited and more prone to frustration than its ability to advance physical technologies. My emphasis will be on the reasons, because the fact of the matter I think is widely agreed upon, although there certainly are some of my colleagues who would object. My orientation, obviously, will be on differences in the nature (on average) of the evolutionary processes at work on physical and social technologies, respectively.

But before I get into the details, I need to lay some groundwork. First, I want to highlight a fact that should be obvious, but sometimes is forgotten. An evolutionary explanation for the ways of doing things—the physical and social technologies—that are prominent at any time presumes that these ways of doing things are replicable to a certain degree. Organizations that are employing them must be able to retain them in close to present form, if they choose. If these firms are profitable and seek to expand, they must be able to reproduce in their new units the ways of doing things that have made them profitable. Other organizations not using those practices must be able to imitate them reasonably reliably if they choose to. The last of these conditions is not necessary in principle for an evolutionary argument to go through, but in fact imitation of technologies that come widely to be regarded as profitable plays a major role in most of the empirical studies of the evolution of technology that I know about. In any case, if the first two conditions do not hold, an evolutionary process cannot effectively select a particular technology, because what is selected at any time can transmute into something else. The requirement for "selective retention" cannot be met.

Biologists have theorized that an evolutionary process needs to operate on reliable "replicators." This is as true for cultural evolutionary processes as for biological evolution.

Second, systematic selection requires that there be reasonably strong connections between the use of a particular set of practices and organizational performance, and that there be reasonably reliable evidence of the efficacy of different ways of doing things. Again, the latter is not necessary in principle, but in fact judgments and conscious choices almost always are a major part of the story of the evolution of technologies, in many cases playing a more important role than simply relative growth of organizations that are using profitable technologies. But either through survival and expansion of the organizations possessing them, or through conscious choices, a way of doing something must be salient to organizational performance to be subject to systematic selection.

In evolutionary biology, to be selected for or against systematically, a trait must have a strong influence on inclusive fitness. An analogous requirement holds in the kind of evolutionary analysis being employed here.

The argument I will develop, of course, is that both of these conditions usually are more favorable to rapid development of physical technologies than of social technologies, for both direct and indirect reasons. I shall develop that argument as follows:

In Section 2 I consider what is known about the ways that physical technologies evolve, a subject on which there has been much more empirical research than on social technologies. This will lead in Section 3 to my argument that, as a rule, social technologies are more difficult to improve through an evolutionary process than physical technologies. I will support my argument with several examples. In the concluding section I reflect upon some of the implications.

2. What Makes Evolutionary Progress Hard or Relatively Easy?

As I have discussed in preceding chapters, over the past half century a large interdisciplinary body of scholarship has developed concerned with understanding the processes through which physical technologies advance over time. In contrast, the body of scholarship that has looked in detail at the development of social technologies—forms of business organization, management practices, market mechanisms and structures, public policies, legal and regulatory structures, and so on—has been limited and scattered. However, it would seem a good bet that the development of social technologies, as the development of physical technologies, usefully can be understood as an evolutionary process.

From this perspective, the key question would seem to be: What are the characteristics that enable the evolutionary progress to be rapid and sustained, or, on the other hand, tend to limit the possibilities of sustained rapid progress? Consideration of this question will set the stage for my argument that in general it is much more difficult to advance social technologies than physical technologies.

First, as Sidney Winter and I argued a long time ago, the competing technologies in question must be sustainable and reproducible. In the language we developed, they must involve a certain amount of "routine." Routines serve as targets for preservation and replication of an activity within an organization that is using them. They also serve as targets for adoption by organizations that presently are not. Technologies for which there is very little in the way of "routine" are, from this point of view, difficult to hold in place, and difficult to imitate. At a particular moment of time one may be "selected" because it is effective in its present form, but then it may change and lose its effectiveness.

Ability to experiment, and to learn from natural experiments, is an essential part of the process through which technologies get improved, but if a technology cannot be held in place or selected sharply, this makes it almost impossible to experiment with it fruitfully in a controlled way. One cannot learn very much from experiments because there is no clear, stable, and reproducible practice that can be associated with good performance or poor. Similarly, not much of durable value can be learned from learning by doing or using. This does not make for rapid progress.

Second, the criteria for better performance, or fitness, that the selection environment enforces must be clear and relatively steady, and competing technologies must differ nontrivially in efficacy under these standards. If the actors using a particular technology gain no significant advantage over those who do not, and if no clear evidence of advantage is available for those who are contemplating choice, evolutionary forces are going to be weak. And if the characteristics that give advantage or are believed to do so vary significantly from period to period, it will be difficult for progress to be cumulative.

Also, as I have noted, technological advance tends to proceed more rapidly when there are a number of minds at work, and many different sources of initiative, and the parties involved are able to learn from and build on each other's successes. That is, competition among organizations or individuals, as well as among technologies, definitely seems to spur progress.

Finally, there obviously are enormous advantages to an innovator in being able to see some distance beyond prevailing practice, and to be able to test with some confidence the likely efficacy of a new design or method without having to build or otherwise put in place a full-scale version and operate it in real time. I argued in preceding chapters that these are exactly the facilitators of invention and innovation provided by an underlying strong science. In contrast, it is much more difficult for a technology to advance if learning is largely limited to what can be acquired by doing or using.

I would like to argue that the strength of understanding in the above sense interacts strongly with the other factors influencing the pace of progress. One of the results of the development of a strong science base supporting a technology often is identification of its key operative elements, and its standardization to some degree. Another useful consequence of strong scientific understanding often is the ability to identify key factors that determine or signal strong or weak performance. Thus a strong science greatly facilitates evaluation. And it often enables innovators to test reliably off-line, with investments short of what would be required for full-scale implementation, and to gain feedback relatively quickly regarding what has the promise of working well and what does not. On the other hand, the development of a strong science base may require that the technology itself be amenable to a certain degree of standardization, and to reliable experimentation.

Also, the motivation for the development of a strong applied science would appear to depend on some consistent notions about the characteristics of good performance of that technology. At the same time, the development and maintenance of a community of people all familiar with a technology and contributing to its cumulative advance also depends on a certain degree of standardization, and broad consistent agreement regarding just what advancement means. This is facilitated greatly if there is a strong applied science or engineering discipline that codifies and teaches the technology.

3. Semisystematic Differences between Physical and Social Technologies

While neither group is homogeneous, and in many activities one can see a mix of physical and social technologies that cannot easily be separated (for example, mass production methods), I want to propose here that all of the conditions associated with sustained and cumulatively significant evolutionary progress tend to be stronger for physical than for social technologies. Physical technologies (or the physical aspects of technologies) generally are easier to specify in detail, to maintain, to replicate reliably, and to experiment with in a way that enables learning; they have more of the "routine" about them. Selection criteria tend to be sharper and steadier, and performance is more easily identified and analyzed. In turn, these characteristics—specificity regarding key aspects of the technology in question and relatively clear criteria of merit—facilitate and encourage abstract analysis and attempts to experiment off-line. It is no happenstance that the sciences underlying physical technologies tend to be much stronger than the sciences underlying social technologies. These same characteristics tend to enable comparability across the experiences of different parties, and the development of a broadly shared analytic point of view on the subject matter.

I will try to support this argument by comparing four relatively well studied cases of innovation, two of them relatively clearly physical technologies—hybrid corn and polio vaccines—and two of them clearly social technologies—quality circles and the M form of business organization. The discussion of these cases is presented in somewhat more detail in the article "Why and How Innovations Get Adopted: A Tale of Four Models" (Nelson, Peterhansl, and Sampat 2005).

Hybrid corn first became available commercially in the 1920s. This achievement was the result of the sustained efforts of many agricultural research workers to develop a better corn seed. The search was facilitated by an increasingly strong scientific understanding of plant biology. In the search, "better" was quite well defined and meant more profitable to grow, all things considered. Those other things to be considered included the opportunity cost of the land and labor involved in growing hybrid corn, the fertilizers and insecticides involved, and other particular characteristics involved in the use of hybrid seeds, as contrasted with the alternatives. The seed itself was a clearly defined thing. And the various activities needed of the farmer involved either the seed itself, or things that needed to be done for or to the plants that grew from the seed. These activities could be routinized to a considerable degree, and could be described in terms of routines to be followed.

Because of the high degree of specificity and routinization involved in using hybrid seeds, the results of growing these hybrids in plots in experimentation stations provided credible evidence to farmers as to the results they likely would achieve if they used hybrids, and took care of their crops in the way recommended by the experimentation stations. Similarly, the experience of one farmer in using hybrids provided highly relevant information to his neighbors, who could, if they wished, buy exactly the same brand of seed and grow their crops using basically the same techniques.

Hybrids originally were made available in only a small number of regions. The particular characteristics of the seed itself needed to be carefully tailored to the soil type and climatic characteristics of the region. A seed that worked well in one region would not necessarily work well in another. However, the success of hybrid seeds in the original regions made agricultural scientists, and seed growers, confident that they could develop hybrids that were suitable to other regions. The techniques of developing, and testing, new hybrids were by then well understood, and indeed quite routine. Hybrids quite rapidly were developed for a wide range of regions and by the 1950s were used by virtually all farmers who grew corn.

The same techniques of creating new and better hybrids in public and private experimentation stations that led to the development of specialized hybrids tailored to the conditions of a wide variety of different regions, also led to the steady improvements of hybrids within each of the regions. The result of all this was a tremendous increase between the 1920s and the 1960s in the total factor productivity of corn production in the United States.

I turn now to the second example: the development of polio vaccines. This innovation depended on identification of the virus involved in polio, or in this case the three different viruses, which occurred in 1949. The broad set of physical techniques for developing a vaccine for infectious illness, once the bacteria or virus causing that illness had been identified, long had been generally known. The underlying sciences and the associated techniques were strong. Thus identification of the viruses set in train several different attempts to develop an effective vaccine for polio.

In the early 1950s Jonas Salk developed what he thought was a promising vaccine, using killed virus. Based on that development, an extensive double-blind set of clinical tests was conducted, and the results clearly showed that the incidence of polio for the treated groups was substantially lower than in the controls. Note that the generally accepted criteria here were very sharp: reduced incidence of the disease, and no noticeable negative side effects. Notice also that the technology itself was well defined. It was a particular vaccine.

In the late 1950s Albert Sabin developed a different vaccine for polio that used live but attenuated virus. Previous experience with vaccines for other diseases indicated that attenuated-virus vaccines tended to give longer immunity than killed-virus vaccines, but there was a risk that the former itself could cause infection. Tests of the Sabin vaccine showed that it was no more dangerous to use than the Salk vaccine. And in addition to the high probability of its giving longer immunity, the Sabin vaccine also had the advantage of being administered orally. In most countries, use of the Sabin vaccine quickly replaced use of the Salk vaccine, which must be injected.

Again note that the criteria were clear and sharp. The fact that the Sabin vaccine could be taken orally was in effect an extra benefit of a physical technology that clearly rated as superior to its predecessor on the generally accepted selected criteria. And note also that the alternatives being evaluated here were sharply different. One used killed virus, and the other attenuated virus. The sharpness of the criteria, the specificity of the technological alternatives, and the strength of the underlying scientific knowledge clearly greatly facilitated off-line research and experiments on nonhuman animals. However, the ultimate comparison was made in a controlled experiment on-line. And the specificity of the technologies and clearness of the criteria also made it possible for many professionals to be involved in the developments in one way or another.

Turning now to our first social technology—quality circles—the history is so incredibly different. Quality circles became fashionable as a social technology to be used within business firms during the early and mid-1980s, a period when Japanese firms were doing extremely well in competition with American firms in certain industries, and American firms and scholars in management were trying to understand the sources of the Japanese prowess, so that American firms could adapt and adopt.

At a very high level of abstraction, the proposition that using quality circles was efficacious could be posed in terms of the long-run profitability of the enterprise. However, the theory about why the use of quality circles would prove profitable for the enterprise involved an amalgam of propositions, some focused directly on the notion that they would help to improve product and process "quality," and through that route improve profitability, and some posed more broadly in terms of the desirability of getting more worker involvement, both objective and subjective, in guiding the management of the enterprise. The core of the quality circle concept generally was agreed to be the regular meeting of small groups of workers, who together would try to get clear on how current practices affected product quality, and to identify changes that would enhance product quality. But it was widely recognized that how individual firms went about doing this did, and probably should, differ significantly from firm to firm.

During the early 1980s there was a surge of articles on the subject, some focused on the Japanese experience and many oriented toward analysis of American firms that had adopted quality circles. These articles recognized that having a quality circle meant different things in different firms. Nonetheless, the orientation was toward trying to evaluate the quantity and quality of the improvements engendered through quality circles. A number of the studies were content with the identification and description of certain specific improvements that they thought could be ascribed to the work of quality circles. Others aimed to do a statistical analysis. Almost all of the latter studies yielded no statistically significant results. In a way this is not surprising because, on the one hand, the independent variable certainly was very heterogeneous, and on the other hand, there was no sharp agreement on exactly how the effectiveness of quality circles should be measured. Partly, at least, because of the absence of real evidence that having a quality circle was efficacious, various studies show a significant decline in the number of articles reporting on or advocating quality circles after the mid-1980s. And it is highly probable that the number of firms that had organized structures that they "called" quality circles diminished as well.

On the other hand, several scholars have proposed that quality circles were part of a general set of developments regarding managerial practice that has moved things in the right direction. Thus Sidney Winter (in Cole and Scott 2000) has argued that the package of proclivities associated with greater concern on the part of firms with the quality of their products, combined with mechanisms to pay detailed attention to the processes in firms that affected product quality, and involvement in the analysis of workers who were part of those processes, undoubtedly was a good thing. Cole and Scott (2000) basically endorse this position by asking the following: "Is it possible that some of the early publicized failures identified by academic researchers, such as quality circles, actually laid the groundwork for some of the later successes? If so, this would suggest that organizational researchers might well examine management fads in a broader time and space framework."

So there very well may have been some real progress made here in an evolving social technology. But if so, the process certainly has been very different from that associated with progress based on a physical technology, and while direct comparison is impossible, because still no one knows how to measure the effect of better-quality management, it is a very safe bet that the cumulative progress achieved under the regime of hybrid corn technology or of polio vaccines has been enormously greater than the cumulative advance achieved under quality management.

As a second example of a new social technology, I want to consider the development and spread of the M form. As Alfred Chandler (1977) tells the story, the M form came into existence in the early part of the twentieth century, as a number of firms that had increased the range of products they produced or the number of markets in which they were active struggled with the management problems of enlarged scale and scope. The standard form of business organization at that time involved a number of functional departments, like finance, marketing, and production, which in turn reported to top management. The enlargement of the variety of things that firms were doing meant that each of these departments had to deal with a more heterogeneous, as well as a larger, set of things. The idea in the M form was to separate companies into divisions, with each division having full responsibility for a small range of products and one or a few markets. Each of the divisions would then have its own functional departments, which now would be able to deal with matters of smaller scale and scope. The function of top management was to monitor the divisions.

It would seem apparent that the adoption of the M form would reduce the complexity and variety of the tasks faced by middle-level management. It also would reorient, and to some extent make more coherent, the task of top management. But there was the question of "the bottom line." To what extent would the adoption of the M form actually increase firm efficiency and profitability?

It was and is virtually impossible to confidently assess the real efficiency advantages associated with the adoption of the M form, for two reasons. First, unlike with a polio vaccine or the use of a hybrid corn seed, controlled experimentation was and is impossible in this case. And with so many other things going on in the environment, and often in the firm, there is no real way that the effect of adoption of the M form, in and of itself, can reliably be estimated. Second, several studies have shown clearly that the M form was different things in different companies, and that even within a given company it tended to change over time. For these reasons, adherence to the notion that large diversified firms should be organized according to the M form became, and remains, something that is justified to a considerable extent as a matter of faith, and by arguments that are much more abstract and simplified than the actual contexts in which firms operate.

It would seem that something like the M form remains the standard mode for organizing large and diversified business. Without doubt, individual businesses learned some things through their experiences with their organizational and managerial structures that has enabled them to get out some of the serious bugs. But to my knowledge, there exists no serious research that has argued that the M form, as a way of organizing large, complex businesses, has been significantly refined and improved over the years so that the structures it has today are significantly more efficient than the structures associated with the M form twenty years ago, or fifty.

4. On the Uneven Improvement of the Ways Things Are Done

From the days of Adam Smith, economists studying economic growth have recognized technological advance as the key driving force. And Smith also recognized the strong interactions between advances in physical technologies and changes in the way work is organized and governed. Economic progress needs to be understood as involving the evolution of both physical and social technologies.

Since the times of Thomas Malthus, economists also have recognized that the advance of technology does not proceed at the same pace in all relevant fields. Malthus saw manufacturing technology as continuing to improve rapidly but agricultural technology as stagnant, with profound long-run consequences for the progress of the human race. He turned out to be far too pessimistic regarding the possibilities for technological advance in agriculture, but the more general point about uneven advance across fields, with the fields advancing most slowly in some cases becoming an increasingly heavy drag on progress, does seem to hold true. Some years ago William Baumol (1967) wrote a fascinating article on just this subject. The growing concern about our apparent limited ability to improve the effectiveness and productivity of education, for example, indicates this problem is real, and very much with us.

Some technologies may be innately more difficult to improve than others because it is very difficult to get quick, sharp feedback on what is effective and what isn't, or because there are major reasons why routinization is difficult or undesirable, or both. Thus an important reason why progress seems to be so slow in dealing with breast and prostate cancers is that it takes a long time to acquire solid information about whether a new treatment actually is saving lives or not. The same problem of slow and difficult-to-interpret feedback certainly is part of the reason why it is proving so difficult to improve educational practice. In addition, in education the heterogeneity of the student population and the varied individual skills of teachers make attempts to "routinize" what is done very difficult, and often counterproductive.

I would like to propose that in today's world the technologies that are proving hardest to advance very often have a large element of the social, and a limited role of the physical. The "service" sectors that were the focus of Baumol's analysis fit this mold, and certainly education does. In Chapter 6, I compared the difficulties we have in learning to improve educational practice with the successes that often have been achieved in medicine, along lines similar to those I followed earlier in this chapter. And I noted that much of the advance we have achieved in medicine has involved the discovery or development of new physical technologies: vaccines, pharmaceuticals, surgical procedures that involve a raft of physical equipment. The cases of limited progress with breast and prostate cancers, and AIDs, tell us that even in fields where there is a lot of physical technology, progress may still be difficult in places. But it is a good bet that if and when progress is made in these areas, the new treatments will involve new physical technologies

As I also noted earlier, in many cases in which significant advance has been achieved in areas where the technology is largely social, this has been the consequence of substituting physical technologies for aspects of the social. The increasing mechanism of mass production that occurred in the period between 1920 and 1960 is one example. The increasing use over the past decade of electronic communication in large complex organizations is another.

But while physical technologies are much easier to advance than social technologies, and while, in many cases, the advance of what were social technologies has involved the introduction of new physical technologies, we remain far from a fully automated society, and there is good reason why we cannot and do not want to go too far down that road. In particular, there are limits to the extent a society ought to want to "automate" its high-level decision and governing processes.

Today some of our most difficult problems involve discovering, inventing, and developing the social technologies needed to make new physical technologies effective. Arguably the lion's share of the strains currently on our health care systems are the result of advances in physical medical technologies that societies have not yet learned how to manage and pay for. The continuing turmoil since 1980 in the organization of the industries involved with telecommunications displays the problem in another guise. In neither of these areas does the relevant social science point clearly to an appropriate organizational solution, although some of my friends in economics argue as if it did. And the spontaneous "evolutionary" processes that are at work—with many approaches tried, and some at any time succeeding while others fail—are not likely to lead to a satisfactory solution in the near future. Just what a selection environment is selecting on is not clear, and successive waves of fads signal that the criteria are not steady either. If something is found that appears to work for a while, it may not be clear what are its key elements, and thus it may be difficult to hold in place. Further, the fact that it works today does not necessarily mean it will work tomorrow.

The two cases of social technologies I used as examples in this chapter are ones for which, in principle at least, there can be and were many alternatives coexisting at any time, and many independent decision-making units. At least in this context, there is a chance of learning by competitive doing and using. However, in many cases the adoption, or abandonment, of a social technology requires collective action, as when certain patterns of action are required or forbidden by law, or where a government agency is a major actor. Thus in the cases above, public policies, and how they change over time, will profoundly influence how our medical care system will evolve and what will happen regarding the way we organize telecommunications. And this makes the process of evolutionary improvement even more difficult.

This problem of evaluating social technologies—more specifically, modes of organizing and governing economic activity—invites and is compounded by the development of ideologies regarding what is appropriate and effective. The role of ideology is likely to be particularly important when the decisions are largely collective and political.

Over the past half century, the idea that market organization is the most appropriate way to organize and govern economic activity has taken strong hold. While there is some empirical evidence supporting this point of view, a characteristic of an ideology is that the notion tends to be applied indiscriminately. In my mind this is what has happened, and it has made designing and choosing modes of organization and governance for activities for which market organization is problematic especially difficult. This concern is the motivation for the last two chapters of this volume.

PART IV

In the previous chapters I have developed two themes. The first is that the driving force behind economic growth has been the coevolution of technologies and institutions. The second is that the processes that improve technologies are much more effective at making progress than the processes through which institutions are changed and new ones introduced.

I have noted that a central reason for the latter is the difficulty of getting sharp, rapid feedback from institutional changes. The effects of actual changes tend to be ambiguous, and difficult to sort out in terms of cause-consequence relationships, leaving lots of room for argument about whether the results of those changes are favorable or unfavorable, and whether the current course is a good one or is in drastic need of change. I have proposed that this is the basic reason why the social sciences, including economics, provide such limited guidance for institutional reform. It is very hard for analysis to identify meaningful, strong, stable relationships there. In various places in this book, I have expressed my concern that the reaction of many of my colleagues in economics to the complexity of the phenomena our subject is supposed to address, and the difficulty of understanding cause-effect relationships in that complex setting, has been to define the discipline in terms of very simple models. But these models do not help us much to understand the reality. And in many cases, I have argued, they actually mislead us.

At the conclusion of Chapter 7, I proposed that this situation leaves the policy debate about appropriate institutions and institutional reform highly vulnerable to fad and ideology. Now, in the concluding chapters of this volume, I argue that this has been what has happened, unfortunately, regarding the policy debate about how to organize various economic activities. At present there is widespread belief that simple market organization is the best institutional form for governing virtually any kind of economic activity. At times this nostrum is useful. But in many cases it is working against effective institutional reform.

In Chapter 8, I discuss this general problem. In Chapter 9, I consider in detail a particular case in point: the recent moves toward making basic scientific research a "market-oriented" activity, which threatens, I argue, to erode the scientific commons.

The Problem of Market Bias
in Modern Capitalist Economies

1. Introduction

The close of the twentieth century saw a virtual canonization of market organization as the best way, indeed the only really effective way, to structure an economic system.[1] This phenomenon was strongest in the United States, and to a somewhat lesser extent the United Kingdom, but was very widespread. The conception of market organization being canonized was simple and pure, along the lines of the standard textbook model in economics. For-profit firms are the vehicles of production. They decide what to produce and how, on the basis of their assessments about what is most profitable. Given what suppliers offer, free choice by customers, who are deciding on the basis of their own knowledge and preferences where to spend their own money, determines how much of what is bought by whom. Competition among firms assures that production is efficient and tailored to what users want, and prices are kept in line with costs. The role of government is limited to establishing and maintaining a body of law to set the rules for the market game, and assuring the availability of basic infrastructure needed for the economy to operate.

Economists of an empirical bent, and political scientists and sociologists who have studied actual modern economies, well recognize the oversimplifications involved in this folk theory. If meant as a positive

* Based on Richard R. Nelson, "The Problem of Market Bias in Modern Capitalist Economies," *Industrial and Corporate Change* 10 (2002): 207–244.

theory of how modern economies actually are structured, it misses the complexity of market organization in many spheres of economic activity, and ignores the wide range of activities involving major investments of resources where markets play a limited role. The theory represses the extensive roles of government in modern economies. More generally, it misses the institutional complexity and variegation of modern economies.[2]

But the folk theory clearly is intended more as a normative statement than as a positive one. And in this role, the theory has been highly successful in recent years.

1.1. The Governance of Particular Sectors and Activities

While the broad ideological argument is focused on "the economy as a whole," it is at the sectoral or activity level that the details of economic organization are worked out. And at this level, today discussion about the way a sector or activity should be structured almost always starts with the presumption that market organization, of a relatively simple kind, is the right solution. This is the "default" solution. In recent years, sectors and activities that had been regulated have been subject to strong pressures for deregulation. Where there is a major public sector role, the pressures are toward privatization. Under this view, competition is always something to be fostered, and arguments for public support of any kind, viewed with suspicion. Propositions to the effect that perhaps market organization is not appropriate for the activity in question tend to be rejected out of hand, and there is a very strong preference to use the market as much as possible, and to keep nonmarket elements to a minimum.

A case can be made that this apparent bias in favor of simple market organization at a sectoral level is, on net, a plus. It points policy discussion right from the start toward a mode of organization that, in fact, has served effectively as a central part of the governing structure over a wide range of activities and sectors. It is associated with bias against governing structures that rely heavily on central planning and top-down command and control, which often have proved problematic or worse in contexts where they have been employed. However, the case for markets can be pushed too far. If the presumption in favor of market organization is accompanied by blindness to the complexity and variegation of modern economies, an ideological resistance to mixed forms of governance, and hostility to structures that make little use of markets, this can be a real problem.

I believe that, at the present time, modern societies are facing a number of challenging and often contentious choices regarding how to organize and govern a variety of activities that together employ a large and growing share of their resources. For some of these, a satisfactory solution likely can be found through market organization that is not too far away from the folk theory. However, in other cases, to make market organization work tolerably well almost surely will require strong and fine-grained regulation, and perhaps a number of other supplementary elements. And for some, it likely will prove best to rely centrally on other basic organizational modes, with markets in an ancillary role.

1.2. Economic Governance as a Political Issue

I use the term *governing structure* to highlight what is at stake in choosing a mode of organization for an activity or an industry—who is to get what, who pays, who is responsible for provision, mechanisms of control—and to call attention to the fact that society can and does have a choice about the matter, a choice that is ultimately political. I note that economists tend to see the governing structure (my terminology) of an industry as involving both a demand side and a supply side. Political scientists recognize a similar distinction between the processes of policy making and administration for the areas of public-sector activity they study. And in the discussion that follows I also will use this rough distinction between demand- and supply-side governance.[3]

Canonical market organization, with potential users deciding how to spend their own money on the demand side, for-profit suppliers on the supply side, and limited regulation, is one form of governance structure. However, it is far from ubiquitous.

First of all, with many goods and services the benefits are spread among the public rather than being private, and here public, generally governmental, processes need to be used to determine how much is wanted, and public funds need to be used to pay for what is procured. National security and public health measures are commonly cited examples. Until recently there was little argument against the proposition that basic scientific knowledge was a public good and its creation and terms of access should be supported publicly. There also are certain activities for which supply is regarded as an innately governmental function. Providing and running the police system and the courts is an obvious example. Structuring elections and developing legislation are others.

Other cases in which society uses collective demand determination machinery, or public provision, are more controversial. Thus there is continuing debate about the extent to which medical care should be funded publicly, as contrasted with privately. Countries differ in the extent to which they consider that rail and airline services provide public as well as private benefits and thus warrant public financial support, direct or indirect. In most countries, most of primary and secondary education is provided through public organizations, an arrangement challenged in the United States by proposals for school vouchers. There is controversy regarding the appropriate role of public spending on and public provision of extra family childcare.

Of course many activities and sectors that generally are thought of as market governed in fact have a quite mixed governing structure. Thus pharmaceuticals production and sales are regulated, and public moneys go into the basic research that pharmaceutical companies draw from in their development work. Most of the old "public utilities"—for example the telephone system and electric power—still are quite regulated, and some, like passenger rail service, are subsidized to some degree. Government programs provide the infrastructure that enables private for-profit airlines to operate: airports and the air traffic control system. The Internet was brought into existence through a combination of private and public efforts. Today society is struggling with the question of in what ways the Internet requires regulation.

In any case, it is a mistake to see the governance issue as being strictly about markets versus government, or about the mix. Childcare, an activity that absorbs an enormous amount of resources, is largely provided by family members, with market institutions and government both playing a secondary role. Not-for-profit organizations principally govern religion, and Little League baseball.

Market organization is a widely used and useful governing structure. However, just as one size shoe does not fit all feet, a single mode of sectoral governance cannot cope with the great variety of human activity.

Modern economies are made up of many very different sectors. There is no way that a single form of organization and governance is going to be appropriate for all of them.

I begin my examination of this issue by reminding the reader that, in historical perspective, the current relatively unchallenged enthusiasm for market organization is rather unusual; in Section 2 I briefly review some aspects of the history of continuing debate. In Section 3 I turn to various theories about the virtues of market organization relative to other forms of governance. It turns out that these are very context dependent, and Sections 4 and 5 consider several lines of argument about what different modes of governance are good for, and develop the case for a mixed economy. In the concluding section I reflect further on why decisions regarding economic governance are so difficult.

2. The Past as Prologue

The presumption and fact that markets play a pervasive role in the governance and organization of economic activity are relatively recent phenomena. A significant expansion in the role of markets occurred first in Great Britain around the beginning of the eighteenth century, and later spread to continental Europe, and the United States, still later to Japan, and recently to large portions of the world. Of course certain kinds of markets have existed from virtually the dawn of history, but until recently markets were central in only a small portion of human activity. It is their pervasiveness, and the broader system legitimating and supporting market organization that came to be called capitalism, that is relatively new on the historical time scale.

With the spread of markets, of production that was largely for sale on markets, and of an economy where either net receipts from sales or wages garnered on labor markets largely determined the access of an individual or family to goods and services, a sphere of economic activity began to emerge in its own right, as a system that was distinct from the broader society and polity. Thus Adam Smith's *The Wealth of Nations* (first published in 1776) is about a market economy, influenced profoundly, to be sure, by the culture and government of the nation containing it, but an object in its own right and with its own basic rules of operation. That book could not have been written a century earlier.

However, it is important to recognize that many activities continued to be outside the market system. Both government and families remained important institutions. Also, throughout the period of ascendancy of capitalism, many sophisticated observers and analysts gave it mixed grades, arguing that there were minuses as well as pluses, and activities in which the market should not be dominant.

While the British "classical school" often is thought of as a strong proponent of markets, as unencumbered as possible, as extended to as wide a range of human activity as is possible, in fact that is not quite accurate. Adam Smith's enthusiasm for markets was nuanced, and he clearly saw a downside. John Stuart Mill did not like many aspects he saw in the rising capitalism of mid-nineteenth-century England. The United States today is regarded as the locus of almost unwashed enthusiasm for unfettered markets. However, Alexander Hamilton, in his *Report on Manufactures,* argued that protection and subsidy were needed if American industry were to survive and prosper. Many of the founders of the American Economic Association, which was established in the late nineteenth century, believed that the capitalism that was emerging in the United States badly needed regulation.

And for all the enthusiasm today for market capitalism of a relatively extensive and unrestricted sort, it is easy to forget that half a century ago, some of the most distinguished scholars were predicting capitalism's demise. In the 1940s Joseph Schumpeter published his classic *Capitalism, Socialism, and Democracy,* and Karl Polanyi, his *The Great Transformation.* Both saw raw capitalism as a system whose time had passed, the former with regret and the latter with relief. Both saw capitalism as it had developed during the first part of the twentieth century as politically unviable in a democracy.

The evidence indicates they were correct, at least at that time, although what happened was not quite what they predicted. In Western Europe, and in the United States, the early postwar era saw major "reforms" in the system. It was widely recognized that the reformed capitalism was significantly different from what it had replaced. The roles of government had expanded greatly. Unemployment insurance became widespread and in many countries quite generous, and similarly Social Security. Public support of education became much more extensive, particularly at the university level, and governments became the principal supporters of scientific research. Many countries expanded the scope of national health insurance, or instituted new programs. Several authors considering the reforms speculated as to whether the new economic system was "capitalism" or something new and different (see, for example, Dahl and Lindblom 1953, Crosland 1956, Bell 1960, Myrdal 1960, Schonfield 1965).

In the United States and United Kingdom, economists increasingly used the term *mixed economy* to describe the system as it was coming to be. The basic themes were well articulated in the 1962 report of the Kennedy administration's Council of Economic Advisors, which contained a number of the country's best known and most respected economists. While market organization was assumed to be the standard way of governing and managing industry, the theory of "market failure," to use a term I will unpack shortly, was very much part of the notion of a mixed economy. Monopoly was recognized as a condition that could negate many of the advantages of market organization, and something to be guarded against by rigorous antitrust law or, where inevitable, to be controlled through regulation in lieu of competition, or through public-sector management. The provision of public goods, such as national security and scientific knowledge, under this view required public support, and in some cases public undertaking. Externalities required regulation or a regime of taxes and subsidies. And government needed to proceed actively to assure that the workings of the economic system did not generate unrelieved poverty.

Of course, these changes in economic policy and, more broadly, changes in the view of what capitalism was and what was needed to make it effective, did not go unchallenged. By the middle or late 1970s, there was loud advocacy for rolling back many of the changes, or at least blocking further moves in these directions. The administrations of Margaret Thatcher in Great Britain and Ronald Reagan in the United States clearly marked a watershed. Since that time the conventional wisdom has been that a simple, lean capitalism is best, and that the earlier chatter about a mixed economy was badly misguided. Thus Daniel Yergin and Joseph Stanislaw (1998) have written about how the marketplace has won out over government in the battle for "the commanding heights" and see the outcome as victory for the right cause, expressing few qualms that the issues might be more complex than the ideological arguments of the victors. Francis Fukuyama (1992) proclaimed a final victory for capitalism (along with liberal democracy) in

The End of History and the Last Man, with hardly a mention of the earlier view that modern economies, while relying heavily on markets, needed to be "mixed."

Mark Blyth (2002) has proposed, in his *Great Transformations: Economic Ideas and Institutional Change in the Twentieth Century,* that there may be a natural cycle regarding popular opinion on the appropriate level and kind of government regulation and involvement more generally, a cycle that involves both policies and ideologies, with a tendency to overshoot in one direction and then, with a lag, reverse directions. He ascribes the turning of the 1980s to an overshooting in a liberal direction during the earlier postwar era. My argument, of course, is that we have overshot again.

As I have emphasized, my principal concern is with how a society governs different economic activities at the level of a sector. My argument is not about macroeconomics, or about whether or not broad reliance on market organization is a reasonable thing. Rather it is that, in the current climate, there is a strong tendency to rely on market organization, of a relatively pure and simple kind, not only in contexts where this can work reasonably well but also where simple market organization is at best problematic.

3. The Case for Market Organization: The Perspective from Economics

Since the days of Adam Smith, British and American economists generally have touted the virtues of the "invisible hand" of market organization. For the most part Smith's argument was qualitative, and supported by a set of empirical cases drawn from his own experiences and those of others. Also, it is important to remember that Smith was making his case for market organization partly as argument against a particular alternative: mercantilism.

Noneconomists seem under the impression that modern economists have built a theoretically rigorous and empirically well supported case for market organization that tightens up the logic of Smith's argument. However, I will argue here that in fact the most commonly cited theoretical argument in modern economics can support little weight, the empirical case for market organization is rough-and-ready, and the persuasive part pragmatic and qualitative rather than rigorous and

quantitative. In my view at least, the arguments for market organization that are most compelling are quite different from that contained
in the standard modern textbook formulation.[4]

That formulation, of course, is that, given a particular set of assumptions, a theoretical model of a market economy yields results that are
"Pareto optimal." An important implication of this line of theoretical
argument is that one need not look at other forms of economic organization, because market organization "can't be beat." Thus this perspective on the virtues of markets does not invite comparative analysis,
except for the purpose of exposing the weaknesses of nonmarket
forms. In any case, that argument is a nonstarter for considering what
are the real advantages of market organization vis-à-vis other forms of
governance.

It is a nonstarter, first of all, because no one really believes that the
model is a close approximation to how a market economy actually
works, or that the real economy actually generates outcomes that even
in principle can't be beat. On the other hand, real market economies
are much richer institutionally than the simple model, and thus theoretical arguments (for example, those contained in market failure theory) may not be an indictment against the actual market economies
that we have. What clearly is needed is careful empirical evaluation of
quite complex alternative governing structures. There has been little
of this kind of hard research. Unfortunately, therefore, analysis of the
pluses and minuses of governing structures that make significant use
of markets has to rest on a mixture of the rather rough comparisons
that history does allow, plus efforts at sensible, if somewhat ad hoc,
theorizing.

Thus while market organization as it actually is does not achieve
"Pareto optimality," most economists and many lay persons would argue that market organization and competition often do seem to generate results that are moderately efficient. There are strong incentives
for firms to produce goods and services that customers want, or can be
persuaded they want, and to produce at as low a financial cost as is possible. Also, under many circumstances competitive market-organized
economic sectors seem to respond relatively quickly to changes in customer demands, supply conditions, and technological opportunities.
Thus, to the extent that producing what customers value is treated as a
plus, and so long as factor prices roughly measure opportunity costs,

there is a strong pragmatic case for market organization, broadly defined, on economic efficiency grounds, at least in certain domains of activity. It is not the case presented in textbook theory. But in my view it is far more persuasive.

3.1. Why Not Top-Down Planning?

The kind of economic governance required would certainly seem to depend on the nature of the salient needs. Thus in wartime, and virtually without protest, capitalist economies have abandoned market governance and adopted centrally coordinated mechanisms of resource allocation, procurement, and rationing. The rationale has been that such economic governance is essential if production is to be allocated to the highest priority needs, and conducted effectively. And by and large there is agreement that remarkable feats of production have been achieved under these arrangements.

The experience with wartime planning has led some analysts to propose that a number of the mechanisms used then would vastly increase economic efficiency during peacetime. However, most knowledgeable analysts have argued against that position, strongly. It is one thing to marshal an economy to concentrate on a central set of agreed-upon high-priority demands over a short period of time, as in wartime production, or in the early years of the communist economies, when the central objective was to build up a few basic industries. It is something else again to have an economy behave reasonably responsively and efficiently in a context of diverse and changing demands, supply conditions, and technological opportunities, over a long time period. The experience with central planning in the ex-communist countries after the era had passed, when building up standard infrastructure sufficed as a central goal, bears out this argument.[5]

However, I would propose that the argument behind the scenes here for market organization is more complex than, and in fact different from, the standard textbook argument that profit-maximizing behavior of firms in competitive market contexts yields economically efficient results. It hinges on the multiplicity, diversity, and unpredictable changeability of wants, resources, and technologies in modern economies that, experience shows, defy the information-processing and resource-allocating capabilities of centrally planned and controlled systems, and also presumes that the chances of appropriate responses to changed conditions are enhanced when there are a number of competitive actors who can respond without going through a process requiring approval by some central authority, or without gaining the approval of a large number of people before acting. Hayek and the modern "Austrian" economists (for example, Kirzner 1979) have stressed the ability of market economies to experiment, to search for unmet needs and unseized opportunities, and have argued that centralized systems are very bad at this. This argument is not what standard textbook theory is about.

I also note that this argument hinges on the desirability of consumer sovereignty, expressed through market choices. It is mute regarding how to mind social or collective demands. More on this shortly.

3.2. A Schumpeterian Perspective

Many observers have proposed that it is in dynamic long-run performance, rather than in short-run efficiency, that market capitalism reveals its greatest strength. As Marx and Schumpeter have stressed, capitalism has been a remarkably powerful engine of economic progress. And here too one can make a rather explicit comparison. Indeed a good case can be made that a central reason for the collapse of the old communist economies was their inability to stay up with and take advantage of the rapid technological progress that was going on in market economics.

But again the characteristics and capabilities of market organization that contribute to technological progress are very different from those that relate to static efficiency, and from the textbook normative model. Schumpeter made a great deal of those differences. Some commentators on Schumpeter have proposed that he did not believe that, in modern capitalism, competition was important. That is not correct. Rather, his argument was that the kind of competition that mattered was not the sort stressed in the economics textbooks, but competition through innovation. The capitalism of his *Capitalism, Socialism, and Democracy* (1942) was an effective engine of progress because competition spurred innovation. His theory places high value on pluralism and multiple rival sources of invention and innovation. However, under this view of what socially valuable competition is all about, the presence of large firms with R & D laboratories as well as some market power was welcomed, despite the fact that such a market structure diverged from the purely competitive one associated with the static theorem about Pareto optimality.

It is interesting that Schumpeter, in his late writings, argued that as science became more powerful, the unruly and inefficient competition of capitalist systems would no longer be needed for industrial innovation, which increasingly could be planned. History has shown him to be very wrong on this point. Centrally planned systems often have achieved strong success in allocating R & D resources where the objectives were sharply defined and the likely best routes to success quite clear. The Manhattan Project and Project Apollo are good examples. However, for the most part potential innovators are faced with the problem of guessing just how much users will value various innovations they might introduce, and also of judging how easy or difficult it would be to develop various alternatives. The answers to these questions seldom are clear. Further, well-informed experts are likely to disagree on the answers. Under these conditions, the competitive pluralism of market-organized R & D systems is a great advantage.

It can be argued that, at least in recent years, the strong performance of market capitalist economies on the industrial-innovation front also has a lot to do with features of modern capitalist economies not highlighted in Schumpeter—for example, public support of university research and training. However, the pluralism, flexibility, and competition of modern capitalism surely are essential aspects of any effective innovation system.

4. The Positive Case for a Mixed Economy: Market Failure Theory

While I find the argument in favor of market organization of economic activity broadly compelling, it is too broad. Its breadth covers up the fact that economies include a large variety of sectors and activities, which have different properties. As proposed earlier, one size shoe does not fit all feet. It is important to consider the details of an activity before deciding whether or not it fits neatly into the simple market shoe.

It is clear that most high-level argument about where market organization works effectively, and where it works poorly, is conducted using the economists' market failure language. Market failure theory takes as its benchmark the theory I discussed earlier, that under the set of assumptions about behavior built into neoclassical economic theory, and given a particular set of context assumptions, market governance of economic activity yields Pareto optimal outcomes. The orientation of market failure theory is to delineate conditions that upset that result.

Because this body of theory is so well known, I can telescope here the standard account of the basic market failure categories. Instead, my emphasis will be on the blurry edges of the standard categories and on some cases that seem to strain the underlying economic theory more generally. In my view, a large share of the current controversies about the role of markets fall into these areas.[6]

4.1. The Public Goods Bestiary

Economists use the public good concept to flag a class of goods and services from which the benefits are collective and communal rather than individual and private. Under this body of conceptualization, a pure public good has two attributes. One is that, unlike a standard private good like a peanut butter sandwich, which can benefit only one consumer (although of course it can be split and shared), a public good provides "atmospheric" benefits that all can enjoy. In the language of economists, public goods are nonrivalrous in use. Your benefiting from a public good in no way diminishes my ability to benefit. The second attribute is that, if a public good or service is provided at all, there is no way to deny access to any person, or to require direct payment for access. Clean air and national security are standard examples of pure public goods. Scientific knowledge often is used as another example. For a neighborhood, the quality of access roads has some public good attributes.

For the procurement of a pure public good, society is virtually compelled to put in place some kind of collective choice mechanism to decide how much to buy, and some kind of a collective revenue source to pay for them. Standard market governance simply will not work. For some "local" public goods, the mechanism can be informal. Thus a neighborhood association may collect voluntary dues for maintenance of access roads. But for public goods that benefit a wide range of people and groups, and to which, if provided, access cannot be blocked, there is no option but to use the machinery of government.

However, pure public goods are rare. And for a variety of goods and services that have some public goods properties, using the market for provision is feasible.

First of all, there is a class of goods and services that, while they are marked by nonrivalry in use, potential beneficiaries can be made to pay for if they are to have access. Access to scientific knowledge or data, for example, can be restricted by secrecy on the part of researchers. In recent years, legal changes have made certain kinds of scientific research results, and certain kinds of data, protectable under patent and copyright law.

Where access can be blocked, there is the option of using market organization for supply, and making individuals and groups pay for what they want to get. The problem with this governance structure is that, if the good or service is nonrivalrous in use, or largely so, use may be restricted when there is no social cost of extending use. The losses here can be small or considerable. Argument about this now is prominent, in the face of moves to use the market more for the support of scientific research, and for scientific data collection and distribution.

Second, and partially related, many goods and services are partly private and partly public, in the sense that there is identifiable benefit to particular individuals, who can be made to pay for access, and at the same time broad atmospheric benefit from the availability or provision of the good or service. Education is a prominent example. Vaccination for contagious diseases is another. It can be argued that mass transport, in addition to generating benefits to the users, also benefits society at large by reducing the congestion and other costs associated with greater use of private transport, were public transport not available.

Society has the choice here to rely largely on market provision, by making the individuals who directly benefit pay the full costs, thus minimizing needed public support. This is the proclivity of the American government these days regarding rail transportation. And we seem to be moving in that direction regarding higher education. However, primary and secondary education continue to be largely publicly financed, even though the benefits to individual students are usually substantial. And vaccination may be required by law.

I now want to turn to a more general point. It is that in many cases the perceived public benefits of a good or service are associated with beliefs about what is appropriate for a society or a polity. Many citizens in a democracy support funding for universal education not because they, or their children, will take advantage of public schools, or because they believe it will reduce the incidence of crime that can affect them, but because they believe that universal free education is a necessary condition for equality of opportunity in a society. Similar arguments have been put forth for public funding of universal preschool child care. Many people clearly believe it is wrong if people in need do not have access to medical care if they cannot afford it. The values at stake here seem different in kind than the utility that an individual might get from a nice steak.

Whether a good or service has significant public good properties clearly depends on how the benefits it yields are viewed. In the cases above, the benefits that are seen as "public" are not easily analyzed in terms of the standard kinds of benefits that are the focus of standard economics. Rather, their "publicness" resides in values defined in terms of perceptions about what makes a society a decent and just one. For this reason, for many goods and services the argument is not about whether innate publicness requires public funding to assure a decent level of provision, but rather whether the good or service should be made available to all, on reasonable or nominal terms, with public moneys footing the bill. That is, a considerable part of the debate is about what goods and services ought to be public.

There are significant costs involved in employing public choice machinery instead of or supplementary to market demand-side machinery. There is, first of all, the question of just how to decide how much is to be provided, in contexts where individuals and groups may value the public provision of the good or service very differently. There is, second, the question of who is to pay. Because of the number of individuals and groups that may try to have a say in these matters, the process is either going to be time-consuming and cumbersome or pruned back and simplified in a way that will certainly outrage certain parties. The outcomes of collective demand-generating processes are inevitably going to be considered by some to be unfair and inefficient. But if a good or service has strong innate public good properties, or is deemed by some as something that ought to be public, this argument is inevitable.

4.2. The Externalities Problem:
Bringing in Broader Interests to the Governing Structure

The externalities concept of economists is meant to refer to products of economic activity that have negative or positive consequences that are not reflected in the benefits and costs perceived by those who engage in the externalities-generating activity. Environmental contamination is an obvious example of a negative "externality" and a clear case where there is a value at stake in the operations of an activity, with no one to represent and fight for it, at least in the simple model of market governance put forth in economic textbooks.

In a famous article written some time ago, Ronald Coase (1960) argued that, if property rights are clear and strong, and the number of interested parties relatively small, in fact markets can deal with these kinds of problems. Those who value clean air or water simply can "buy" behavior that respects those values from the potential polluter. The problem arises when those who care about the values, which could be neglected, are dispersed. In this case some kind of collective-action machinery is needed to bring them in. A good way to think about regulation or a tax on pollution is to see these measures as the result of governance machinery that has brought in a broader range of interests and values bearing on decision making in an activity or sector than would be there under simple market organization.

The general problem for society is to delineate the range of interests that should be represented, their relative influence, and the mechanisms through which they can operate to make their values felt. The latter can range from public interest advertising, or boycotts, which can proceed without direct access to governmental machinery, to lawsuits that involve general governmental apparatus, to particular pieces of special regulation and associated control machinery.

As suggested earlier, one of the major advantages of market governance of an activity or sector is that this tends to avoid the costs and inefficiencies of central planning. One of the reasons for its flexibility and responsiveness to certain kinds of needs is that simple market governance tends to count a rather narrow range of interests. Yet it is hard to identify an activity, or a sector, where there are not some values at stake that go beyond the direct interests of the customers and the suppliers. Severe externalities from an activity clearly call for amending simple market organization to give those interests an effective voice. On the other hand, the greater the number of interests and values that have to come to some collective conclusion before action is taken, or that have a veto power over change, the more cumbersome the governance system. The question, of course, is where to draw the line.

4.3. The Costs of Competition and the Problem of Private Monopoly

The benefits of competition are part of virtually all arguments extolling the advantages of market organization. Of course one can have competition without having for-profit firms. Indeed there are a number of proposals for reforming primary and secondary education based on giving parents and students a wider range of school choice, and providing stronger incentives to schools to attract and hold students, that don't necessarily involve introducing for-profit schools into the supply side of the picture. Some of those who oppose this kind of reform, or doubt its advantages, argue that parents and students do not in general have the knowledge or motivation to make good choices in such a setting, and that stimulating competition among schools would invite catering to ill-informed tastes. There are similar arguments, pro and con competition, regarding choice of medical plans and doctors. I will consider this set of issues in more detail shortly.

Here I want to flag the problem that, in a number of activities or sectors, there are significant economies of scale of provision relative to the size of the market, or strong advantages to having an internally coordinated system, or both. Activities with these characteristics are called by economists "natural monopolies." If a sector or an activity is a natural monopoly, competition is not a desirable or a viable element of a governing structure. This traditionally had been the assumption regarding the range of sectors that have been called "public utilities," including prominently the telephone system, electric power, and railroads. Up until recently, public utilities tended to be operated as government corporations in much of Europe, and as franchised private but regulated corporations in the United States.

Over the past quarter century there have been strong pressures to denationalize, or deregulate, the old public utilities. Often this argument has been associated with the proposition that in fact these activities no longer are natural monopolies, if they ever were. However, in many cases it has turned out that the generation of competition has proved very difficult or very costly. And as a result, customers now tend to face a relatively unregulated private monopoly, as contrasted with a regulated or public one.

American economists are inclined to rationalize the use of antitrust law to prevent undue market power from arising, and regulation to deal with cases where there is natural monopoly, on the grounds that monopolists tend to charge too high a price. It is clear, however, that much of the force behind the policies to break up or rein in monopolies, or to regulate them closely, has to do with concerns that arise when private bodies gain considerable power over people's lives, a matter that may involve but also may transcend being forced to pay monopoly prices. Economists are inclined to rationalize the fact that governments not only fund but directly control activities related to national security and the criminal justice system by the fact that these activities yield "public goods." But it probably is at least as relevant that there is near consensus that it would be highly dangerous to place the power over these activities in private hands. While clearly there is widespread concern about undue governmental powers, in the arena of public utilities there is concern about unregulated private power as well.

I propose that concern about the lack of accountability to the public of those who have private power over activities and services that many people believe are of vital importance to them lies at the heart of the current debate about how to govern activities like telephone service, electricity generation and distribution, urban water supply, the railroad system, urban mass transport. I think that to ignore this aspect of the debate about how to govern these sectors is to miss the point. However, as with the issue of regulation to deal with externalities, the key question for regulation of industries where monopoly or a highly concentrated structure is inevitable, is where to draw the line.

4.4. The Issue of Uneven Expertise and Agency

Economists have become more interested recently in how asymmetric information between buyer and seller, or, more generally, lack of the expertise to judge quality on the part of customers, complicates the workings of markets. I propose that a number of the current controversies about the efficacy of market organization, about regulation of market supply, and about alternatives to market supply reflect this issue.

The problem clearly is fundamental in medical care. The medical community long has professed that, while doctors sell their services on the market, they most emphatically do not try to maximize their profits but rather prescribe in the patients' interests. Analysts have observed that this may be true to some extent, but still the capabilities of patients to choose among physicians or physician groups remains problematic. Thus the questions of what information needs to be provided to those choosing among doctors or plans and what controls there should be on advertising are important matters in considering the role that competition should play in the provision of medical care. And there is the question of whether, even under suitable regulatory constraints, competition among health plans and physicians for patients is a useful component of the governing structure, or whether competition may even be on net pernicious.

The same issues of course come up in arguments over the wisdom of adopting a voucher plan, and school competition, in education. There is considerable resistance on the part of many citizens, not simply public-school teachers, to the notion that for-profit schools should receive public support and can act as useful competitors to public schools. Similar issues are involved in the debate about the rules and regulations that should be required of extra family child care, and whether or not to encourage for-profit firms in that line of activity.

My point here is not that those who oppose simple market organization in areas where there is considerable consumer ignorance have a fully persuasive argument for heavy regulation or nonmarket provision. These alternatives to market organization have their own liabilities. Rather, it is that where one cannot count on informed customers to make good choices, the argument in favor of lean market organization is problematic.

4.5. The Peculiar Bias of Market Failure Theory

I want to conclude this survey of market failure theory by pointing out a bias built into that theory. By the way it is formulated, market failure theory carries a heavy normative load, to the effect that markets are preferred to other forms of governance unless they are basically flawed in some sense. Thus the only reason why government should provide for national security and protect citizens from crime is that markets can't do these jobs very well. Parents need to take care of children because of market failure. As one reflects on it, the argument that we need government because markets sometimes "fail" seems rather strange, or at least incomplete. Can't one make a positive case for government, or families, for that matter, as a form that is appropriate, even needed, in its own right?

5. The Functions of the State and the Community

5.1. Values of the Collective

Of course there is an ancient body of theorizing that puts forth a positive case for government. In much of its early incarnation, and some of its more recent, the state is viewed as the structure through which values are defined at the level of the community, and decisions regarding the community as a whole are made. Reflect on Plato's discussion in *The Republic,* or Hegel's discussion of the good state, which is defined in terms of the quality of its justice and the character of its citizens. This formulation of the role of the state of course does not resolve the issue of differences among individuals who comprise the state. Indeed disputes about values are likely to be even more heated than disputes involving choices that affect economic interests differently. And the issue of how to decide may be even more contentious. Plato saw the answer in government by philosophers. For better or worse, modern societies are stuck with democratic process.

A liberal position on how to deal with value differences within the population would be to keep the state out of it, and to try to avoid forcing the values of one group upon another. But in many cases there is no way to do that. Abortion either is legal or it is not.

This theory clearly captures a lot of the flavor of contemporary debates about matters like the right to life and the right to choose, the commitment of a society to ideals of equal opportunity and fairness, and whether there should be universal health insurance regardless of ability to pay. Arguments about these matters involve beliefs about appropriate collective values, or values of the collective, that transcend those of particular individuals. Under this theory, in these areas at least, the state, which defines the collective, is the natural vehicle of governance in contexts where a collective position on something has to be taken one way or another. In these areas the state may choose to use markets to further some collective values, but the purpose being served is a public purpose, and the responsibility for furthering it ultimately is a state responsibility.

5.2. Providing the Contest for a Fruitful Civil Life and Economy

Another, but not mutually exclusive, body of theorizing about the state focuses not so much on collective values but on the state as the necessary vehicle to set the context for fruitful private lives and actions. From at least the time of Hobbes, and Locke, theories about the need for a strong state have involved, centrally, the proposition that an effective state is needed for individuals to lead secure, decent, and productive lives. Originally this body of theorizing had little to do with economics, much less the role of the state in market economies. Thus Hobbes's case for a strong state to establish and enforce a clear body of law is posed in terms of the need to avoid the "war of every man against every man." While his case involved security of property, this was not its central orientation. With Locke, the orientation is more toward security of property, but his great writings were before capitalism emerged as a recognizable economic system.

The argument for a strong state here is an argument for a single ultimate source of legal authority and police power. In the language of market failure theory, it is a natural monopoly argument as well as a public good argument. But the orientation to these issues in the political philosophy literature is that these are natural, basic functions of the state; they don't simply fall to the state by default, because of some kind of market failure.

A closely related proposition is that the state has principal responsibility for assuring the provision of needed basic infrastructure, physical as well as legal. While the emphasis in Adam Smith's *The Wealth of Nations* was on the need for a reliable government and legal system for an economy to work decently, as economies grew more complicated, provision of basic services soon became viewed as a responsibility of the state.

Of course the question of what is infrastructure that needs to be provided, for markets to work well, and what markets themselves can be expected to provide often is not an easy one. But this issue is not generally argued out strictly under the concepts of market failure theory. Consider activities like providing a system of contract law, building and maintaining a road system, or a railroad system, or supporting the development of basic scientific knowledge. These activities can be viewed as public goods, in the sense of market failure theory, with the market failure stemming from the fact that their benefits are to a considerable extent collective rather than individual, and hence that for-profit firms would have great difficulty collecting for their provision on a conventional market. Or they can be considered as "needed infrastructure" that governments are, by their functions, responsible for getting provided. While the former theory sees the reason for government provision or overview and control in the inability of markets to do an adequate job, the latter sees provision of such goods and services as a central responsibility of government, even if they could be provided through market mechanisms. And where market mechanisms in fact are used as part of the machinery for provision, the latter perspective sees government as still responsible for overseeing the operation, at least to some degree.

5.3. The State and the Community

Several of the theories of the state referred to above rest heavily on the concept of a natural community of individuals, families, and more extended social structures, tied to each other by community bonds. Under this conception, the state is the vehicle through which the community makes collective decisions and takes coordinated collective action, when that is appropriate. But from another point of view, it is clear that much of the decision making and action taking of the community does not involve state-mediated collective action. Indeed, assuring that the state does not interfere too much in the life of the civil community has been a central issue in Anglo-American political theory.

I believe it is fruitful, and illuminating, to view the economy as an aspect of community life, rather than as a set of institutions that stand separate.[7] From this perspective, *the economy* is the term used to denote and focus attention on the activities of the community that use scarce resources to achieve human purposes. It is clear that much of economic activity in this broad sense does not involve markets, in the standard sense of that term.

Adam Smith is mostly known today, particularly among economists, for his *The Wealth of Nations*. There he stressed the value of the "invisible hand" of market mechanisms. The orientation of his *Theory of Moral Sentiments* (1853) was quite different in a number of ways. There he stressed the extended empathy that humans in a community have for each other, along with feelings of rivalry, and sometimes of hostility. Extended empathy can be a powerful ingredient in a governing structure, and in some cases an ingredient that can be deemed vital for effective governance. But extended empathy is not what markets are about. Thus, to pick up on an earlier theme, the family is the standard governance structure for child care, and for many other economic activities, not because of simple market failure, but because the family can be counted on (mostly) to hold the extended empathy toward its children that seems essential to good care. Similarly, there are a wide variety of other activities involving members of the community that neither formal governments nor markets play a central role in governing, but that are instead governed by neighborhood groups, voluntary associations, clubs, and the like.

Karl Polanyi was in a long line of social analysts who saw the extension of markets as an enemy of society, a destroyer of communal modes of governance. This is not a market failure argument. It is an argument that markets should be fenced off from certain kinds of activities.

The reality, but even more the myth, of the community structure that was undermined by market capitalism included, first, the idea that the community took care of its own, and second, that each community member, depending on his or her status, had certain rights as well as certain obligations. With the rise of the modern state, formal government gradually took on responsibility for taking care of its citizens, and for assuring their basic rights. Over time, arguments about the appropriate domain of such rights have moved from political rights to economic rights.

Thus under traditional democratic theory, all citizens of a state ought to have the right to vote, the right to equal treatment under the law, and a variety of freedoms of action regarding personal matters. Access to these basic rights of citizenship were seen as something that should not be rationed through markets, and for which government had a fundamental responsibility. During the nineteenth century, government also came to be charged with protecting those who were regarded as too weak to protect themselves from market arrangements that would hurt them: thus child labor laws were passed, and laws limiting hours of work for certain classes of labor. A right of all citizens to a free public education, to a minimal level at least, gradually came to be recognized. The core arguments of modern welfare-state theories add to these venerable political and protective rights a set of rights to access to certain kinds of goods and services. This decoupling of access to a considerable range of goods and services from the normal market process is the hallmark of the modern welfare state.[8]

Note that the proposition here regarding the role of government has a family resemblance to that associated with the position that government is responsible for needed infrastructure. The difference is that the orientation is not so much to what is needed to make the economy work as to what is needed to make a society viable. Also, note that in both theories there is a strong notion of collective values. While the base values in this theory are associated with individual well-being, the notion that society is simply a collection of individuals and families who have their own independent wants and purposes misunderstands this perception of what human societies are. *Solidarity* is a word often used by advocates of this position. From another (sometimes closely related) tradition, we all are our brothers' keepers.

6. Economic Governance as a Continuing Challenge

Arguments about appropriate governing structures are difficult for many reasons. In the first place, there often are significant conflicts of interest and differences in views regarding the salient values at stake. Since a central aspect of a governing structure involves the mechanism that determines which interests and values count, it is easy to see why this may be a contentious issue. And the question of who is responsible for supply, and under what set of rules, often involves contenders with strong interests in how that question is resolved. Reflect on the conflicts involved in proposals in the United States for a "patient's bill of rights" in dealing with managed-care organizations, or in proposals for a voucher scheme for publicly funded education. Deregulation of the electric power system and the telephone system was supported strongly by certain firms and interests, and a tightening of regulation would be strongly resisted by those interests.

The problem is difficult not just because of competing interests and values, but also because of real uncertainties—the better term might be ignorance—regarding the consequences of adopting one governance scheme or another. As I have argued, given the analytic limitations of the social sciences, or the complexity of the subject matter, or both, it simply is impossible to foresee reliably the consequences of a patient's bill of rights or a voucher scheme for public education. The developing argument about whether and how to regulate spam and pornography on the Internet is made additionally complicated by the fact that it is impossible to forecast how different regulatory regimes will in fact work.

Further, for better or for worse, decisions that lead to the establishment of and changes in a governance structure almost always are made in a highly decentralized manner, and much of the action is by private parties doing things they think are in their best interest. The current modal structure and the range of variants of managed health care in the United States is largely the result of decisions made by, on the one hand, organizations seeing potential profit in managed care, or striving to reorganize their managed care operation so as to make it profitable, and, on the other hand, individuals and organizations with a responsibility to fund health care, who had to make decisions regarding with whom to do business.

Of course in this case and others, the evolution of public programs and policies is an important part of the story. The ratification of a governance structure or changes in one ultimately is a political decision, even if that decision does not involve new law. However, given the way issues arise and are dealt with in a democracy, policies are made and remade piece by piece. Thus today the U.S. Congress is treating the issues of patients' rights and insurance coverage for pharmaceutical costs as if they were separate issues. The issues of school reform and reform of regulation of public utilities are complicated by the fact that there are many government agencies that will have a say, some at the national level, some at the state level, and, in education, some at the local level.

Some analysts would blame the problems societies have had in developing coherent and effective governing structures for areas like medical care, or the Internet, on this fragmentation. However, from another point of view this decentralization and the serial nature of the policy-making process largely has protected us from grand coherent plans, the reach of which could extend well beyond what can be well predicted.[9] While ex ante analysis can serve to rule out certain proposals as obviously inadequate in certain areas, the development of governance structures for various activities has to rely to a considerable extent on evaluation of experience with attempts to reform.

It would be nice if experience with prevailing systems and their variants provided sharp, clear feedback on what is working and what is not, so as to guide the next round of adjustments. However, even putting aside the fact that the interests and values of different parties might lead them to evaluate the same thing differently, and even where there is agreement that the current regime is unsatisfactory in certain ways, it may be extremely difficult to identify just what aspect of the current regime is causing the problem, or how to fix it. While ex post evaluation of a reform may be somewhat easier than ex ante prediction of the effects of that reform, it still is very difficult.[10]

In such a context, a general broad belief in the efficacy of market organization undoubtedly is on net a plus, given the broad experience societies have had with market organization and the alternatives. However, it is a mistake to think that simple markets are the solution to all of our economic governance problems. To make market organization work decently well in certain contexts requires quite complex ancillary governing structures. And market organization is simply poorly suited for governing certain kinds of activities. It is important to develop a thoughtful understanding of the complexities and limits of market organization.

Notes

1. For a statement in this spirit, see Fukuyama (1992) and Yergin and Stanislaw (1998).
2. Mowery and Nelson (1999) describe in detail the involvement of gov-

ernment programs in sectors conventionally thought of as "market organized." See also Hollingsworth and Boyer (1997). North (1990) and Hodgson (1999a) stress the institutional complexity of modern economies.

3. For a good discussion, see Lipsey, Courant, and Ragan (1998), chap. 3.

4. The discussion that follows develops some of the themes I first introduced in my 1981 article, "Assessing Private Enterprise: An Exegesis of Tangled Doctrine."

5. Lindblom's discussion of these issues in his *Politics and Markets* (1977) is particularly good.

6. Of the many expositions of the many facets of market failure theory, I find Stiglitz (1986) especially fine. See also Lipsey, Courant, and Ragan (1998), chap. 18.

7. This is very much the position taken by Lindblom (2001).

8. Esping-Anderson (1990) provides a broad and incisive picture of the modern welfare state. See also Goodin et al. (1999).

9. The dangers of detailed planning where understanding is limited has been stressed by Hayek and Lindblom.

10. See Rivlin's discussion (1971).

CHAPTER 9

The Market Economy
and the Scientific Commons

1. Introduction

One major point developed in the preceding chapter was that many important clusters of economic activity operate under mixed structures of organization and governance, involving both market and nonmarket elements. A second point was that the ascendancy in recent years of a strong and often undiscriminating pro-market ideology has placed the nonmarket parts of our economic system at risk. Both of these points are illustrated vividly in the case of basic scientific research.

Clearly modern capitalism has proved a remarkably powerful engine of technological progress. Much of the attention to its workings has focused, appropriately, on the business firms and entrepreneurs, operating in a market setting, who are the central actors in developing and introducing new products and processes. At the same time it is widely recognized that the power of market-stimulated and guided invention and innovation often is dependent on the strength of the science base from which they draw (Nelson 1993, Mowery and Nelson 1999). This science base largely is the product of publicly funded research, and the knowledge produced by that research is largely open and available for potential innovators to use. That is, the market part

---

* Based on Richard R. Nelson, "The Market Economy and the Scientific Commons," *Research Policy* 33 (2004): 455–471.

of the capitalist engine rests on a publicly supported scientific commons.

The message of this chapter is that the scientific commons is becoming privatized. While the privatization of the scientific commons up to now has been relatively limited, there are real dangers that, unless halted soon, important portions of future scientific knowledge will be private property and fall outside the public domain, and that could be bad news both for the future progress of science and for technological progress. The erosion of the scientific commons will not be easy to stop. Here I want to call the alarm, and to suggest a strategy that has some promise.

But before I get on with that task, I need to clear some intellectual underbrush. A number of influential philosophers and sociologists of science have put forth a set of views, a theory, about the scientific enterprise that until recently has served well to protect the scientific commons. However, this theory no longer is adequate to the task, because the way it characterizes the nature of the scientific enterprise does not fit modern perceptions and the reality. Also, under the theory, it is hard to understand why privatization and markets are encroaching on the commons and, if they are, what is the matter with that. It is important, therefore, to scrutinize this theory.

A key element of the theory is that the work of scientists doing basic research is and should be motivated by the search for understanding, and that the practical payoffs that often come from successful research are largely unpredictable. Vannevar Bush (1945) is one among many proponents of public support of science who put forth this theme, and argued that it would be a mistake to look to likely practical payoffs as a guide to where scientific funds should be allocated. Serendipity is the reason why scientific research often has a practical payoff, and the chances of serendipity are greatest when bright and dedicated scientists are free to attack what they see as the most challenging scientific problems in the way they think most promising.

For this reason, decisions regarding what questions to explore, and the evaluation of the performance of individual scientists and broad research programs, should mostly be in the hands of the scientists working in a field. Indeed for the government or the market to intrude too much into how scientific research resources are allocated would be to kill the goose that lays the golden egg. In the terms used by Michael Polanyi (1967), society should appreciate and protect "the Republic of Science."

An associated belief or ideal is that the results of scientific research are and should be published and otherwise laid open for all to use and evaluate. As Robert Merton (1973) argued, the spirit of science is "communitarian" regarding access to the knowledge and technique it creates. All scientists should be free to test the results of their fellows and to find them valid or not supported, and to build on those results in their own work. Because the results of scientific research are laid in the public domain for testing and further development, the bulk of scientific knowledge accepted by the community is reliable (as John Ziman [1978] has emphasized) and scientific knowledge is cumulative. These are basic reasons why the scientific enterprise has been so effective as an engine of discovery. And economists often have argued that keeping science open is the most effective policy for enabling the public to draw practical benefits from it.

My position in this chapter is that the argument for keeping basic science open is fundamentally correct, but it is in danger of being forgotten, or denied. A good share of the reason is that, as originally put forth, this part of the argument seemed a natural consequence of the other aspects of the theory: that the practical payoffs from scientific research were not predictable but largely came about through serendipity, and that the allocation of scientific resources should be guided not by anticipation of particular practical payoffs but rather by the informed judgments of scientists regarding the most important problems to work on. Keeping scientific findings in the public domain, with reward to the scientist being tied to the acclaim of his or her fellows, along with public funding of research based on peer review of the scientific promise of the proposal and the scientist, then would seem an important part of an incentive and control system for fostering productive science (for a discussion along these lines, see Dasgupta and David 1994).

However, the notion that academic scientists have no idea and do not care about the practical problems that their research might illuminate never has been fully true. In this era of biotechnology it is obvious, if it was not before, that both the funders and the undertakers of research often have well in mind the possible social and economic payoffs from what they are doing. But if in fact much of scientific research is consciously aimed, at least broadly, at problems the solution to which can have major, and broadly predictable, practical value, what is the case against harnessing market incentives to the undertaking of research and to the use of research results? In particular, why should the privatization of these kinds of research results be viewed as a problem?

The case for open scientific knowledge clearly needs to be reconstructed to recognize explicitly that much of scientific research in fact is oriented toward providing knowledge useful for the solution of practical problems, that the applications of new scientific findings often are broadly predictable, and that this is why control over scientific findings in some cases is financially valuable property. I think there is a case for keeping basic scientific knowledge open, even under these conditions. To privatize basic knowledge is a danger both for the advance of science and for the advance of technology. I will develop my argument as follows.

Section 2 is concerned with how technological advance draws from science. Without denying the role of serendipity, I will argue that, for the most part, science is valuable as an input to technological change these days because much of scientific research is in fields that are oriented to providing knowledge that is of use in particular areas. These are the scientific fields that Donald Stokes (1996) saw as being in "Pasteur's Quadrant," where the research aims for deep understanding but the field itself is oriented toward achieving practical objectives, like improving health, or achieving better understanding of the properties of materials, or achieving a powerful theory of computing.

However, a strong base of scientific understanding should be understood as making more powerful the innately evolutionary processes that are involved in the advance of technology, rather than eliminating the need for multiple competitive sources of innovation. To restrict access to basic science is to cut down significantly on the number of parties who can effectively invent in a field.

In Section 3 I discuss the rise and erosion of the idea that public support of open science is warranted because the expected returns arc high but the areas of return are so uncertain that market mechanisms will not suffice. I begin by briefly reviewing the ideological and political debates that occurred after World War II that led to broad consensus regarding the value of public support of open, autonomous science. As I noted, that rhetoric stressed that the payoffs from science were almost completely unpredictable, and thus the allocation of funds to science should not be influenced by perceptions of social needs. The publicly supported science system that actually developed was in fact much more oriented to facilitating making progress on important practical problems than that rhetoric allowed, and this is now obvious.

I do not want to argue that most academic researchers working in, for example, the biomedical sciences define their goals as dealing with particular diseases. Much of the most important work in such fields is quite fundamental in nature, in the sense that it explores basic processes and phenomena, without a clearly defined, specific, practical objective in mind. However, the fundamental questions and appealing lines of research in sciences in Pasteur's Quadrant are strongly influenced by perceptions of what kind of knowledge is relevant to problem solving in a field. Thus one of the reasons why cell biology now is such a fashionable field is the belief that basic understanding won here might just unlock the cancer puzzle or enable us to understand better how receptors work.

This perception of how the modern science system actually works has eroded the notion that it is important to keep science open. I believe that this is a serious mistake.

While perceptions of possible applications of research are not as vague as proposed in the earlier rhetoric about serendipity, the actual paths to application of apparently promising scientific discoveries are in fact very uncertain. Understandings that come from science seldom lead immediately or directly to the solution of practical problems. Rather, they provide the knowledge and the tools to wrestle with them more effectively. I propose that, for just this reason—that the findings of basic science set the stage for follow-on applications work—for society to get maximal benefit from its support of basic science, there must be open access to scientific research results. Open access permits many potential inventors to work with new knowledge. Privatization restricts access to only those whom the owner allows to make use of it. This is why some of the recent developments are so worrisome.

In Section 4 I discuss the current situation and the dangers in more detail. Then I turn to a number of measures that I believe have some promise as attacks on the problem.

2. The Coevolution of Practice and Understanding

Virtually everybody these days appreciates that the power of modern technological innovation depends to a considerable extent on its ability to draw from modern science. But there is little general understanding, and there are some quite wrong beliefs, about the nature of the science-technology links. Understanding these links correctly is a precondition, I believe, for having an effective discussion about what public policy toward science ought to be. This certainly is so regarding the current controversies about patenting in science. Thus this section discusses what scholars studying technological advance know about these issues.

I have argued that technologies need to be understood as involving both a body of practice, manifest in the artifacts and techniques that are produced and used, and a body of understanding, which supports, surrounds, and rationalizes the former. For technologies that are well established, an important part of the body of understanding supporting practice generally is grounded in the empirical experience of practitioners regarding what works and what doesn't, things that sometimes go wrong, reliable problem-solving methods, and so on. However, in recent times virtually all powerful technologies have had strong connections with particular fields of science. These connections, of course, are central to the discussion in this chapter.

There is a widespread belief that modern fields of technology are, in effect, applied science, in the sense that practice is directly drawn from scientific understanding, and that advancing technology essentially is a task of applying scientific knowledge to achieve better products and processes. This task requires scientific expertise but in most cases is relatively routine once the target is specified. Indeed in his *Capitalism, Socialism, and Democracy* (1942), Schumpeter argued that by the mid-twentieth century this was largely the case, and that the kind of competition among firms that had over the prior century made capitalism such a powerful engine of progress no longer was necessary. With strong science, technological advance could be planned. Schumpeter's views were in accord with those of many prominent scientists of his day, and today.

Yet, as I proposed earlier, careful studies of how technological advance actually proceeds in this modern era clearly show that the process defies planning in any detail, and competitive exploration of multiple paths remains an essential part of it. Technological advance remains an evolutionary process because, while strong science provides tools for problem solving, it seldom points directly to a viable solution. If anything, strong science increases the advantages to society of having many competent actors striving to improve the art.

Technological practice and understanding tend to coevolve, with advance of understanding sometimes leading to effective efforts to improve practice, and advance in practice sometimes leading to effective efforts to advance understanding. Thus the germ theory of disease developed by Pasteur and Koch, by pointing clearly to a certain kind of cause, led to successful efforts to get certain diseases (now known to be caused by external living agents) under control. Maxwell's theory of electromagnetism led to Hertz, Marconi, and radio. But in many cases advances in practice come first, and lead to efforts to understand scientifically. The discovery by Shockley and his team at Bell Laboratories that a semiconducting device they had built as an amplifier worked, but not in the way they had predicted, led him to understand that there was something wrong, or incomplete, about the theory in physics regarding the electrical characteristics of semiconductors, which in turn led to his own theoretical work, and a Nobel Prize. Rosenberg (1996) has argued that a number of the most challenging puzzles science has had to face have been made visible by or been created by new technologies, and the puzzles of why they work as they do.

Much of the development of modern science should be understood as the result of institutionalized responses to these challenges and opportunities. Quite often specialized fields of applied science or engineering developed out of the experience of more generally trained scientists working on the problems of a particular technology or industry. Thus the field of metallurgy came into existence as chemists worked on problems of quality control in the rapidly growing steel industry (Rosenberg 1998). As the industries producing chemical products expanded, chemical engineering developed as a field of research as well as an area for teaching. The physics of mechanical forces long had been useful for civil engineers designing buildings and bridges. But with the new physics of electricity and magnetism, a whole new set of science-based industries was launched. As complex electrical "systems" came into place, the new field of electrical engineering grew up. Later on, the invention of the modern computer would spawn the field of computer science. Stronger knowledge in chemistry and biology led to the development of a collection of specialized fields involved in agricultural research. Fields like pathology, immunology, and cardiology grew up for teaching and research at medical schools.

All of these fields of science are in Pasteur's Quadrant. Research done here often probes for quite deep understanding. But the fields as a whole, and broad programs of research in the fields, are dedicated quite explicitly to solving particular kinds of practical problems and advancing bodies of practical technology. I have developed this story at considerable length because in much of the writing on science and the institutions governing science, these applied sciences tend to be ignored. However, in the United States, Western Europe, and Japan, they account for the lion's share of the resources going into the support of science.

Popper (1959), Campbell (1974), Ziman (1978), Kitcher (1993), and other scholars of the advancement of science have stressed that science is a system of knowledge. The test that guides whether new reported findings or theories are accepted into the corpus of accepted knowledge is: Is it valid? Is it true? Popper and his followers have argued that there can be no firm, positive answer to these questions. The ability to stand up under attempts at refutation, or (probably more commonly) for apparent implications to hold up when they are explored, may be the best humans can hope for. But in any case, from this philosophical perspective the quest in science is for understanding in its own right. And there certainly is a lot of truth to this position as a characterization of the nature of scientific debates.

On the other hand, as Vincenti and others who have reflected on the similarities and differences between technological and scientific knowledge have argued, the central test for technological knowledge is: Is it useful? Technological knowledge is part of a cultural system that is concerned with achieving practical ends, rather than with knowledge for its own sake. The objective is to get something that works, or works better, and "understanding" is important only insofar as it helps in that effort.

However, the selection criteria for new science and for new technology cannot be kept sharply separate for sciences in Pasteur's Quadrant. In these fields, an important and often stringent testing ground for science is provided by those who think they see how it might be applied in practice. And failure to understand why something works is a strong motivation for scientific research.

By far the greater part of modern scientific research, including research done at universities, is in fields where practical application is central in the definition of a field. And, not surprisingly, these are the fields on which efforts to advance technology mostly draw. Two recent surveys (Klevorick et al. 1995; Cohen, Nelson, and Walsh 2002) have asked industrial R & D executives to identify the fields of academic research that contributed most to their successes in R & D. The fields they listed were exactly those discussed above.

The most recent of these studies (Cohen, Nelson, and Walsh) also asked about the kind of research output that was most valuable to industry, and the most important pathways through which industry gained access. Contrary to much of the current discussion, prototype technologies were not rated an important output of academic research for most industries (biotechnology is an exception), but rather general research results and research techniques (and even in biotechnology these kinds of research outputs were rated as useful much more often than prototypes). Relatedly, in most industries the respondents reported that the most frequent use of university research results was in problem solving in projects, rather than in triggering the initiation of projects.

In most industries the respondents said that the most important pathway through which people in industry learned of and gained access to what was coming out of public research was through publications and open conferences. Put another way, today industry gets most of its benefit from academic science through open channels. In their more narrowly focused but more detailed study of the pathways through which research results of the MIT departments of mechanical and electrical engineering get to industry, Agrawall and Henderson (2002) arrive at a similar conclusion.

I want to conclude this section by again stressing that in all the fields of technology that have been studied in any detail, including those where the background science is very strong, technological advance remains an evolutionary process. Strong science makes that process more powerful but does not reduce the great advantages of having multiple paths explored by a number of different actors. From this perspective, the fact that most of scientific knowledge is open, and available through open channels, is extremely important. This enables there to be, at any time, a significant number of individuals and firms who possess and can use the scientific knowledge they need to compete intelligently in this evolutionary process. The "communitarianism" of scientific knowledge is an important factor contributing to its productivity in downstream efforts to advance technology.

3. The Governance of Public Science

World War II and the period just after marked something of a watershed in broad public and political recognition of the important role that public science plays in technological progress, particularly in the United States and the United Kingdom. To be sure, much earlier visionaries, such as Francis Bacon, had argued for support of science as a means through which societies could progress materially. Scholars, like Don Price (1962), David Hart (1998), and David Guston (2000), have described the earlier history of debate about science policy in the United States. But it was the World War II experience, when government-supported and focused R & D was so successful, both in the development of weapons that won the war and in the development of medical capabilities that greatly reduced casualties both from wounds and from infectious diseases, compared with earlier wartime experiences, that gripped the public's attention. The title of the Vannevar Bush report (1945) advocating a major postwar program in the United States in support of science caught the spirit—*Science, the Endless Frontier.*

In both the United States and the United Kingdom, the discussion about the appropriate postwar role of public science was structured and constrained, for the most part, by recognition of the central role played by companies with their own R & D capabilities in the process of technological advance; the point of view was implicitly Schumpeterian. While there were exceptions, the discussion was not about contesting that role. Rather, the focus was on the system of public science, done in universities and public laboratories, that was separate from the corporate system but strongly complementary, and that needed public support. The argument of those who advocated stronger government support was that such support would make the overall system of innovation more powerful.

In both the United Kingdom and the United States, the debate about the governance of public science squared off along much the same lines. In Britain, J. D. Bernal, a distinguished physicist, and a socialist, argued (1939) for a government program in which the allocation of public funds to science would be strongly guided by the weighing of social needs, and the support program as a whole would be closely monitored by the government. To this point of view Michael Polanyi, a distinguished philosopher of science, took strong exception, advocating a largely self-governing "Republic of Science" (1967), which would be publicly funded, but in which the scientific community itself would set priorities and decide on what was good science.

In the United States, Bush's manifesto *Science, the Endless Frontier* argued strongly for a self-governing scientific community, but with national priorities playing a role in setting broad research directions, at least in certain areas. In particular, national security and health were singled out as areas in which the overall research budget and broad research priorities needed to be made through political and governmental processes. But given the funding within those broad areas, the scientists themselves were to have basic discretion for devising the research programs they thought most appropriate. Government nonscientists were not to meddle. Regarding the role of public science in supporting economic progress more broadly, Bush saw the government's role as supporting basic research, with the science system as self-governing, with respect to both identification of the broad fields of greatest promise and the details of allocating funds and carrying out research.

There is no question but that, like Polanyi's response to Bernal, Bush's articulation of a basically self-governing community of science was put forth in good part to counter, to block, proposals for a postwar publicly supported science system that would involve much more political and government control of the allocation of resources. U.S. Senator Harley Kilgore took much the same position as did J. D. Bernal in the United Kingdom. Bush believed that Kilgore's proposal would destroy the creativity and power of science, and that it would be far better to have the top scientists running the show.

There also is no question but that Polanyi and Bush felt it was of extreme importance that governments support fields like theoretical physics and mathematics, where perceptions of potential practical payoff had little to do with the way the fields unfolded, although they provided important knowledge and technique that helped to win the war.

Hence the emphasis on serendipity, and the unpredictability of areas of potential payoff. It is almost certain that both men knew well that much of scientific research was not of this kind but rather was in fields where perceptions of practical problems played a significant role in defining the broad agenda, if not the short-run priorities of resource allocation. However, the rhetoric of Polanyi and Bush obscured the fact that most of science is in Pasteur's Quadrant.

It is not surprising, therefore, that in both the United States and Great Britain it turned out that mission-oriented agencies became the primary government supporters of basic research. In the United States the Department of Defense funded basic work in computer and materials science and electrical engineering. The Atomic Energy Commission (later the Department of Energy) has had principal responsibility for funding high-energy physics. The National Institutes of Health (NIH) became the primary funder of university research in the biomedical sciences. The National Science Foundation, the only significant research-funding agency in the United States without a mission other than support of science, always has been a small supporter relative to the mission-oriented agencies. The lion's share of the research done in the United States, funded by government and undertaken in universities and public laboratories, is in fields in Pasteur's Quadrant.

This fact both solves the puzzle of why science has contributed so much to technological advance and enables one to understand better why Vannevar Bush (and most of his science-trained followers writing about science policy) had such strong faith in the ability of the scientific community to steer their efforts in socially productive directions. But this recognition also signals that the lines between basic science and applied science are fuzzy, not sharp. And it raises the question of where the publicly supported Republic of Science ought to leave off and the market begin. It is fair to say that for the most part the postwar debates were somewhat ad hoc about this. Thus Bush recognized a central role for market-organized and induced R & D, and saw public science as providing inputs to that market system, but also as being separate. However, he provided little in the way of coherent argument about where one stopped and the other began. Indeed, despite its obvious importance, outside of economics this question has aroused little analytical interest.

Economists have grappled with the question of the appropriate spheres of government activity in the science and technology system using two theoretical concepts: externalities and public goods. The externalities concept is about benefits (and costs) of private economic activity that those who make the relevant decisions do not see as benefits (or costs) to them. Here economists have highlighted the "spillovers" from industrial R & D, information and capabilities created by a firm's efforts to create better products and processes that it cannot fully capture, and hence that benefit other firms, including competitors. In general, the analyses by economists oriented toward the externalities from R & D have served not as a base for arguments for a domain of public science, but rather for arguments that industrial R & D in some instances should be encouraged by favorable tax treatment and perhaps subsidies of various kinds, to reduce private costs. Indeed, the policy discussion proceeding under the conception that research yields externalities naturally tends to be pulled toward devising policies that will make the results of R & D more proprietary, less public. An important part of the current policy discussion in fact is oriented in just this way.

The public good concept of economists is much more directly relevant to analysis of the appropriate domain of public science, or at least of the range where "communalism of knowledge" should apply. For our purposes here, the most salient aspect of the economists' public good concept is that a public good is "nonrivalrous in use." Unlike a standard economic good, like a peanut butter sandwich, which either you or I can eat but not both (although we can split it), a public good can be used by all of us at the same time without eroding the quality for any of us.

Knowledge is a canonical case of something that is nonrivalrous in use in this sense, and this is not a proposition conjured up by economists. The notion that I can tell you what I know, and then you will know it and I will too, almost surely has been widely understood by sophisticated persons for a long time. There is no "tragedy of the commons" for a pure public good like knowledge. And to deny access to it, or to ration it, can result in those denied doing far less well than they could if they had access. In the case in point, if access to certain bodies of scientific knowledge or technique were withheld from certain researchers, they might be effectively barred from doing productive R & D in a field.

Now the fact that something is nonrivalrous in use does not mean that its use cannot be restricted. However, until relatively recently it was broadly assumed that it was difficult to restrict access to scientific knowledge. Certainly scientific knowledge could not be patented. This effectively took science outside the domain where market incentives could work. Indeed the presumption that the returns to scientific research could not be appropriated was a central part of the argument for why public funding was necessary.

However, over the past quarter century two key developments have challenged this view of basic science. First, the courts have ruled that at least some of the results of basic research can be patented. And second, about the same time that the implications of these rulings were becoming evident, Congress passed the Bayh-Dole Act of 1980, which strongly encouraged universities to take out patents on their research results where they could, on the basis of a (not well supported) argument that this would help firms that could make practical use of the results do so under a protective license. (For a detailed account, see Eisenberg 1996.) The first of these developments significantly increased the incentives for for-profit firms to engage in the areas of basic research where the results can be patented, and to try to make a business of licensing patented research results to other firms that can make use of them. The second has brought about profound changes in the way universities give access to their research results. As a result, important areas of science are now much more under the sway of market mechanisms than used to be the case. And in particular, in some important fields of science important bodies of scientific understanding and technique now are private property rather than part of the commons.

A widespread reaction has been, "So what is the problem with that?" There is a strong presumption these days that if market organization can and will do a job, that obviously is a good thing. From this point of view, the main argument that needs to be made for government support of basic research is that the long-run benefits to society are high, and that for-profit firms have little incentive to do much of it because of the difficulties in establishing property rights, as well as the long time lags and great uncertainties involved in moving from research results to commercial product. If these barriers to market organization are lowered for some reason, let the market move in.

I note that knowledge of an effective product design or a production process, what customarily is considered as technological knowledge, shares with scientific knowledge the property of being nonrivalrous in use. Yet society relies largely on the market to induce R & D aimed at creating new products and production processes, and there is little dispute that granting patents on product and process inventions is reasonable social and economic policy. So why not allow patents on the stuff of basic science, if that will induce the market to move in?

My response is that the outputs of scientific research almost never themselves are final products, or even close, but have their principal use in further research, some to advance the science further, some to follow leads that may enable a useful product or process to be found and developed. But in both cases, there is considerable uncertainty about the best paths to pursue. Progress calls for exploration of a number of paths. My concern is not with patents on the outputs of scientific research that are directly useful or close to that, so long as the scope of the patent is limited to that particular use. It is about not hindering the ability of the scientific community, both that part interested in advancing the science further and that part interested in trying to use knowledge in the search for useful products, to work freely with and from new scientific findings.

I do not know of a field of science in which knowledge has increased cumulatively and, through cumulative advance, dramatically, that has not been basically open. It is easy to argue that scientists never have fully followed the canons of science identified and laid out by Robert Merton: universalism, communitarianism, disinterestedness, and organized skepticism. Scientists are well known to keep their work secret until they are ready to publish. There certainly is a lot of self-interest, opportunism, hostility, and downright deviousness and lying that one observes in the histories of the progressive sciences. A scientific paradigm held by the elite in a field can hold intellectual tyranny. It is valuable to bring new organizations into the basic research scene, and in some cases for-profit business firms have explored paths that the academic community snubbed.

But on the other hand, a careful reading of important scientific controversies, for example the argument about the nature of combustion at the start of the nineteenth century, or the nature of the genetic code, or whether the expansion of the universe is decelerating or accelerating, shows the importance and the power of a public science system in which, by and large, all participants have access to much the same set of facts, and to the debates about whether new proposed facts or theories arc valid, are open to all working in a field. One cannot come away from reading Horace Judson's *The Eighth Day of Creation* (1996), a history of the development of molecular biology as a field of science, without respecting the power of open science to progress.

This is equally true for sciences that are strongly in Pasteur's Quadrant. Roy Porter's history of medical knowledge and practice, *The Greatest Benefit to Mankind* (1997), gives case after case when progress was made through a system in which researchers were free to try to replicate or refute the arguments and findings of others.

While my argument above has focused on the advantages of an open science for the advancement of science, much of my discussion in Section 2 was concerned with developing a case for why open science is important to technological progress. These arguments of course are mutually reinforcing. Keeping the body of scientific knowledge largely open for all to use, in the attempts to advance science and in the attempts to advance technology, is in my view an extremely important matter. Its importance is not recognized adequately in the current discussions.

4. The Importance of Protecting the Scientific Commons

The major expansion of patents into what used to be the realm of science is well documented. I am persuaded that there is enough of a potential problem here to call the alarm. However, I confess that the evidence that there already is a problem—that access to scientific research results having high promise of enabling solutions of important practical problems is being sharply restricted by patent holders—presently is very limited. The most detailed study that has been done of this is by Walsh, Arora, and Cohen (2002). (Their study involved interviews with a number of researchers in the biomedical field, asking about whether their research had been hindered by patent rights that blocked access to certain paths they wanted to explore.)

Scholars studying this potential problem have identified at least two different kinds of situations in which the presence of patents can hinder research. (For a general discussion, see Merges and Nelson 1990.) One of these is the problem caused by patents on "research tools" (see National Research Council 1997), where research techniques of widespread use in a field, materials that are inputs to a wide range of research endeavors, or key pathways for research (like the use of a particular receptor), are patented, and the patent holder aggressively prosecutes unlicensed use or reserves exclusive rights to further research using the tool. The second, highlighted recently by Heller and Eisenberg (1998) is focused on contexts where development of or advance toward a useful product or technique may involve transgressing on several patents held by different parties.

The latter problem, that of the need to assemble a large number of permissions or licenses before being able to go forward, was found by the Walsh, Arora, Cohen interviews and case studies not to be particularly important as of yet. Regarding research tools, a number of the more important general-purpose ones are available to all who will pay the price, and while in some cases there were complaints about the price, at least they were available.

On the other hand, the study did identify a number of instances in which the holder of a patent on an input or a pathway (for example, a receptor) that was important in a particular field of exploration did not widely license, and in some cases sought to preserve a monopoly on use rights. It is clear that in a number of the cases, the patented finding had been achieved through research at least partially funded by the government. This policy well may have been reasonable from the point of view of the patent holders. But the burden of this chapter is that it is not good from the point of view of society, seeking to maximize the benefits of publicly funded research.

The authors of the study take a cautious position regarding the implications of their findings. I find them sufficient evidence to indicate that there is a real problem here, or there will be soon, and it is time to think about what can be done to contain it.

There are two broad policy arenas that bear on this issue, to which I want to call attention here. One is intellectual property rights law. The other is the policies of universities and public laboratories regarding their research findings, and government policy regarding the university research it funds. My discussion below is oriented to what is needed, in my view at least, to preserve an appropriately wide area of public scientific knowledge.

4.1. Can We Protect the Republic of Science through Patent Law?

I find that many people are puzzled when they learn that patents are being taken out on genes or gene codes, or more generally are intruding into the realm of science. There is a widespread belief that scientific facts or principles or natural phenomena are not patentable. Indeed, the courts have endorsed this position strongly, as a general philosophical principle.

But the problem is that the lines between natural substances and principles and man-made ones are blurry, not sharp. Nearly a century ago a landmark patent-law case was concerned with whether purified human adrenalin was a natural substance and hence not patentable (although the process for purification certainly was patentable) or whether the fact that adrenalin never was pure in its natural state meant that the purified substance was man-made and hence patentable. The decision was the latter, and while it can be argued that the decision was unfortunate, one certainly can see the logic supporting it. In any case, the precedent set in the case has held through the years (*Parke-Davis & Co. v. H. K. Mulford & Co.*, 1911). Recent patents on purified proteins and isolated genes and receptors are couched in terms that highlight something that man has created or modified from its natural state.

A recent article by Bar-Shalom and Cook-Deegan (2002) is concerned with the consequences of a patent granted on a monoclonal antibody (antibodies are natural substances, but particular antibodies cloned by a particular process have been judged to be not natural) that binds to a particular antigen (a natural substance) on the outer surface of stem cells, and hence is capable of recognizing such cells and serving as a basis for processes that would isolate stem cells. The patent also claimed "other antibodies" that can recognize and pick out that antigen. The latter part of the claim in effect establishes ownership of the antigen. The authors argue, correctly in my view, that the inclusion in the patent claims of all "other antibodies" meant that the patent was unreasonably broad and should have been pruned back by the patent office and the courts. However, one can clearly see the blurry lines here between the natural and the artificial. And the patentee could well argue that the "invention" was a method of recognizing a particular antigen (such a method would seem to fall within the bounds of patentability) and the particular antibody actually used was just an exemplar. In the case in question this patent was licensed exclusively to a particular company and, in turn, was later used effectively to close down another company that had achieved a process capable of isolating stem cells, earlier than the licensee, using a method that was judged to infringe.

Putting the issue of undue patent scope aside for the moment, the problem of determining the patentability of a research output whose future use is largely in further research seems almost inevitable for research in Pasteur's Quadrant, for obvious reasons. The original work in question was done by an oncologist at Johns Hopkins University. The research clearly was fundamental and at the same time was aiming for understandings and techniques that would be useful in dealing with cancer.

The problem becomes even more complicated in scientific fields that are concerned with advancing understandings of technologies, fields like computer science and aeronautical engineering. Thus Walter Vincenti (1990) describes at some length the research done at Stanford during the 1920s that aimed to develop good engineering principles (reliable if rough "laws") that would guide the design of aircraft propellers. The results of this research were laid open to the general aviation design community and were not patented. But had the researchers had the motivation, they probably could have posed their results in terms of processes useful in propeller design, which might have been patentable then and likely would be today. A significant portion of the work within the modern field of computer science is concerned with developing concepts and principles that can help improve design. Up until recently, at least, little of this work seems to have been patented, but portions of it clearly could be.

In each of these cases, the research outputs were (are) at once important inputs to a flow of future research and useful inputs for those who are focused on solving practical problems. In much of this chapter I have been arguing that, because of the latter, there are major general economic advantages if those understandings and techniques are part of the general tool kit available to all those working to advance practice in the area. The obvious objection is that the ability of the discoverer or developer of these understandings and techniques to control their use is an important incentive for the research that creates them. I would reply that, at least in the case of research at universities, funded by government grants, this usually is not the case. I will discuss university policy shortly.

But to return to the present discussion, I am not optimistic about how much of the problem can be dealt with by patent law. The focus here is on patent law on research outputs that provide tools for advancing a science or technology, as contrasted with a final product or process per se. Here one can urge several things of the patent office and the courts. But the problem of innately blurry lines will remain.

First, one can urge that more care be taken not to grant patents on discoveries that largely are of natural phenomena, by requiring a strong case that the subject matter of the patent application or patent is "artificial," and by limiting the scope of the patent to elements that are artificial (more on the patent scope problem shortly). Demaine and Fellmeth (2003) make a similar argument, that patents should be allowed only on outputs of research that are a "substantial transformation" from the natural. The lines here are blurry. But the slope clearly is slippery, and a strong argument can be made that the dividing line has been let slip too far and leaning hard in the other direction is warranted. In the case of purified natural substances, this would call for a greater proclivity to limit the patent to the process and not allow the purified product per se to be patented.

Second, one can urge a relatively strict interpretation of the meaning of "utility" or usefulness. This issue is particularly important for patent applications and patents that argue very broadly that the research result in question can be useful in efforts to achieve something obviously useful—a case for usefulness once removed. But the problem here is that the direct usefulness then is as an input or a focus of research, and this is the kind of generic knowledge and capability I have been arguing is important to keep open and in the public domain. A stricter interpretation would require a more compelling demonstration of significant progress toward a particular practical solution than seems presently required, and, particularly if combined with the suggestion below about reining in patent scope, would be a major contribution to protecting the commons.

Third, there is the issue of the allowed patent scope. There is a strong tendency of patent applicants to claim practice far wider than they actually have achieved. The description above of a claim covering "all antibodies" that identify a particular substance is a case in point. While there are obvious advantages to the patentee of being able to control a wide range of possible substitutes to what has actually been achieved, there are great advantages to society as a whole of not allowing such broad blocking of potential competitive efforts. I believe that getting the patent office and the courts to understand the real economic costs of granting patents that are too broad is of the highest priority.

I have argued the special importance of not allowing patents to interfere with broad participation in research going on in a field. One way to further this objective would be to build some kind of an explicit research exemption into patent law, analogous to the fair use exemptions in copyright law. Indeed there is a long history of statements by judges to the effect that use in pure research is not a violation of a patent. Universities clearly have been clinging to this theory to justify their freedom of research.

A recent decision of the Court of Appeals for the Federal Circuit (*Madey v. Duke University*, October 2002) has changed the situation. In a ruling on an infringement suit against Duke, the court argued that doing research, basic or applied, was part of the central business of a university, and that the university benefited in terms of funding as well as prestige from the research it did. Thus university interests, not simply scientific curiosity, were at stake in the research. Therefore, it was quite reasonable under the law for a patent holder to require that the university take out a license before using patented material in research. After this ruling, it is highly likely that patent holders will act more aggressively when they believe that university researchers may be infringing on their patents. While there is a chance that the Supreme Court will reverse, that is not a good bet. It now looks as if an exemption for use in basic research will come into place only if there is new law.

However, under current university policies, a case for such new law is not easy to make. Among other things, there clearly is the problem of how to delineate basic research. As I have been highlighting, much of university research is in Pasteur's Quadrant, where in many cases there are practical objectives as well as the goal of advancing basic understanding. And in recent years universities have been patenting their research results.

Discussions with industry executives suggest that, until recently, industry often gave university researchers a de facto research exemption. Now they often are very reluctant to do so. In many cases they see university researchers as direct competitors to their own research efforts aimed to achieve a practical result that is patentable. And they feel themselves burdened by the requirement to take out licenses to use university research results that are patented, and see no reason why they shouldn't make the same demands on universities. In my view, the obstacles to a serious research exemption are largely the result of university policies.

Of the several proposals for a research exemption that have circulated recently, I find one of the most interesting to be that put forth by Rochelle Dreyfuss (2004). In what follows, I amend it slightly. Under the Dreyfuss proposal, a university or nonprofit research organization (under one version of her proposal, any research organization) would be immune from prosecution for using patented materials in research if (1) those materials were not available on reasonable terms (this is my amendment), and (2) if the university or other research organization agreed not to patent anything that came out of the research (or if they did patent, to allow use on a nonexclusive royalty-free basis; my amendment). Certainly there could be some difficulty in determining, if the matter were brought up, whether the patented material was available at reasonable terms, or just what "reasonable" means, but in many of the most problematic cases this proposal is designed to fix, the answer is that they are not available at all. In some cases it would not be easy to determine whether a patent emanated from a particular research project or from some other activity. But these problems do not seem unusually difficult compared with other matters often litigated. And it is likely that, for the most part, if a research organization proceeded under this law, there wouldn't be much litigation and there would be much reduced fear of such.

After the Duke decision, the road to a university research exemption almost surely must go through Congress. The advantage of a proposal like that made by Dreyfuss is that it would trade open access to research results for university researchers for agreement by university researchers not themselves to add to the problem of patents in science. The principal obstacle to such a deal, I believe, is the universities themselves.

4.2. Will Universities Defend the Scientific Commons?

I believe the key to ensuring that a large portion of what comes out of future scientific research will be placed in the commons is staunch defense of the commons by universities. Universities almost certainly will continue to do the bulk of basic scientific research. If they have policies of laying their research results largely open, most of science will continue to be in the commons. However, universities are not in general supporting the idea of a scientific commons, except in terms of their own rights to do research. In the era since Bayh-Dole, universities have become a major part of the problem, avidly defending their rights to patent their research results and license as they choose.

Derek Bok (2003) has argued persuasively that the strong interest of universities in patenting is part and parcel of trends that have led universities to embrace commercial activities in a variety of areas, in athletics, for example, as well as science. Earlier I proposed that Bayh-Dole, and the enhanced interest in universities for patenting, should be regarded as one aspect of a broad, increased public acceptance of the importance of intellectual property rights.

But these factors do not make the problem any less significant, only harder to deal with.

The current zeal of universities for patenting represents a major shift from the universities' traditional support of open science. This does not mean that traditionally university research was largely distanced from practical applications. There long have been many university research programs designed to contribute to economic development (see Rosenberg and Nelson 1994). Since the late nineteenth century, university research has played a major role in the development of American agricultural technology. The hybrid seed revolution that was key to the dramatic increases in productivity achieved during the half century after 1930 in corn and other grain production was made possible by work at agricultural experimentation stations that explored basic concepts and techniques of hybridization. These basic techniques were made public knowledge. Universities also made available on generous terms the pure lines of seeds they developed, to serve as the basis for commercial efforts to design and produce hybrids. University-based research on plant nutrition and plant diseases and pests helped companies identify and design effective fertilizers and insecticides. Very little of this university research was patented.

American engineering schools and departments have had a long tradition of doing research to help industry. As noted earlier, chemical and electrical engineering were developed as scientific fields largely within universities. Earlier I recounted Stanford's role in developing principles of propeller design. Several universities played key roles in developing the early electronic computers. There was some patenting of devices that came out of university engineering research, but there was also an apparent continuing commitment to contribute to the advance of basic engineering understanding as the common property of the professions.

American medical schools also long have been contributors to technical advance in medicine and the enhanced ability of doctors to deal with human illness. Medical schools occasionally have been the sources of particular new medical devices and new pharmaceuticals, although this was not common prior to the rise of biotechnology and modern electronics. And while patents were sometimes taken out on particular products (streptomycin, identified by a team led by a Rutgers University scientist, is a good example), by and large until the 1980s there was little patenting, and many medical schools had an articulated policy of dedicating research results to the public commons.

The sea change, or the schizophrenia, began to emerge as a result of several developments (see Mowery et al. 2001). First, during the 1970s and 1980s there was a broad general ideological change in the United States in attitudes toward patents, from a general hostility in the 1930s and the early postwar years to a belief that patents were almost always necessary to stimulate invention and innovation. Actually, several empirical studies provide evidence that in many industries patents are relatively unimportant as a stimulus to R & D (see Cohen, Nelson, and Walsh 2000). However, much of the argument for Bayh-Dole concentrated on pharmaceuticals, and patent protection was and continues to be important for pharmaceuticals companies.

Second, there was the rise of molecular biology as a field of science and the development of the principal techniques of biotechnology, which for a variety of reasons made university biomedical research a much more likely locus of work leading to pharmaceuticals or potential pharmaceuticals, and to techniques that could be used in such work. Third, as noted, several key court decisions made many of these developments patentable. The apparent possibility of substantial income from university research clearly attracted some university officials, and university scientists. The patenting of the Cohen-Boyer gene-splicing process, and the quick flow of substantial revenues to the two universities that held the rights, provided a strong signal that there now was substantial money that could be brought in from licensing university inventions.

The Cohen-Boyer patent was granted prior to the passage of Bayh-Dole. The Bayh-Dole Act legitimated, even warranted, university patenting. And universities have not been slow in adopting policies in which patenting anything that can be patented is the rule.

In my view, there is nothing wrong per se with universities patenting what they can from their research output. In some cases such patenting may actually facilitate technology transfer, although in many cases it is a good bet that technological transfer is not enhanced but instead the university is simply earning money from what it used to make available for free (see the cases studies in Colyvas et al. 2002). The cases that worry me are ones in which the university is licensing exclusively or narrowly a development that is potentially of wide use, or it is limiting to one or a few companies the right to take a particular development further in circumstances where there still is sufficient uncertainty regarding how best to proceed, which makes participation by a number of companies in that endeavor socially desirable. The argument that unless an exclusive license is given no one will try to advance seems particularly dubious for research tools of wide application, and for findings that appear to open up possibilities for new research attacks on diseases where a successful remedy clearly would find a large market. The Cohen-Boyer patent was licensed to all comers, and there were plenty of them. The report by Colyvas et al. (2002) gives several examples showing the willingness of pharmaceuticals companies to work from university research findings that appeared to point toward promising treatments, without receiving an exclusive license.

I do not see a major problem if access to certain parts of the commons requires a small fee. What I want is for universities to recognize that, for research results of these sorts, if they patent them, they have an obligation to license them to all who want to use them, at reasonable fees. (Similarly, with respect to "research tools" created by industry research and patented, my difficulty is not so much with those where use is open but users are charged a fee, provided the fee is not too high; it is with those that are not made widely available.) Bok

(2003, p. 143), recognizing this same problem, proposes that the major universities come to an agreement to license widely and easily, not exclusively, research results that basically are inputs to further research. However, a policy of open licensing of research results of certain kinds is not likely to be adopted voluntarily by universities, because this practice will not always be seen as maximizing expected revenues from intellectual property. And that is what many universities are aiming for now.

The recent report signed jointly by a number of university presidents and chancellors, and foundation presidents (Atkinson et al. 2003) shows the tension here. The authors (their focus is the field of agricultural research) clearly recognize the problem that can be and has been caused by university patents that block or cause high transaction costs for downstream research to advance agricultural technologies, and announce the establishment of a "Public Sector Intellectual Property Resource for Agriculture," which would make access easier. But the authors stop far short of agreeing to a general policy of open licensing of university research results that set the stage for downstream applied R & D.

Universities will not give up the right to earn as much as they can from the patents they hold unless public policy pushes them hard in that direction. I see the key in reforming Bayh-Dole. The objective here, it seems to me, is not to eliminate university patenting but to establish a presumption that university research results, patented or not, should as a general rule be made available to all who want to use them, at very low transaction costs and reasonable financial costs. This would not be to foreclose exclusive or narrow licensing in those circumstances where that is necessary to gain effective technology transfer. Rather, it would be to establish the presumption that such cases are the exception rather than the rule.

There is nothing in Bayh-Dole that explicitly encourages exclusive or narrow licensing, but nothing discourages it either, and the rhetoric associated with the legislation pushed the theory that, generally, dedicating research results to the public commons did not encourage use. There is nothing in the legislation that says universities should use their patenting and licensing power to maximize university income, but there is little in the language that discourages that. What is needed, I believe, is language that recognizes much better than the current language does that much of what comes out of university research is most effectively disseminated to users if placed in the public domain, and that exclusive or restricted licensing may deter widespread use, at considerable economic and social cost.

The act as currently written does include the statement that the objective of the act is "to ensure that inventions made by nonprofit organizations . . . are used in a manner to promote free competition and enterprise without unduly encumbering future research and discovery." However, apparently presently this clause has no teeth. I propose that this statement of objective be highlighted, and supplemented by the proposition that in general this objective calls for licensing that will achieve the widest possible use. Exclusive or narrow licensing by a university should require an explicit rationale. The willingness of firms to take up university research results without an exclusive license should be regarded as evidence that an exclusive license is not appropriate.

Such language would encourage universities to move in the right direction on their own, by strengthening the hand of those at universities who believe that universities should be contributing to the scientific and technological commons. At the present time, such university researchers and administrators seem to be bucking the law as well as internal interests. It also would provide legitimacy to government agencies funding university research to press for licensing that allows broad access. The recent tussle between the National Institutes of Health and the University of Wisconsin regarding stem cell patents illustrates the value of such an amended Bayh-Dole. In this case, the university originally had in mind arranging an exclusive license for a firm, and that would have been very profitable for the university. The NIH in effect indicated that unless the university licensed widely and liberally, it would consider the university's licensing policies when evaluating future research proposals. The university then went along with the license policies advocated by NIH. Several legal scholars have proposed that, under the current law, the NIH in this case was skating on thin ice. There is nothing in the law that explicitly calls for open licensing. And had the NIH been forced to follow its bark with a bite, it might well have been taken to court.

Or consider how the case analyzed by Bar-Shalom and Cook-Deegan (discussed in Section 4.1) might have gone, had the amendment I am proposing been in place. It is likely that the NIH recognized quite early in the game the value of allowing more than one company to work with the new technique for identifying stem cells, and of allowing widespread research use, and would have balked at the exclusive license that was given had it felt itself on a firm footing for doing so. Later the NIH was asked to open use of the patented technique under the "march in" provisions of Bayh-Dole, but did not do so because, according to the way the legislation is written, such a step clearly is exceptional. It would have been in a far stronger position to accede to the request to open up use if the language I propose were in the legislation.

Many university administrators and researchers certainly would resist such an amendment, on the grounds that it would diminish their ability to maximize financial returns from their patent portfolio. As I observed above, the principal support for university patenting with freedom to license as they wish now comes from universities and is based on their perception of their own financial interests; the case for it on grounds that this facilitates technology transfer no longer is credible. If pressed hard, the case that the current policy is against the public interest should carry the day. And it is interesting that, if universities were so constrained in their licensing policies, that might dampen their resistance to a research exemption of the sort proposed by Dreyfuss, since the financial costs to them of agreeing not to patent or not to charge for licenses would be diminished.

My message in this chapter is that our scientific commons is in danger, the costs of having it erode further are likely to be high, and we ought to move to protect it. What I have proposed is a strategy for protecting the commons.

The case of the encroachment of market elements into the scientific commons is important in its own right, but it also serves to highlight, by making concrete, several of the basic themes I have been pressing over the course of this book. One is the importance of understanding technological advance as an evolutionary process. This perspective calls attention to the importance of having a variety of competitive sources of new technology, and puts a spotlight on the social and economic costs of restricting access to the scientific knowledge that is necessary for productive research and problem solving in a field.

A second theme is the importance of institutional structures, both in supporting and molding the advance of technology, and in enabling its fruitful use, and the variety of institutional forms we use for organizing and governing economic activity. In many cases, including the one considered in this chapter, nonmarket institutions have evolved and proved effective.

A third is the weakness of our ability to understand institutions and how they work, much less to design them effectively, as compared with our understanding of physical technologies. This weakness in our knowledge leaves institutional change vulnerable to fads and ideologies, and, at the present time, to undiscriminating belief in the efficacy of market organization.

If I were asked to put one item at the top of the agenda for growth theory that I laid out in Chapter 1, it would be study of economic institutions: their variety, how they work, and how they evolve. This is where I now am concentrating my own efforts. I invite others to join me.

REFERENCES

INDEX

References

Abernathy, William, and James M. Utterback (1975). "A Dynamic Model of Process and Product Innovation." *Omega* 3 (6): 639–656.

Abramovitz, M. (1952). "Economics of Growth." In B. Haley, ed., *A Survey of Contemporary Economics*, vol. 2, 132–178. Homewood, IL: Published for the American Economic Association by Richard D. Irwin, Inc.

—— (1956). "Resource and Output Trends in the United States since 1870." *American Economic Review* 46 (May): 5–23.

—— (1986). "Catching Up, Forging Ahead, and Falling Behind." *Journal of Economic History* 46 (2): 385–406.

—— (1989). *Thinking about Growth*. Cambridge: Cambridge University Press.

Abramovitz, M., and P. David (1994). *Convergence and Deferred Catch Up*. Center for Economic Policy Research Publication 401 (Aug.), Stanford University.

Aghion, P., and P. Howitt (1990). "A Model of Growth through Creative Destruction." *Econometrica* 60: 323–351.

Agrawall, A., and R. Henderson (2002). "Putting Patents in Context: Exploring Knowledge Transfer at MIT." *Management Science* 48: 44–60.

Alchian, A., and H. Demsetz (1973). "The Property Rights Paradigm." *Journal of Economic History* 33: 16–27.

Aldrich, Howard (1979). *Organizations and Environments*. Englewood Cliffs, NJ: Prentice Hall.

Allen, R. C. (1987). "Collective Invention." *Journal of Economic Behavior and Organization* 4: 1–24.

Amsden, A. (1989). *Asia's Next Giant: South Korea and Late Industrialization*. New York: Oxford University Press.

Anderson, Esben (1994). *Evolutionary Economics*. London: Pinter.

Anderson, Philip W., Kenneth J. Arrow, and David Pines, eds. (1988). *The Economy as an Evolving Complex System*. Redwood City, CA: Addison-Wesley Publishing Company.

Aoki, Masahiko (1990). "Towards an Economic Model of the Japanese Firm." *Journal of Economic Literature* 28 (Mar.): 1–27.

Arora, A., and A. Gambardella (1994). "The Changing Technology of Technological Change: General and Abstract Knowledge and the Division of Innovative Labor." *Research Policy* 23: 523–532.

Arthur, W. Brian (1988a). "Competing Technologies: An Overview." In G. Dosi et al., eds., *Technical Change and Economic Theory*, 590–607. London: Pinter.

——— (1988b). "Self-Reinforcing Mechanisms in Economics." In Philip W. Anderson, Kenneth J. Arrow, and David Pines, eds., *The Economy as an Evolving Complex System*, 9–31. Redwood City, CA: Addison-Wesley.

Atkinson, R., et al. (2003). "Public Sector Collaboration for Agricultural Management." *Science* 301 (July 11): 174–175.

Axelrod, R. (1997). *The Complexity of Cooperation*. Princeton: Princeton University Press.

Bacon, R., and W. Eltis (1976). *Britain's Economic Problem: Too Few Producers*. London: Macmillan.

Barkow, J. H., L. Cosmides, and J. Tooby, eds. (1992). *The Adapted Mind: Evolutionary Psychology and the Generation of Culture*. New York: Oxford University Press.

Bar-Shalom, A., and R. Cook-Deegan (2002). "Patents and Innovation in Cancer Therapeutics: Lessons from CellPro." *The Milbank Quarterly* 80 (Dec.): 637–676.

Basalla, George (1988). *The Evolution of Technology*. Cambridge: Cambridge University Press.

Baum, Joel A. C., and Jitendra V. Singh (1994). *Evolutionary Dynamics of Organizations*. New York: Oxford University Press.

Baumol, W. (1967). "Macroeconomics of Unbalanced Growth: The Anatomy of the Urban Crisis." *American Economic Review* 57 (June).

——— (1986). "Productivity Growth, Convergence and Welfare: What the Long-Run Data Show." *American Economic Review* 76 (Dec.): 1072–1085.

Baumol, W., R. Nelson, and E. Wolff (1994). *Convergence of Productivity*. Oxford: Oxford University Press.

Bell, D. (1960). *The End of Ideology*. Cambridge, MA: Harvard University Press.

Bernal, J. D. (1939). *The Social Functions of Science*. London: Routledge and Kegan Paul.

Bijker, Wiebe (1995). *Of Bicycles, Bakelites, and Bulbs*. Cambridge, MA: MIT Press.

Bijker, Wiebe E., Thomas P. Hughes, and Trevor J. Pinch (1987). *The Social Construction of Technological Systems*. Cambridge, MA: MIT Press.

Blyth, M. (2002). *Great Transformations: Economic Ideas and Institutional Change in the Twentieth Century*. New York: Cambridge University Press.

Bok, D. (2003). *Universities and the Marketplace.* Princeton: Princeton University Press.

Boyd, Robert, and Peter J. Richerson (1985). *Culture and the Evolutionary Process.* Chicago: University of Chicago Press.

Bresnahan, T., and M. Trajtenberg (1995). "General Purpose Technologies: Engines of Growth." *Journal of Econometrics* 65: 93–108.

Bucciarelli, L. (1994). *Designing Engineers.* Cambridge, MA: MIT Press.

Burgelman, R. (1994). "Fading Memories." *Administrative Sciences Quarterly* 39: 24–56.

Bush, V. (1945). *Science, the Endless Frontier.* Washington, DC: National Science Foundation.

Campbell, Donald (1960). "Blind Variation and Selective Retention in Creative Thought as in Other Knowledge Processes." *Psychological Review* 67: 380–400.

———— (1965). "Variation and Selective Retention in Socio-Cultural Evolution." In H. R. Barringer, G. I. Blakston, and R. W. Mack, eds., *Social Change in Developing Areas: A Reinterpretation of Evolutionary Theory.* Cambridge: Shenkman.

———— (1974). "Evolutionary Epistemology." In P. A. Schilpp, ed., *The Philosophy of Karl Popper,* 413–463. LaSalle, IL: Open Court.

Casella, Alessandra, and Bruno S. Frey (1992). "Federalism and Clubs: Towards an Economic Theory of Overlapping Political Jurisdictions." *European Economic Review* 36 (2–3): 639–646.

Cavalli-Sforza, Luigi, and Marcus Feldman (1981). *Cultural Transmission and Evolution: A Quantitative Approach.* Princeton: Princeton University Press.

Chandler, Alfred D. (1962). *Strategy and Structure: Chapters in the History of Industrial Enterprise.* Cambridge, MA: Harvard University Press.

———— (1977). *The Visible Hand: The Managerial Revolution in American Business.* Cambridge, MA: Harvard University Press.

———— (1990). *Scale and Scope: The Dynamics of Industrial Capitalism.* Cambridge, MA: Harvard University Press.

Chiaromonte, Francesca, and Giovanni Dosi (1993). "Heterogeneity, Competition, and Macroeconomic Dynamics." *Structural Change and Economic Dynamics* 4: 39–63.

Chomsky, N. (1988). *Language and Problems of Knowledge: The Managua Lectures.* Cambridge, MA: MIT Press.

Christensen, Clayton, and Richard Rosenbloom (1995). "Explaining the Attacker's Advantage: Technological Paradigms, Organizational Dynamics, and the Value Network." *Research Policy* 24: 233–257.

Clark, A. (1997). *Being There: Putting Brain, Body, and World Together Again.* Cambridge, MA: MIT Press.

Clark, Norman, and Calestous Juma (1987). *Long Run Economics: An Evolutionary Approach to Economic Growth.* London: Pinter.

Coase, R. (1937). "The Nature of the Firm." *Economica* 4: 386–405.

—— (1960). "The Problem of Social Cost." *Journal of Law and Economics* 3: 1–44.

Cohen, Wesley M., and Daniel A. Levinthal (1989). "Innovation and Learning: The Two Faces of R & D." *Economic Journal* 99 (Sept.): 569–596.

Cohen, W., R. Nelson, and J. Walsh (2000). "Patenting Their Intellectual Assets: Appropriability Conditions and Why U.S. Manufacturing Firms Patent or Not." National Bureau of Economic Research Working Paper 7522, Boston.

—— (2002). "Links and Impacts: The Influence of Public Research on Industrial R and D." *Management Science* 48: 1–23.

Cole, R., and W. R. Scott, eds. (2000). *The Quality Movement and Organization Theory.* Thousand Oaks, CA: Sage.

Colyvas, J., et al. (2002). "How Do University Inventions Get Into Practice?" *Management Science* 48: 61–72.

Commons, J. (1924). *Legal Foundations of Capitalism.* New York: Macmillan.

—— (1934). *Institutional Economics.* Madison: University of Wisconsin Press.

Conlisk, John (1989). "An Aggregate Model of Technical Change." *Quarterly Journal of Economics* 104 (4): 787–821.

Constant, E. W. (1980). *The Origins of the Turbojet Revolution.* Baltimore: Johns Hopkins University Press.

Cool, Karel, and Dan Schendel (1988). "Performance Differences among Strategic Group Members." *Strategic Management Journal* 9 (3): 207–223.

Cooter, Robert D., and Daniel L. Rubinfeld (1989). "Economic Analysis of Legal Disputes and Their Resolution." *Journal of Economic Literature* 27 (3): 1067–1097.

Cowan, R., and D. Foray (1997). "The Economics of Codification and the Diffusion of Knowledge." *Research Policy* 26: 595–622.

Crawford, S., and E. Ostrom (1995). "A Grammar of Institutions." *American Political Science Review* 89: 582–600.

Crosland, C. A. R. (1956). *The Future of Socialism.* London: Jonathan Cape.

Cuban, L. (1986). *Teachers and Machines: The Classroom Use of Technology since 1920.* New York: Teachers College Press.

Cyert, R., and J. March (1963). *A Behavioral Theory of the Firm.* Englewood Cliffs, NJ: Prentice Hall.

Dahl, R., and C. E. Lindblom (1953). *Politics, Economics, and Welfare.* New York: Harper and Brothers.

Dasgupta, P., and P. David (1994). "Towards a New Economics of Science." *Research Policy* 23: 487–522.

David, P. (1985). "Clio and the Economics of QWERTY." *American Economic Review Papers and Proceedings* 75 (2): 332–337.

—— (1991). "Computer and Dynamo: The Modern Productivity Paradox in a Not-Too-Distant Mirror." In *Technology and Productivity: The Challenge for Economic Policies*. Paris: OECD.

—— (1992). "Heroes, Herds and Hysteresis in Technological History." *Industrial and Corporate Change* 1 (1): 129–179.

Davis, Lance E., and Douglass North (1971). *Institutional Change and American Economic Growth*. Cambridge: Cambridge University Press.

Dawkins, R. (1976). *The Selfish Gene*. Oxford: Oxford University Press.

Day, Richard H., and Gunnar Eliasson (1986). *The Dynamics of Market Economies*. Amsterdam: North Holland.

DeBresson, Chris (1987). "The Evolutionary Paradigm and the Economics of Technological Change." *Journal of Economic Issues* 21 (2): 751–762.

Demaine, L., and A. Fellmeth (2003). "Natural Substances and Patentable Inventions." *Science* 300 (May 30): 1375–1376.

Demsetz, Harold (1967). "Towards a Theory of Property Rights." *American Economic Review Papers and Proceedings* 57 (2): 347–359.

Denison, E. F. (1962). *The Sources of Economic Growth in the United States and the Alternatives before Us*. New York: Committee For Economic Development.

—— (1968). *Why Growth Rates Differ: Postwar Experience in the Nine Western Countries*. Washington: Brookings Institution.

—— (1979). *Accounting for Slower Economic Growth*. Washington: Brookings Institution.

Dennett, D. (1995). *Darwin's Dangerous Idea*. New York: Simon and Schuster.

Dertouzos, M., R. Lester, and R. Solow (1989). *Made in America*. Cambridge, MA: MIT Press.

Diamond, P., D. Macfadden, and M. Rodriguez (1972). "Identification of the Elasticity of Substitution and the Bias of Technical Change." In D. Macfadden, ed., *An Econometric Approach to Production Theory*. Amsterdam: North Holland.

Domar, E. (1963). "On Total Factor Productivity and All That." *Journal of Political Economy* 71 (Dec.): 568–586.

Donald, M. (1991). *Origins of the Modern Mind*. Cambridge, MA: Harvard University Press.

Dosi, Giovanni (1982). "Technological Paradigms and Technological Trajectories: A Suggested Interpretation of the Determinants and Directions of Technical Change." *Research Policy* 11 (3): 147–162.

—— (1988). "Sources, Procedures, and Microeconomic Effects of Innovation." *Journal of Economic Literature* 26 (3): 1120–1171.

Dosi, Giovanni, Richard Nelson, and Sidney Winter, eds. (2000). *The Nature and Dynamics of Organizational Capabilities.* Oxford: Oxford University Press.

Dosi, Giovanni, David Teece, and Sidney Winter (1992). "Towards a Theory of Corporate Coherence: Preliminary Remarks." In Giovanni Dosi, Renato Giannetti, and Pier Angelo Toninelli, eds., *Technology and Enterprise in a Historical Perspective,* 185–211. Oxford: Clarendon Press.

Dosi, Giovanni, et al., eds. (1988). *Technical Change and Economic Theory.* London: Pinter.

Douglas, Mary (1986). *How Institutions Think.* Syracuse: Syracuse University Press.

Dreyfus, H. L., and S. E. Dreyfus (1986). *Mind over Machine: The Power of Human Intuition and Expertise in the Era of the Computer.* New York: Free Press.

Dreyfuss, R. (2004). "Protecting the Public Domain in Science: Has the Time for an Experimental Use Exemption Arrived?" *Arizona Law Review* 46: 457–471.

Durham, William H. (1991). *Coevolution: Genes, Culture, and Human Diversity.* Stanford: Stanford University Press.

"Economic Report of the President together with the Annual Report of the Council of Economic Advisors" (Jan. 1962). Washington, DC: U.S. Government Printing Office.

Edmondson, A., R. Bohmer, and G. Pisano (2001). "Disrupted Routines: Team Learning and Technology Implementation in Hospitals." Working Paper 00-003, Harvard Business School.

Eggertsson, Thrainn (1990). *Economic Behavior and Institutions.* Cambridge: Cambridge University Press.

—— (1999). "The Emergence of Norms in Economics: With Special Reference to Economic Development." Manuscript, Max Planck Institute for Research into Economic Systems.

Eisenberg, R. (1987). "Property Rights and the Norms of Science in Biotechnology Research." *Yale Law Review* 97: 177–231.

—— (1996). "Public Research and Private Investment: Patents and Technology Transfer in Government-Sponsored Research." *Virginia Law Review* 82: 1163–1727.

Eisenberg, R., and R. Nelson (2002). "Public vs. Proprietary Research: A Useful Tension?" *Daedalus* 131: 89–102.

Elliot, Donald (1985). "The Evolutionary Tradition in Jurisprudence." *Columbia Law Review* 85 (Jan.): 38–94.

Elster, J. (1989a). *The Cement of Society.* Cambridge: Cambridge University Press.

—— (1989b). *Solomonic Judgements.* Cambridge: Cambridge University Press.

Enos, J. (1962). "Invention and Innovation in the Petroleum Refining Industry." In R. Nelson, ed., *The Rate and Direction of Inventive Activity*. Princeton: Princeton University Press.

Esping-Anderson, G. (1990). *The Three Worlds of Welfare Capitalism*. London: Oxford University Press.

Fabricant, S. (1954). *Economic Progress and Economic Change*. Thirty-fourth Annual Report of the National Bureau of Economic Research. New York: NBER.

Fligstein, Neil (1990). *The Transformation of Corporate Control*. Cambridge, MA: Harvard University Press.

Fontana, W., and Leo W. Buss (1992). "What Would Be Preserved If the Tape Were Played Twice." Mimeo, Santa Fe Institute.

Freeman, Christopher (1982). *The Economics of Industrial Innovation*. London: Penguin.

———— (1991). "The Nature of Innovation and the Evolution of the Productive System." In *Technology and Productivity: The Challenge for Economic Policies*, 303–314. Paris: OECD.

Freeman, C., and F. Louca (2001). *As Time Goes By: From the Industrial Revolutions to the Information Revolution*. New York: Oxford University Press.

Freeman, C., and C. Perez (1988). "Structural Crises of Adjustment, Business Cycles, and Investment Behavior." In Giovanni Dosi et al., eds., *Technical Change and Economic Theory*. London: Pinter.

Friedman, Daniel (1991). "Evolutionary Games in Economics." *Econometrica* 59 (2): 637–666.

Friedman, Milton (1953). *Essays in Positive Economics*. Chicago: University of Chicago Press.

Fukuyama, F. (1992). *The End of History and the Last Man*. New York: Avon.

Gavetti, Giovanni, and Daniel Levinthal (2000). "Looking Forward and Looking Backward: Cognitive and Experiential Search." *Administrative Science Quarterly* 45: 113–137.

Gelijns, A. (1991). *Innovation in Clinical Practice: The Dynamics of Medical Technology Development*. Washington, DC: National Academy Press.

Gelijns, A., N. Rosenberg, and A. Moskowitz (1998). "Capturing the Unexpected Benefits of Medical Research." *New England Journal of Medicine* 339 (Sept. 3): 693–698.

Gilfillan, S. C. (1935). *Inventing the Ship*. Chicago: Follett.

Gilson, Ronald J., and Mark J. Roe (1993). "Understanding the Japanese *Keiretsu*: Overlaps between Corporate Governance and Industrial Organization." *Yale Law Journal* 102 (4): 871–906.

Goldberg, V. (1976). "Commons, Clark, and the Emerging Post-Coasian Law and Economics." *Journal of Economic Issues* 10: 877–894.

Gollop, F. M., and D. W. Jorgenson (1980). "U.S. Productivity Growth by

Industry." In J. W. Kendrick and B. N. Vacara, eds., *New Developments in Productivity Measurement and Analysis*. Series in Studies in Income and Wealth 44. Chicago: University of Chicago Press.

Goodin, R., et al. (1999). *The Real Worlds of Welfare Capitalism*. Cambridge: Cambridge University Press.

Gort, Michael, and Steven Klepper (1982). "Time Paths in the Diffusion of Product Innovations." *Economic Journal* 92 (367): 630–653.

Gould, Stephen J. (1980). *The Panda's Thumb: More Reflections on Natural History*. New York: Norton.

——— (1985). *The Flamingo's Smile: Reflections in Natural History*. New York: Norton.

Granovetter, Mark (1985). "Economic Action and Social Structure: The Problem of Embeddedness." *American Journal of Sociology* 91 (3): 481–510.

Griliches, Z. (1957). "Hybrid Corn: An Exploration in the Economics of Technological Change." *Econometrica* 25 (Oct.): 501–522.

——— (1980). "R & D and the Productivity Slowdown." *American Economic Review* 70 (May): 343–348.

——— (1994). "Productivity, R & D, and the Data Constraint." *American Economic Review* 84 (Mar.): 1–23.

Grossman, G. (1989). "Quality Ladders in the Theory of Growth." National Bureau of Economic Research Working Paper 3099.

——— (1994). "Endogenous Innovation in the Theory of Growth." *Journal of Economic Perspectives* 8: 23–44.

Grossman, G., and E. Helpman (1989). "Comparative Advantage and Long-Run Growth." *American Economic Review* 79: 796–815.

Guston, D. (2000). *Between Politics and Science*. Cambridge: Cambridge University Press.

Hagarty, S. (2000). "Characterizing the Knowledge Base in Education." In *Knowledge Management in the Learning Society*. Paris: OECD.

Hall, P., and R. Taylor (1994). "Political Science and the Four New Institutionalisms." Manuscript, Harvard University Center for European Studies.

Hannan, Michael, and Glenn R. Carroll (1992). *Dynamics of Organizational Populations*. New York: Oxford University Press.

Hannan, Michael, and John Freeman (1989). *Organizational Ecology*. Cambridge, MA: Harvard University Press.

Harrington, M. (1997). *The Other America*. New York: Collier.

Hart, D. (1998). *Forged Consensus*. Princeton: Princeton University Press.

Hayek, Friedrich (1967). *Studies in Philosophy, Politics, and Economics*. London: Routledge and Kegan Paul.

——— (1973). *Law, Legislation, and Liberty*, vol. 1: *Rules and Order*. London: Routledge and Kegan Paul.

——— (1988). *The Fatal Conceit: The Errors of Socialism.* Chicago: University of Chicago Press.

Hegel, G. (1967). *Hegel's Philosophy of Right,* trans. F. M. Knox. London: Oxford University Press.

Heller, M., and R. Eisenberg (1998). "Can Patents Deter Innovation? The Anticommons in Biomedical Research." *Science* 280 (May 1): 698–701.

Henderson, Rebecca (1993). "Underinvestment and Incompetence as Responses to Radical Innovation: Evidence from the Photolithographic Alignment Equipment Industry." *Rand Journal of Economics* 24 (2): 248–270.

Henderson, Rebecca, and Kim Clark (1990). "Architectural Innovation: The Reconfiguration of Existing Product Technologies and the Failure of Established Firms." *Administrative Sciences Quarterly* 35 (1): 9–30.

Hendriks-Jansen, H. (1996). *Catching Ourselves in the Act: Situated Activity, Interactive Emergence, Evolution, and Human Thought.* Cambridge, MA: MIT Press.

Hirshleifer, Jack, and Juan Carlos Martinez-Coll (1988). "What Strategies Can Support the Evolutionary Emergence of Cooperation?" *Journal of Conflict Resolution* 32 (2): 367–398.

Ho, S. (1980) "Small-Scale Enterprises in Korea and Taiwan." World Bank Staff Working Paper 384. Washington, DC: World Bank.

Hobday, M. (1995). *Innovation in East Asia: The Challenge to Japan.* London: Edward Elgar.

Hodgson, Geoffrey M. (1988). *Economics and Institutions.* Cambridge: Polity.

——— (1991). "Economic Evolution: Intervention contra Pangloss." *Journal of Economic Issues* 25 (2): 519–533.

——— (1991/92). "Thorstein Veblen and Joseph Schumpeter on Evolutionary Economics." ZIF Research Group, Biological Foundations of Human Culture. Germany: University of Bielefeld.

——— (1993). *Economics and Evolution: Bringing Life Back into Economics.* Cambridge: Polity Press.

——— (1994). "The Return of Institutional Economics." In N. Smelser and R. Swedberg, eds., *The Handbook of Economic Sociology,* 58–76. Princeton: Princeton University Press.

——— (1998). "The Approach of Institutional Economics." *Journal of Economic Literature* 36: 166–192.

——— (1999a). *Economics and Utopia.* London: Routledge.

——— (1999b). *Evolution and Institutions: On Evolutionary Economics and the Evolution of Economics.* Cheltenham: Edward Elgar.

——— (2001). *How Economics Forgot History.* New York: Routledge.

——— (2004). *The Evolution of Institutional Economics.* New York: Routledge.

Holland, John H., et al. (1986). *Induction: Processes of Inference, Learning, and Discovery.* Cambridge, MA: MIT Press.

Hollingsworth, J. R., and R. Boyer (1997). *Contemporary Capitalism: The Embeddedness of Institutions.* Cambridge: Cambridge University Press.

Holmstrom, B., and J. Tirole (1989). "The Theory of the Firm." In R. Schmalensee and J. Tirole, eds., *Handbook of Industrial Organization.* New York: North Holland.

Hughes, Thomas P. (1983). *Networks of Power: Electrification in Western Society, 1880–1930.* Baltimore: Johns Hopkins University Press.

Hull, David (1988). *Science as a Process.* Chicago: University of Chicago Press.

——— (2001). *Science and Selection.* Cambridge: Cambridge University Press.

Hutchins, E. (1996). *Cognition in the Wild.* Cambridge, MA: MIT Press.

Iwai, Katsuhito (1984a). "Schumpeterian Dynamics, Part I." *Journal of Economic Behavior and Organization* 5 (2): 159–190.

——— (1984b). "Schumpeterian Dynamics, Part II." *Journal of Economic Behavior and Organization* 5 (3–4): 321–351.

Jablonka, Eva, and John Ziman (2000). "Biological Evolution: Processes and Phenomena." In John Ziman, ed., *Technological Innovation as an Evolutionary Process.* Cambridge: Cambridge University Press.

Jepperson, R. (1991). "Institutions, Institutional Effects, and Institutionalization." In W. Powell and P. DiMaggio, eds., *The New Institutionalism in Organizational Analysis,* 63–82. Chicago: University of Chicago Press.

Johnson-Laird, P. N. (1983). *Mental Models: Towards a Cognitive Science of Language, Inference, and Consciousness.* Cambridge, MA: Harvard University Press.

Jorgenson, D. W. (1986). "The Great Transition: Energy and Economic Change." *Energy Journal* 7: 1–13.

Jorgenson, D. W., and Z. Griliches (1967). "The Explanation of Productivity Growth." *Review of Economic Studies* 34 (July): 249–283.

Jorgenson, D. W., Z. Griliches, and B. Fraumeni (1980). "Substitution and Technical Change in Production." Harvard Institute of Economic Research, Discussion Paper 752, March.

Judson, H. (1996). *The Eighth Day of Creation: Makers of the Revolution in Biology,* expanded ed. Plainview, NY: Cold Spring Harbor Laboratory Press.

Kaldor, N. (1957). "A Model of Economic Growth." *Economic Journal* 67 (Dec.): 591–624.

Kaldor, N., and J. Mirrlees (1962). "A New Model of Economic Growth." *Review of Economic Studies* (June).

Kandori, Michihiro, George J. Mailath, and Rafael Rob (1993). "Learning, Mutation, and Long-Run Equilibria in Games." *Econometrica* 61 (1): 29–56.

Katz, Michael, and Carl Shapiro (1994). "Systems Competition and Network Effects." *Journal of Economic Perspectives* 8: 93–116.

Kealey, T. (1996). *The Economic Laws of Scientific Research*. London: Macmillan.

Kendrick, J. W. (1956). "Productivity Trends: Capital and Labor." *Review of Economic Statistics* 38 (Aug.): 248–257.

——— (1973). *Postwar Productivity Trends in the United States, 1918–1969*. National Bureau of Economic Research. New York: Columbia University Press.

Kendrick, J. W., and E. Grossman (1980). *Productivity in the United States: Trends and Cycles*. Baltimore: Johns Hopkins University Press.

Kim, J. I., and L. J. Lau (1994). "The Sources of Economic Growth in the East Asian Newly Industrialized Countries." *Journal of Japanese and International Economics*, 235–271.

Kim, L. (1997). *Imitation to Innovation: The Dynamics of Korea's Technological Learning*. Boston: Harvard Business School Press.

Kirzner, I. M. (1979). *Perception, Opportunity, and Profit*. Chicago: University of Chicago Press.

Kitcher, Philip (1993). *The Advancement of Science*. New York: Oxford University Press.

Klepper, Steven (1993). "Entry, Exit, Growth, and Innovation over the Product Cycle." Manuscript, Carnegie-Mellon University.

Klepper, Steven, and Elizabeth Graddy (1990). "The Evolution of New Industries and the Determinants of Market Structure." *Rand Journal of Economics* 21 (1): 27–44.

Klevorick, A., et al. (1995). "On the Sources and Significance of Interindustry Differences in Technological Opportunities." *Research Policy* 24: 185–205.

Kline, S. (1995). *Conceptual Foundations for Multidisciplinary Thinking*. Stanford: Stanford University Press.

Knight, F. (1921). *Risk, Uncertainty, and Profit*. Boston: Houghton Mifflin.

Kreps, D. (1990). "Corporate Culture and Economic Theory." In J. Alt and K. Shepsle, eds., *Perspectives on Positive Political Economy*. Cambridge: Cambridge University Press.

Krugman, Paul (1994). "The Myth of Asia's Miracle." *Foreign Affairs* 73 (Dec.): 62–78.

Kuhn, Thomas S. (1970). *The Structure of Scientific Revolutions*. Chicago: University of Chicago Press.

Kuttner, R. (1997). *Everything for Sale: The Virtues and Limits of Markets*. New York: Knopf.

Kwasnicki, Witold (1996). *Knowledge, Innovation, and Economy: An Evolutionary Exploration*. Cheltenham, England: Edward Elgar.

Lakatos, Imre (1970). "Falsification and the Methodology of Scientific Research Programmes." In Imre Lakatos and Alan Musgrave, eds., *Criticism and the Growth of Knowledge,* 91–196. New York: Cambridge University Press.

Landes, D. (1970). *The Unbound Prometheus.* London: Cambridge University Press.

Landes, William M., and Richard A. Posner (1987). *The Economic Structure of Tort Law.* Cambridge, MA: Harvard University Press.

Lane, David (1993). "Artificial Worlds and Economics." *Journal of Evolutionary Economics* 3 (11): 89–108.

Langlois, Richard N., ed. (1986). *Economics as a Process: Essays in the New Institutional Economics.* New York: Cambridge University Press.

—— (1989). "What Was Wrong with the Old Institutional Economics and What Is Still Wrong with the New?" *Review of Political Economy* 1: 270–298.

—— (1992). "Transaction Cost Economics in Real Time." *Industrial and Corporate Change* 1 (1): 99–127.

—— (1995). "Do Firms Plan?" *Constitutional Political Economy* 6: 247–261.

—— (1999). "Knowledge, Consumption, and Endogenous Growth." Manuscript, University of Connecticut.

Latour, Bruno (1986). *Science in Action.* London: Milton Keynes.

Lazonick, William (1990). *Competitive Advantage on the Shop Floor.* Cambridge, MA: Harvard University Press.

Lerner, B. (2001). *The Breast Cancer Wars.* New York: Oxford University Press.

Levinthal, Daniel (1997). "Adaptation on Rugged Landscapes." *Management Science* 43: 934–950.

Lewontin, Richard C. (1974). *The Genetic Basis of Evolutionary Change.* New York: Columbia University Press.

Lindblom, C. E. (1959). "The Science of Muddling Through." *Public Administration Review* 19: 79–88.

—— (1977). *Politics and Markets.* New York: Barre Books.

—— (2001). *The Market System: What It Is, How It Works, and What to Make of It.* New Haven: Yale University Press.

Lipsey, R., P. Courant, and C. Ragan (1998). *Economics.* New York: Addison-Wesley.

Lowi, T. (1969). *The End of Liberalism.* New York: Norton.

Lucas, R. E. B. (1988). "On the Mechanisms of Economic Development." *Journal of Monetary Economics* 22: 3–42.

—— (1993). "Making a Miracle." *Econometrica* 61 (Mar.): 251–272.

Lumsden, Charles J., and Edward O. Wilson (1981). *Genes, Mind, and Culture.* Cambridge, MA: Harvard University Press.

Magnusson, Lars, ed. (1994). *Evolutionary and Neo-Schumpeterian Approaches to Economics.* London: Kluwer Academic.

Malerba, Franco, and Luigi Orsenigo (1993). "Industry Evolution and

Artificial Worlds." Paper presented for the Workshop on Artificial World Models, Nov. 11–14, Santa Fe Institute, Santa Fe, NM.

—— (1994). "The Dynamics and Evolution of Industries." Manuscript, Department of Economics, Bocconi University.

Malerba, Franco, et al. (1999). "History-Friendly Models of Industry Evolution: The Computer Industry." *Industrial and Corporate Change* 8: 1–36.

Mansfield, E. (1968). *Industrial Research and Technological Innovation: An Econometric Analysis.* New York: Norton.

Mansfield, E., J. Rapoport, and A. Romeo (1977). *The Production and Application of New Industrial Technology.* New York: Norton.

Mansfield, E., J. Rapoport, and J. Schnee (1971). *Research and Development in the Modern Corporation.* New York: Norton.

March, James G., and Herbert A. Simon (1958). *Organizations.* New York: Wiley.

Marshall, Alfred (1948). *Principles of Economics,* 8th ed. London: Macmillan.

Marx, K. (1932). *Capital.* New York: Modern Library.

Matthews, R. (1986). "The Economics of Institutions and the Sources of Growth." *Economic Journal* 96: 903–918.

Maynard-Smith, J. (1982). *Evolution and the Theory of Games.* Cambridge: Cambridge University Press.

Mayr, Ernst (1988). *Toward a New Philosophy of Biology.* Cambridge, MA: Harvard University Press.

McGuire, Patrick, Mark Granovetter, and Michael Schwartz (1993). "Thomas Edison and the Social Construction of the Early Electrical Industry in the United States." In Richard Swedberg, ed., *Explorations in Economic Sociology.* New York: Russell Sage.

Merges, R., and R. Nelson (1990). "The Complex Economics of Patent Scope." *Columbia Law Review* 90: 839–916.

Merton, R. (1973). *The Sociology of Science: Theoretical and Empirical Investigations.* Chicago: University of Chicago Press.

Metcalfe, Stanley (1988). "The Diffusion of Innovation: An Interpretative Survey." In Giovanni Dosi et al., eds., *Technical Change and Economic Theory,* 560–589. London: Pinter.

—— (1992). "Variety, Structure, and Change: An Evolutionary Perspective on the Competitive Process." *Revue D'economie Industrielle* 59: 46–61.

—— (1998). *Evolutionary Economics and Creative Destruction.* New York: Routledge.

Metcalfe, Stanley, and Michael Gibbons (1989). "Technology, Variety and Organization." In Richard S. Rosenbloom and Robert A. Burgelman, eds., *Research on Technological Innovation, Management and Policy,* vol. 4: 153–193. Greenwich, CT: JAI Press.

Milgrom, Paul, and John Roberts (1990). "The Economics of Modern Manufacturing." *American Economic Review* 80 (3): 511–528.

Mill, J. S. (1961). *Principles of Political Economy.* New York: Augustus Kelley. (First published 1848.)

Mokyr, Joel (1990). *The Lever of Riches.* New York: Oxford University Press.

Mowery, D., and R. Nelson (1999). *The Sources of Industrial Leadership.* New York: Cambridge University Press.

Mowery, D., and N. Rosenberg (1979). "The Influence of Market Demand on Innovation: A Critical Review of Some Recent Studies." *Research Policy* 8: 102–153.

Mowery, D., et al. (2001). "The Growth of Patenting and Licensing by American Universities." *Research Policy* 30: 99–119.

Mueller, Dennis (1989). *Public Choice II.* Cambridge: Cambridge University Press.

Mueller, Dennis, and John Tilton (1969). "Research and Development Costs as Barriers to Entry." *Canadian Journal of Economics* 2 (4): 570–579.

Murmann, P. (2003). *Knowledge and Competitive Advantage: The Coevolution of Firms, Technology, and National Institutions.* Cambridge: Cambridge University Press.

Murnane, R., and R. Nelson (1984). "Production and Innovation When Techniques Are Tacit: The Case of Education." *Journal of Economic Behavior and Organization* 5: 353–373.

Murnane, R., N. Sharkey, and F. Levy (2002). "Can the Internet Help Solve America's Education Problems?" In P. Graham and N. Stacey, eds., *The Knowledge Economy and Postsecondary Education.* The Committee on the Impact of the Changing Economy on Postsecondary Education. Washington, DC: National Academy Press.

Myrdal, G. (1960). *Beyond the Welfare State.* London: Duckworth.

Nachbar, John (1992). "Evolution in the Finitely Repeated Prisoner's Dilemma." *Journal of Economic Behavior and Organization* 19 (3): 307–326.

National Research Council (1997). *Intellectual Property Rights and Research Tools in Molecular Biology.* Washington, DC: National Academy Press.

——— (1999). *How People Learn: Bridging Research and Practice.* Washington, DC: National Academy Press.

Nelson, Katherine (1996). *Language in Cognitive Development.* Cambridge: Cambridge University Press.

Nelson, Katherine, and Richard Nelson (2002). "On the Nature and Evolution of Human Know-how." *Research Policy* 31: 719–733.

Nelson, Richard R. (1964). "Aggregate Production Functions and Medium-Range Growth Projections." *American Economic Review* 54: 575–606.

——— (1973). "Recent Exercises in Growth Accounting: New Understanding or Dead End." *American Economic Review* 63: 462–468.

——— (1977). *The Moon and the Ghetto*. New York: Norton.

——— (1981). "Assessing Private Enterprise: An Exegesis of Tangled Doctrine." *Bell Journal of Economics* 12: 93–111.

———, ed. (1993). *National Innovation Systems: A Comparative Analysis*. New York: Oxford University Press.

——— (1994). "What Has Been the Matter with Neoclassical Growth Theory?" In G. Silverberg and L. Soete, eds., *The Economics of Growth and Technical Change*. Aldershot, England: Edward Elgar.

——— (1995). "Recent Evolutionary Theorizing about Economic Change." *Journal of Economic Literature* 33 (Mar.): 48–90.

——— (1998). "The Agenda for Growth Theory: A Different Point of View." *Cambridge Journal of Economics* 22: 497–520.

——— (2000). "Knowledge and Innovation Systems." In *Knowledge Management in the Learning Society*. Paris: OECD.

——— (2002). "The Problem of Market Bias in Modern Capitalist Economies." *Industrial and Corporate Change* 10: 207–244.

——— (2003a). "On the Uneven Evolution of Human Know-how." *Research Policy* 32: 909–922.

——— (2003b). "Physical and Social Technologies and Their Evolution." *Economie Appliquée* 61: 13–31.

——— (2004). "The Market Economy and the Scientific Commons." *Research Policy* 33: 455–471.

Nelson, Richard, and Howard Pack (1999). "The Asian Miracle and Modern Growth Theory." *Economic Journal* 109: 416–436.

——— (2003). "Factors behind the Asian Miracle: Entrepreneurship, Education, and Finance." In L. Paganetto and E. Phelps, eds., *Finance, Research, Education, and Growth*. New York: Palgrave.

Nelson, R., A. Peterhansl, and B. Sampat (2005). "Why and How Innovations Get Adopted: A Tale of Four Models." *Industrial and Corporate Change* 13: 679–701.

Nelson, R., and N. Phelps (1966). "Investment in Humans, Technological Change, and Economic Growth." *American Economic Review* 56 (May): 69–75.

Nelson, Richard, and Nathan Rosenberg (1993). "Technical Innovation and National Systems." In Richard R. Nelson, ed., *National Innovation Systems: A Comparative Study*, 3–22. New York: Oxford University Press.

Nelson, Richard, and Bhaven Sampat (2001). "Making Sense of Institutions as a Factor Shaping Economic Performance." *Journal of Economic Behavior and Organization* 44: 31–54.

Nelson, Richard, and Sidney Winter (1974). "Neoclassical vs. Evolutionary Theories of Economic Growth: Critique and Prospectus." *Economic Journal* 84 (Dec.): 886–905.

———— (1977). "In Search of a Useful Theory of Innovation." *Research Policy* 6 (1): 36–76.

———— (1982). *An Evolutionary Theory of Economic Growth*. Cambridge, MA: Harvard University Press.

Nelson, R., and E. Wolff (1997). "Factors behind Cross-Industry Differences in Technical Progress." *Structural Change and Economic Dynamics* 18: 205–220.

Nelson, R., and G. Wright (1992). "The Rise and Fall of American Technology Leadership: The Postwar Era in Historical Perspective." *Journal of Economic Literature* 30 (Dec.): 1–64.

Newell, A., and H. Simon (1972). *Human Problem Solving*. Englewood Cliffs, NJ: Prentice Hall.

North, Douglass C. (1981). *Structure and Change in Economic History*. New York: Norton.

———— (1990). *Institutions, Institutional Change, and Economic Performance*. Cambridge: Cambridge University Press.

———— (1994). "Economic Performance through Time." *American Economic Review* 84: 359–368.

North, D., and J. Wallis (1994). "Integrating Institutional Change and Technical Change in Economic History: A Transaction Cost Approach." *Journal of Institutional and Theoretical Economics* 150: 609–624.

Odagiri, H., and A. Goto (1997). *Technology and Industrial Development in Japan*. New York: Oxford University Press.

Olson, M. (1971). *The Rise and Decline of Nations: Public Goods and the Theory of Group Action*. Cambridge, MA: Harvard University Press.

Ostrom, E. (1991). *Governing the Commons: The Evolution of Institutions for Collective Action*. Cambridge: Cambridge University Press.

———— (1998). "A Behavioral Approach to Rational Choice Theory of Collective Action." *American Political Science Review* 92: 1–22.

Owen, R. (1991). *A New View of Society and Other Writings*. Harmondsworth, England: Penguin.

Pack, H. (1987). *Productivity, Technology, and Industrial Development*. New York: Oxford University Press.

Pack, H., and L. E. Westphal (1986). "Industrial Strategy and Technological Change: Theory vs. Reality." *Journal of Development Economics* 22: 87–128.

Pavitt, K. (1987). "On the Nature of Technology." Lecture given at the University of Sussex, England, June 23.

Penrose, Edith (1952). "Biological Analogies in the Theory of the Firm." *American Economic Review* 42 (5): 804–819.

Perez, Carlotta (1983). "Structural Change and the Assimilation of New Technology in the Economic and Social System." *Futures* 15: 357–375.

Perrow, Charles (1986). *Complex Organizations: A Critical Essay*, 3rd ed. Glenview, IL: Scott Foresman.

Petroski, Henry (1992). *The Evolution of Useful Things*. New York: Knopf.

Pinker, S. (1994). *The Language Instinct: How the Mind Creates Language*. New York: Morrow.

Piore, Michael J., and Charles F. Sabel (1984). *The Second Industrial Divide: Possibilities for Prosperity*. New York: Basic Books.

Plato (1961). *The Republic*. New York: Pantheon.

Plotkin, Henry (1982). *Learning, Development, and Culture: Essays in Evolutionary Epistemology*. New York: Wiley.

—— (1994). *Darwin Machines and the Nature of Knowledge*. Cambridge, MA: Harvard University Press.

Polanyi, K. (1944). *The Great Transformation*. Boston: Beacon Press.

Polanyi, Michael (1958). *Personal Knowledge: Towards a Post-Critical Philosophy*. London: Routledge and Kegan Paul.

—— (1967). "The Republic of Science." *Minerva* 1: 54–73.

Pollard, S. (1981). *Peaceful Conquest: The Industrialization of Europe, 1760–1970*. Oxford: Oxford University Press.

Popper, Karl (1959). *The Logic of Scientific Discovery*. New York: Basic Books.

—— (1968). *Conjectures and Refutations: The Growth of Scientific Knowledge*. New York: Harper Torchbooks.

Porter, R. (1997). *The Greatest Benefit to Mankind*. New York: Norton.

Posner, Michael, ed. (1990). *Foundations of Cognitive Science*. Cambridge, MA: MIT Press.

Posner, R. (1981). *The Economics of Justice*. Cambridge, MA: Harvard University Press.

—— (1992). *Economic Analysis of Law*. Boston: Little, Brown.

Powell, Walter W., and Paul J. DiMaggio (1991). "The Iron Cage Revisited: Institutional Isomorphism and Collective Rationality in Organizational Fields." In W. Powell and P. DiMaggio, eds., *The New Institutionalism in Organizational Analysis*, 63–82. Chicago: University of Chicago Press.

Price, D. (1962). *Science and Government*. Oxford: Oxford University Press.

Prigogine, Ilya, and Isabelle Stengers (1984). *Order Out of Chaos*. London: Fontana.

Rivlin, A. (1971). *Systematic Thinking for Social Action*. Washington: Brookings Institution.

Rodrik, D. (1994). "Getting Interventions Right: How South Korea and Taiwan Grew Rich." Manuscript, Columbia University.

Romanelli, Elaine (1991). "The Evolution of New Organizational Forms." *Annual Review of Sociology* 17: 79–103.

Romer, Paul (1990). "Endogenous Technological Change." *Journal of Political Economy* 98: 71–102.

—— (1991). "Increasing Returns and New Developments in the Theory of Growth." In William Barnett et al., eds., *Equilibrium Theory and Applications*, 83–110. Cambridge: Cambridge University Press.

—— (1992). "Idea Gaps and Object Gaps in Economics Development." Paper prepared for the World Bank Conference, How Do National Policies Affect Long-Run Growth? Washington, DC, March 9.

—— (1994). "The Origins of Endogenous Growth." *Journal of Economic Perspectives* 8: 3–22.

Rosenberg, Nathan (1969). "The Direction of Technological Change: Inducement Mechanisms and Focusing Devices." *Economic Development and Cultural Change* 18: 1–24.

—— (1974). "Science, Innovation, and Economic Growth." *Economic Journal* 84: 90–108.

—— (1976). *Perspectives on Technology.* Cambridge: Cambridge University Press.

—— (1982a). "How Exogenous Is Science?" In N. Rosenberg, *Inside the Black Box: Technology and Economics.* Cambridge: Cambridge University Press.

—— (1982b). "Learning by Using." In N. Rosenberg, *Inside the Black Box: Technology and Economics.* Cambridge: Cambridge University Press.

—— (1996). "Uncertainty and Technological Change." In R. Landau et al., eds., *The Mosaic of Economic Growth.* Stanford: Stanford University Press.

—— (1998). "Technological Change in Chemicals." In A. Arora, R. Landau, and N. Rosenberg, *Chemicals and Long-Run Economic Growth.* New York: John Wiley.

—— (2001). "Engineering Knowledge." Manuscript, Stanford University.

Rosenberg, Nathan, and Luther E. Birdzell (1986). *How the West Grew Rich.* New York: Basic Books.

Rosenberg, Nathan, and Richard Nelson (1994). "American Universities and Technological Advance in Industry." *Research Policy* 23: 323–348.

Rosenkopf, Lori, and Michael Tushman (1994). "The Coevolution of Technology and Organization." In Joel A. C. Baum and Jitendra V. Singh, eds., *Evolutionary Dynamics of Organizations.* New York: Oxford University Press.

Ruben, P., and M. Bailey (1992). "A Positive Theory of Legal Change." Manuscript, Department of Economics, Emory University.

Rumelt, Richard P. (1991). "How Much Does Industry Matter?" *Strategic Management Journal* 12 (3): 167–185.

Rutherford, M. (1994). *Institutions in Economics: The Old and the New Institutionalism*. Cambridge: Cambridge University Press.

Ruttan, V., and V. Hayami (1984). "Towards a Theory of Induced Institutional Innovation." *Journal of Development Studies* 20: 203–223.

Sabel, Charles, and Jonathan Zeitlin (1993). "Stories, Strategies, Structures: Rethinking Historical Alternatives to Mass Production." Manuscript.

Sahal, Devendra (1981). *Patterns of Technological Innovation*. Reading, MA: Addison-Wesley.

Saviotti, Paolo. (1996). *Technological Evolution, Variety, and the Economy*. Cheltenham, England: Edward Elgar.

Saviotti, Paolo, and J. Stanley Metcalfe, eds. (1991). *Evolutionary Theories of Economic and Technological Change*. Reading, MA: Harwood Academic.

Saxenhouse, G. (1974). "A Tale of Japanese Technological Diffusion in the Meiji Period." *Journal of Economic History* (Mar.): 149–165.

Scherer, F. M. (1983). "R & D and Declining Productivity Growth." *American Economic Review* 73 (May): 215–218.

Schmookler, J. (1952). "The Changing Efficiency of the American Economy." *Review of Economic Statistics* 34 (Aug.): 214–231.

——— (1966). *Invention and Economic Growth*. Cambridge, MA: Harvard University Press.

Schoemaker, Paul J. (1986). "The Evolution of Rules." In Richard N. Langlois, ed., *Economics as a Process*, 117–133. New York: Cambridge University Press.

——— (1991). "The Quest for Optimality: A Positive Heuristic of Science?" *Behavioral and Brain Sciences* 14 (2): 205–245.

Schonfield, A. (1965). *Modern Capitalism*. London: Oxford University Press.

Schotter, Andrew (1981). *The Economic Theory of Social Institutions*. Cambridge: Cambridge University Press.

Schumpeter, Joseph A. (1934). *The Theory of Economic Development*. Cambridge, MA: Harvard University Press.

——— (1939). *Business Cycles*. New York: Prentice Hall.

——— (1942). *Capitalism, Socialism, and Democracy*. New York: Harper and Row.

Scott, W. Richard (1991). "Unpacking Institutional Arguments." In W. Powell and P. DiMaggio, eds., *The New Institutionalism in Organizational Analysis*, 164–182. Chicago: University of Chicago Press.

——— (1992). *Organizations: Rational, Natural, and Open Systems*, 3rd ed. Englewood Cliffs, NJ: Prentice Hall.

Shepsle, K., and B. Weingast (1982). "Institutionalizing Majority Rule: A Social Choice Theory with Policy Implications." *American Economic Review* 72: 367–371.

Shockley, William (1950). *Holes and Electrons in Semiconductors.* New York: Van Nostrand.

Shubik, M. (1975). "The General Equilibrium Model Is Incomplete and Not Adequate for the Reconciliation of Micro and Macroeconomic Theory." *Kyklos* 28: 545–573.

Silverberg, Gerald. (1987). "Technical Progress, Capital Accumulation, and Effective Demand: A Self-Organizing Model." In David Batten, John Casti, and Borje Johnsen, eds., *Economic Evolution and Structural Adjustment,* 116–144. Berlin: Springer-Verlag.

Silverberg, Gerald, Giovanni Dosi, and Luigi Orsenigo (1988). "Innovation, Diversity and Diffusion: A Self-Organizing Model." *Economic Journal* 98 (Dec.): 1032–1054.

Simon, Herbert (1947). *Administrative Behavior.* New York: Free Press.

Simon, Herbert, and Charles Bonini (1958). "The Size Distribution of Business Firms." *American Economic Review* 48 (Sept.): 607–617.

Smelser, Neil, and Richard Swedberg, eds. (1994). *Handbook of Economic Sociology.* Princeton: Princeton University Press.

Smith, A. (1853). *The Theory of Moral Sentiments.* London: Henry G. Bohn.

——— (1937). *The Wealth of Nations.* New York: Modern Library. (First published 1776.)

Sober, Elliott, ed. (1984). *Conceptual Issues in Evolutionary Biology.* Cambridge, MA: MIT Press.

Soete, Luc, and Roy Turner (1984). "Technology Diffusion and the Rate of Technical Change." *Economic Journal* 94 (Sept.): 612–623.

Solow, Robert M. (1956). "A Contribution to the Theory of Economic Growth." *Quarterly Journal of Economics* 70 (Feb.): 65–94.

——— (1957). "Technical Change and the Aggregate Production Function." *Review of Economics and Statistics* 39 (Aug.): 214–231.

——— (1959). *Investment and Technical Change in Mathematical Methods in the Social Sciences.* Stanford: Stanford University Press.

Solow, R. M., J. Tobin, and C. E. von Weizacher (1966). "Neoclassical Growth with Fixed Factor Propositions." *Review of Economic Studies* 33 (Apr.): 79–115.

Spencer, Herbert (1887). *The Factors of Organic Evolution.* London: Williams and Norgate.

Stiglitz, J. (1986). *Economics of the Public Sector.* New York: Norton.

——— (1989). "Learning to Learn, Localized Learning, and Technological Progress." In P. Dasgupta and P. Stoneman, eds., *Economic Policy and Technological Performance.* Cambridge: Cambridge University Press.

Stokes, Donald (1996). *Pasteur's Quadrant: Basic Science and Technological Innovation.* Washington: Brookings Institution.

Sugden, Robert (1989). "Spontaneous Order." *Journal of Economic Perspectives* 3 (4): 85–97.

Swan, T. W. (1956). "Economic Growth and Capital Accumulation." *Economic Record* 32 (Nov.): 334–361.

Teece, D. (1993). "The Dynamics of Industrial Capitalism: Perspectives on Alfred Chandler's Scale and Scope." *Journal of Economic Literature* 31: 199–225.

Teece, D., and G. Pisano (1994). "The Dynamic Capabilities of Firms: An Introduction." *Industrial and Corporate Change* 3: 537–556.

Terleckyj, N. (1960). "Sources of Productivity Advance: A Pilot Study of Manufacturing Industries, 1899–1953." PhD diss., Columbia University.

Tinbergen, J. (1942). "Zur Theorie der Langfristegen Wirtschaftsentwichlung." *Weltwirtschaftsliches Archiv* 55.

Titmuss, R. (1997). *The Gift Relationship*. New York: New Press.

Tucker, C. (1998). "The Role of Government in Supporting Technological Advance." PhD diss., Columbia University.

Tushman, Michael L., and Philip Anderson (1986). "Technological Discontinuities and Organizational Environments." *Administrative Sciences Quarterly* 31: 439–465.

Tushman, Michael L., and Elaine Romanelli (1985). "Organizational Evolution: A Metamorphosis Model of Convergence and Reorientation." *Research in Organizational Behavior* 7: 171–222.

Tushman, Michael, and Lori Rosenkopf (1992). "Organizational Determinants of Technological Change: Toward a Sociology of Technological Evolution." *Research in Organizational Behavior* 14: 311–347.

Utterback, James (1994). *Mastering the Dynamics of Innovation*. Boston: Harvard Business School Press.

Utterback, James, and Fernando Suarez (1993). "Innovation, Competition, and Market Structure." *Research Policy* 22 (1): 1–21.

Varela, F. J., E. Thompson, and E. Rosch (1991). *The Embodied Mind*. Cambridge, MA: MIT Press.

Veblen, Thorstein (1898). "Why Is Economics Not an Evolutionary Science?" *Quarterly Journal of Economics* 12: 373–397.

——— (1899). *The Theory of the Leisure Class: An Economic Study of Institutions*. New York: Macmillan.

——— (1915). *Imperial Germany and the Industrial Revolution*. New York: Macmillan.

——— (1958). *The Theory of Business Enterprise*. New York: Mentor Books.

Verspagen, Bart (1992). "Endogenous Innovation in Neoclassical Growth Models: A Survey." *Journal of Macroeconomics* 14 (Fall): 631–662.

Vincenti, Walter (1990). *What Engineers Know and How They Know It.* Baltimore: Johns Hopkins University Press.

———— (1994). "The Retractable Airplane Landing Gear and the Northrup Anomaly: Variation-Selection and the Shaping of Technology." *Technology and Culture* 35: 1–33.

Von Tunzelmann, G. N. (1995). *Technology and Economic Progress.* Aldershot, England: Edward Elgar.

Walsh, J., A. Arora, and W. Cohen (2002). "The Patenting and Licensing of Research Tools and Biomedical Innovation." Paper prepared for the STEP Board of the National Academy of Sciences, Washington DC.

Westphal, L., L. Kim, and C. Dahlman (1985). "Reflections on Korea's Acquisition of Technological Capability." In N. Rosenberg and C. Frischtak, eds., *International Technology Transfer.* New York: Praeger.

Williamson, Oliver E. (1975). *Markets and Hierarchies: Analysis and Antitrust Implications.* New York: Free Press.

———— (1985). *The Economic Institutions of Capitalism.* New York: Free Press.

———— (1995). *The Mechanisms of Governance.* Oxford: Oxford University Press.

Wilson, E. O. (1975). *Sociobiology: The New Synthesis.* Cambridge, MA: Harvard University Press.

Winter, Sidney (1964). "Economic 'Natural Selection' and the Theory of the Firm." *Yale Economic Essays* 4 (1): 225–272.

———— (1984). "Schumpeterian Competition in Alternative Technological Regimes." *Journal of Economic Behavior and Organization* 5 (3–4): 287–320.

———— (1986a). "Comments [Rationality of Self and Others in an Economic System: Adoptive Behavior and Economic Theory]." *Journal of Business,* Part 2, 59 (4): S427–S434.

———— (1986b). "The Research Program of the Behavioral Theory of the Firm: Orthodox Critique and Evolutionary Perspective." In Benjamin Gilad and Stanley Kaish, eds., *Handbook of Behavioral Economics,* vol. A, 242–245. Greenwich, CT: JAI Press.

———— (1988). "On Coase, Competence and the Corporation." *Journal of Law and Economics* 4: 163–180.

———— (2000). "Organizing for Continuing Improvement." In R. Cole and W. R. Scott, eds., *The Quality Movement and Organization Theory.* Thousand Oaks, CA: Sage.

Witt, Ulrich (1989). "The Evolution of Economic Institutions as a Propagation Process." *Public Choice* 62 (2): 155–172.

————, ed. (1993). *Evolutionary Economics.* London: Edward Elgar.

Womack, J., D. Jones, and D. Roos (1990). *The Machine That Changed the World.* New York: Macmillan.

World Bank (1993). *The East Asian Miracle: Economic Growth and Public Policy.* Oxford: Oxford University Press.

Yergin, D., and J. Stanislaw (1998). *The Commanding Heights.* New York: Simon and Schuster.

Young, A. (1995). "The Tyranny of Numbers: Confronting the Statistical Realities of the East Asian Growth Experience." *Quarterly Journal of Economics* 110 (3): 641–680.

Young, H. Peyton (1993). "The Evolution of Conventions." *Econometrica* 61 (1): 57–84.

Ziman, John (1968). *Public Knowledge.* Cambridge: Cambridge University Press.

——— (1978). *Reliable Knowledge.* Cambridge: Cambridge University Press.

———, ed. (2000). *Technological Innovation as an Evolutionary Process.* Cambridge: Cambridge University Press.

Index